Mormons at the Met

Mormons at the Met

by
Glen Nelson

illustrations by
Annie Poon

Mormon Artists Group
New York 2012

for my mother and father
who gifted me with music

Contents

Mormons at the Met

INTRODUCTION

I SAT IN THE AUDIENCE of the Metropolitan Opera in New City on the night of January 5, 1996, and I watched the tenor Richard Versalle fall to his death onstage. The performance had just begun when he died. It was the Met premiere of Leoš Janáček's *The Makropulos Case*, an opera about a woman named Emilia Marty who is given a potion to extend life 300 years. Jessye Norman was to sing the starring role. The young American, David Robertson, was making his debut as the orchestra's conductor. The rarely-performed opera is all about death and the value of life. It contains a suicide, an attempted murder, and finally a declaration from the 337-year old Marty that if life lasts too long, it loses its value. At the end of the opera, exhausted with life, she offers the secret elixir to anyone who will take it. No one will touch it except to destroy it, and as the formula burns, she sinks to the floor and dies.

Opera is about dying, in a way. There are comic operas too, but the majority of works in the repertoire are tragedies—far more than movies, for example—and audiences go to the opera for a hard look at mortality. Characters die at the opera house every night; this night was very different, obviously. Vítek, the tenor role played by Versalle, is a law clerk who sets off the action of *The Makropulos Case* by discovering an unresolved legal case that is nearly one hundred years old.

As soon as the curtain went up, I felt uncomfortable. The scene was set in a law office, and at stage left, there was a ladder that stretched up to the rafters in front of a wall of file drawers. The ceiling above the Met stage is enormous. The proscenium arch itself is fifty-four feet wide and forty feet high. I don't know exactly how long the ladder was, but it must have been 20 or 30 feet. It was designed to look endless. Vítek started to climb the ladder, and as he ascended higher and higher, he opened file drawers, all the while singing.

Nothing appeared amiss as Versalle sang the line, "Too bad you can live only so long." He then fell backwards off the ladder, and he landed on his back, with his head crashing against the stage floor. In my section of the audience, none of us had ever seen this opera, and we weren't entirely sure the fall was un-scripted. We just sat and waited. The orchestra continued playing briefly. And then I heard the conductor yell to the stage, "Richard? Richard!" Someone rushed in from the wings, and the curtain came down.

The house lights came up. A stunned reaction all around— the performance was only a few minutes old. I was there with my wife, Marcia. We didn't know what to do. From where we were, up in the balcony, we couldn't see much movement in the audience below. A few people stood in the aisles, but the majority stayed where they were in their seats waiting for whatever would come next. It felt like a very long time before a voice sounded out over a microphone that Richard Versalle had been taken to the hospital for treatment and that there would be an intermission. I don't remember all of the details of that night; some of it I've tried to forget, but I do distinctly remember feeling angry. I thought that the set design and stage direction were irresponsibly hazardous. It looked to me like Versalle had slipped and fallen to his death.

After 45 minutes passed without any update, a Met official announced that the performance was cancelled. Ticketholders were instructed how to get replacement tickets, but I already knew that I wouldn't be coming back to see that opera. I couldn't. The following performance of *The Makropulos Case* was a Saturday matinee, and it was dedicated to Versalle, age 63, who, the papers reported, died of a heart attack onstage. A blizzard blanketed the city with snow overnight, and the matinee performance was cancelled, too.

I had witnessed two other men die here in New York in the ten years since I moved from a farm town in Southern Utah. The first casualty was hit by a bus in Times Square at the intersection of Broadway and 42nd Street. I was standing diagonally across the street at the time. The other death was a man my wife and I saw jump from a high ledge of Macy's Department Store near Herald Square on 35th street, to the encouraging chorus of fools below.

Inside the Met, people have died both onstage and in the audience. I was listening to a radio broadcast from the Met on Saturday January 23, 1988—a performance of *Macbeth*—when an 82-year old singing coach named Bantcho Bantchevsky committed suicide by jumping from the Family Circle Balcony down four stories to the orchestra level. His body fell into empty seats and then rolled into the aisle.

It's rare to have a performer die onstage, but it has happened before at the Metropolitan. The most famous tragic event was the death of Leonard Warren, a great American baritone and a native New Yorker. He had sung 662 performances at the Met before he took the stage on March 4, 1960 in *La forza del destino*, of all things, at the age of 48. The performers that night included some legends: Renata Tebaldi, Richard Tucker, and Jerome Hines. Thomas Schippers conducted. Raymond A. Ericson later wrote about that night in *Musical America*:

In the middle of Act II (as given at the Metropolitan), the duet for Mr. Warren and Mr. Tucker, "Solenne in quest'ora" (Swear to me in this solemn hour) brought another crescendo of applause and bravos. Mr. Warren then was left onstage alone to sing the recitative that begins "Morir! Tremenda cosa!" (To die! Tremendous moment!). How ominous this phrase was to prove!

Mr. Warren continued into the superb aria that follows, "Urna fatale" (O fatal pages), and he had never seemed in better form as his remarkable voice rode the long legato phrases and soared excitingly through the cadenzas to the climactic high notes. At the end, he stood quietly until the shouts of approval had died away. Moving to stage left he completed his next few lines of recitative and then fell forward heavily, as if he had tripped.

Roald Reitan, as the Surgeon, entered, singing his single phrase, "Lieta novella, e salvo" (Good news I bring you, I saved him). No response came from Mr. Warren, as Thomas Schippers, the conductor, waited with upstretched arms to bring the orchestra in.

Uncertainty and wonder gripped everyone for a few seconds, and the audience stirred uneasily. Mr. Reitan then went quickly over to Mr. Warren, knelt by his side. The audience did not know that Mr. Reitan raised Mr. Warren's head slightly, that the stricken baritone uttered faintly the word "Help!" and then went limp. The audience was only aware of Mr. Reitan's looking anxiously into the wings and at Mr. Schippers, and of a voice in the auditorium saying clearly, "Bring the curtain down!"

...About 10:30, warning bells rang in the lobbies, and the audience filed back to their seats. [General Manager] Mr. Bing reappeared before the curtain, his expression grave.

"This is one of the saddest days in the history of opera," he began. "I will ask you please to stand," he continued, as the shaken audience uttered gasps of disbelief, "In memory of one of our greatest performers, who died in the middle of one of his greatest performances." After the audience had arisen, some of the members openly sobbing, Mr. Bing concluded: "I am sure you will agree with me that

it would not be possible to continue with the performance."
Slowly, a dazed and saddened public departed.[1]

This is a morbid way to introduce an upbeat book, I know, but
for me opera is serious business. I have always responded to it
viscerally. Other people my age grew up laughing at opera—at
Elmer Fudd in drag singing Wagner to Bugs Bunny, "Kill the
wabbit, kill the wabbit!" and at television commercials parodying
Pagliacci, "No more Rice Krispies! We've run out of Rice
Krispies!" Not me. My mother was a singer. She sang small parts
in *Carmen* and *Rigoletto* in our town's college productions. On
Saturdays, as we cleaned our house, we played the reel-to-reel
tapes of Broadway musicals and light operas that my parents
recorded from television broadcasts. We heard them over and
over, along with recordings of the operas my mother performed.
I knew the music by heart. One of my childhood toys was the set
of castanets that Mom used as a stage prop in her *Carmen* days.

There was no opera company close to us on our farm, so I saw
no live performances, but for some reason, I was surrounded at
home by the elements of opera—painting, dance, music, and theater—and both of my parents encouraged me and my four siblings to appreciate the arts. Their message to us seemed to be
this: there is more in this world than sheep and hay.

My dad played trombone in a community band as a young
man, and he supported an uncle who was a painter and ce-
ramist by purchasing all of his works that he could afford. My

mother was an expert tailor, weaver and quilter who raised sheep for their wool, and then she could shear, card, spin, dye and weave it into fabric and then make a suit out of it without a pattern. My parents assumed that all of us would make the most of ourselves one way or another. I started to take piano lessons in first grade. My oldest brother, Mark, learned to paint. My oldest sister, Kris, was a cellist. Another sister, Rhea, played the piano, and my other brother, Ray, sang and was a ballet dancer in high school, when he wasn't playing football, basketball, and baseball.

I stepped into the Metropolitan Opera house for the first time on a college school trip when I was 18 years old. The performance was *Tosca*, and it wasn't a particularly good performance, now that I think about it. I was there with a group of students who wanted to be anywhere else but listening to an opera, and we were viewing the opera from the worst seats in the place. But for me it became a beacon somehow, and I knew I would return.

When a friend came back to New York a few years later to audition for opera apprenticeships, I traveled with him, and we went to the Met again. This time, I heard Placido Domingo sing *Otello* one night, and then I returned the very next evening for an opera I'd never heard of, Alban Berg's *Wozzeck*. Freezing outside in mid-January, the house was less than half full. We had standing room tickets, but the ushers told us to take a seat wherever we wanted.

We ended up near the aisle in the center of the orchestra for a searing performance of a story so bleak that I thought razor blades should be included in each playbill program. I had never heard anything like it, and as importantly, I had never felt anything like it. The drama on stage was the opposite of the silly, trite, dismissible clichés associated with opera stories. If I hadn't been hooked on opera before that night, I certainly was after it.

I moved to New York to go to graduate school after serving a mission for the Church of Jesus Christ of Latter-day Saints (LDS) in Costa Rica and Panama. I couldn't afford to go out very often. I remember walking into Tower Records two blocks north of the opera house on a Saturday afternoon. In the basement where classical music records were kept, the clerks had turned on the live, Texaco Radio Broadcast from the Met. I recognized the music immediately. It was *Tosca*, and the voice over the air had the unmistakable ping of Luciano Pavarotti. It was the first act, and the painter Cavaradossi was laboring in the church on a portrait of the Madonna that he paints to resemble his girlfriend, Tosca. He began his aria, "Recondita Armonia", (Remembered harmony) and to my surprise, the entire store started to sing along—men and women. At first, under their breath, but gradually with more abandon, just like Luciano, until we all sang the ending, "Tosca, sei tu" (Tosca, it's you) together. To the radio audience's applause, we laughed and went our separate ways, but I knew that the homesickness I was feeling for my farm town wouldn't last long. Opera, as strange as it seems for a young Utah boy, had become a bridge to something else.

My father passed away on November 6, 2006, a victim of the atomic testing fallout in the Nevada desert of the 1950s. People in Southern Utah call the delayed-onset cancers caused by the testing Downwinder's Syndrome. My dad, tending his herd of sheep, used to sit atop the mesas northeast of the Mojave and watch the mushroom clouds billow and drift over him, just as many of the locals did. My mother died of a related cancer, too, in September 2010.

Late in life, I brought her to New York and gave her a ticket to a performance at the Metropolitan Opera of *Rigoletto*. It was the same opera she had sung in college. I met her outside after the performance. She was still in tears. Mom related to me that as soon as the orchestra began playing the overture, fifty years melted away. She remembered every word and every note of the score she sang a half-century earlier. It was as if she were back in school, she said. She had been a sophisticated girl from Salt Lake City who followed her voice teacher down to a tiny agricultural college in the middle of nowhere, and there met a gangly farmer boy, married, and raised a family. It was where she would die, a few hundred feet from the adobe brick house where her husband was born.

At the end of a personally tumultuous year in 2011, I happened to look at a season brochure for the Metropolitan Opera. On its back pages was printed the roster of singers for the new season, 2011-12. I started to notice names of singers I knew, not only from seeing them onstage but from seeing them in church.

There were six LDS singers engaged to perform roles in the up-coming season.

I had the idea to write about a season at the Met with an eye on these Mormon singers, as a tribute to my parents. I could go to the performances and describe them. I could explain how these vocalists arrived professionally. Some of the six are friends whom I've known for several years. I assumed that seeing them would remind me of other LDS singers in the Met's history, and the whole thing might end up being a snapshot of a unique, operatic Mormon moment. There has never been a time when so many LDS opera singers are poised to enjoy significant careers in opera. At the very least, it would be a nice excuse to spend some evenings in a place that feels, if not sacred to me, like home.

August 2011
New York City

CHAPTER 1

I HAVE A PLAN FOR THE SEASON. Six LDS singers are set to perform roles at the Met, and I intend to hear all of them. They are Ginger Costa-Jackson, mezzo-soprano; Wendy Bryn Harmer, soprano; Erin Morley, soprano; Tamara Mumford, mezzo-soprano; Nicholas Pallesen, baritone; and Nina Warren, soprano. All of them have sung roles at the Met before, except for Pallesen, but he sang at the National Council Grand Finals Concert in 2007 at the Met. He hasn't sung in a Met production yet; this could be the year of his debut. Most of the LDS vocalists will be singing in multiple operas. Four of the six have been offered roles, and the other two are covers, that is, understudies for roles. At the moment, they have no idea whether they'll go on or not. Depending on the fate of others, they may be performing too.

I want to do more than to hear each of the singers once. They have multiple roles throughout the season. If I can figure out the logistics, I plan to hear every singer in every one of their opera assignments. It's not entirely crazy. I won't be in the audience each time they walk on stage—each opera during the Met season is performed about 10 times.

The six singers' roles this season are as follows: for Tamara Mumford: the role of Mark Smeaton in *Anna Bolena* on opening night; Flosshilde, a Rhinemaiden in *Götterdämmerung* in January, and then again in the spring in *Das Rheingold* and *Götter-*

dämmerung in three complete *Ring* cycles, for a total of 24 performances. For Ginger Costa-Jackson: the role of Rosette in *Manon* beginning in March, 9 performances, and covering the role of Smeaton. For Erin Morley: the role of Woglinde, another of the Rhinemaidens, in *Götterdämmerung* and *Das Rheingold*, and the Forest Bird in *Siegfried*, 15 performances. For Nicholas Pallesen: covering the role of Lysander in *The Enchanted Island* beginning on New Year's Eve, potentially 10 performances. For Nina Warren: covering the role of Brünnhilde in all of the *Ring* cycle, potentially 14 performances in *Die Walküre*, *Siegfried*, and *Götterdämmerung*. And for Wendy Bryn Harmer: Gutrune in *Götterdämmerung*, Emma in *Khovanshchina* in February, Freia in *Das Rheingold*, and Ortlinde in *Die Walküre*, for a total of 21 performances.

I live five blocks from the opera house. I can figure this out. The performances are scattered throughout the entire season, but in the final weeks when Wagner's *Ring* cycle is underway, one or more of these singers will be performing nearly every night, and two and even three LDS singers will be onstage together. In addition to attending these performances, I plan to catalog the season generally as it is reported in newspapers, magazines, and online websites, and broadcast on TV and in movie theaters. I want to delve into the business side of the Met's operations as well, and follow the ups and downs of the Met's financial stability and the health of its performing artists. I want to understand how an opera performance comes to be.

All of this goes beyond fandom. It is more than a question of the singers' celebrity. I can't put their achievements in perspective without knowing what is at stake. The Met is a multi-million dollar entity, a gigantic machine that is driven by forces as disparate as unions, wealthy patrons, and starving artists. I can't know what it means to be a Mormon singer at the Met—or even a Mormon listening to Mormon singers singing at the Met—unless I examine the contortions of its internal politics, the interactions of its public and private life, and the analysis of its successes and failures, and its coverage in the press. All of these factors intersect in questions of Mormonness and its assimilation and cultural development.

I'm going to have to roll up my pant cuffs and wade through a lot of data. All of it will be filtered by my perceptions of things, but I'm not afraid of subjectivity. I want to learn and report. And I want to react to what I see and hear. How does it feel to be on the audience side of the footlights for an entire season? That's what I want to know. And backstage, what does it take to keep this institution up and running? Does it matter to anybody that there are suddenly this many singers who are LDS at the Met? Maybe it shouldn't matter. It is difficult to put the achievement in context for someone who isn't an opera fan. Imagine having six Mormon painters in exhibitions at the Museum of Modern Art in one year, or six LDS baseball players in the World Series. This is unprecedented.

As I grew up, I knew many musicians, but I never imagined

that I'd meet a professional opera singer who was a Mormon. There's another way to say it: I didn't think it was possible to be a Mormon and sing at the Metropolitan. It was outside of my experience. But here we are in 2011, and there will be many nights of Mormons at the Met. Does it mean anything special to these singers to have fellow Mormons as colleagues? And what does it say to me about my religious culture to have artists of this caliber on display to the world? Does their existence have the potential to affect Mormon culture?

To be honest, I have no idea what I'm getting myself into. I have a feeling that I will come to think of myself a little differently, somehow, by the end of the season. At the very least, it's going to be quite a commitment. The idea comes to mind to estimate how many hours I'll be spending in the Met audience this season and how much money I'll pay for tickets. I decide not to make a tally.

I haven't met all of the LDS singers. Four of the six (Morley, Pallesen, Harmer, and Warren) live or have lived in the boundaries of our Manhattan congregations—Mormons call these units wards. Mumford lives in Connecticut. I don't know where Costa-Jackson is based. It's entirely possible that at the end of the season I will not have met all these vocalists. I know that Wendy Bryn Harmer is originally from Roseville, California. She made her Met debut in *Le nozze di Figaro* in 2005. She has performed at the Met 109 performances since then. She lives in Manhattan, according to her website, "with her husband and dogs." She graduated from The Boston Conservatory and attended apprentice programs in San Francisco, St. Louis and Villecroze, France. She has won a lot of competitions, awards, and grants, including prizes from Teatro alla Scala and The Marilyn Horne Foundation. I have heard her perform maybe a half-dozen roles at the Met. She's also been a soloist with orchestras and other organizations, including the Mormon Tabernacle Choir.

Tamara Mumford is from Sandy, Utah and is a graduate of Utah State University. She made her debut at the Met in 2006 in *Luisa Miller* and has sung 108 performances to date. Again, an impressive bio for a young singer, she's making a name for herself all over the place, both as an opera singer and as a recitalist. Her Carnegie Hall debut took place in 2005. She is active in music festivals, particularly the Marlboro summer festival. I wouldn't call her a new music specialist, exactly, but in addition to the opera roles at the Met, she's actively involved in 20th and 21st century music. Her recordings include a project at Yale with Naxos Records performing the complete songs of Charles Ives, and last summer, she gave the American premiere of Han Werner Henze's *Phaedra* in Philadelphia.

Erin Morley's debut at the Met came a bit later, in 2008, in *Manon Lescaut*. She has sung 38 performances there before the beginning of this season. A Salt Lake City native, she graduated from The Juilliard School and then completed a master's degree from Eastman School of Music. I know Erin because she lived in our congregation for years. I've followed her career, which began with performances at Wolf Trap, Santa Fe Opera, Carnegie Hall (with the Cleveland Orchestra), Chicago Symphony, and the Mormon Tabernacle Choir. Like the other singers, she has been lauded with many prizes and foundation grants.

Ginger Costa-Jackson made her Met debut in the Opening Night Gala of 2008 in *Manon*, and she has sung 37 performances in the house. She was born in Palermo, Italy and grew up in Utah. She has performed with the Utah Festival Opera, Glimmerglass Opera, Gran Teatre del Liceu (Barcelona), and at Carnegie Hall with the Collegiate Chorale. Her website is titled "Opera's Three Soprano Sisters." It features Ginger and her two younger sisters who are students and just beginning their careers: Marina, a lyric soprano who began studies at Utah State University in 2008, and Miriam, a coloratura soprano who, "at age 15 was the youngest singer Director Michael Ballam had ever hired to sing with the Utah Festival Opera."

Nicholas Pallesen lived in our stake as well—there are fourteen wards and branches that comprise a borough-wide unit in Manhattan called a stake—and so we know each other a little bit. He is originally from Riverside, California. He's sung with the New York City Opera, Baltimore Concert Opera, and Shreveport Opera. He's a graduate of the Juilliard Opera Center, and he was an apprentice at Santa Fe Opera and Opera Theatre of St. Louis. All of these singers have very impressive stamps of approval in the forms of awards. Pallesen's website notes his successes, "Mr. Pallesen is a winner of the Giulio Gari, the Sullivan

Foundation, the Opera Index, Shreveport Opera Singer of the Year, the National Federation of Music Clubs Competitions, Bel Canto Foundation, and the Rochester Oratorio Society Classical Idol competitions. He has also won awards from the George London Foundation, the Loren L. Zachary Society, the Liederkranz Foundation, the Gerda Lissner Foundation, the Licia Albanese-Puccini Foundation, the Opera Birmingham Competition, the Santa Fe Opera, and a Richard Gold Career Grant from the Shoshana Foundation, among others." To be honest, I don't know what all of these citations mean. But I notice, as I review the up-and-coming singers in the opera landscape today, they have many of the same affiliations. They are checklists of approval.

Nina Warren's Met debut took place in 1992 in Wagner's *Die Walküre.* At the time, she was living in our ward. At the Met, she sang 25 performances between 1992 and 1994, and then she decamped to Europe where she and her husband and three children lived until recently, when they moved back to her native California. I remember the first time I heard her voice. It was like a trumpet, and that was something of a surprise; she was this petite woman with such an enormous soprano voice. At the time in the early 1990s, she was everywhere, singing Tosca and other starring roles at the New York City Opera, and just beginning to take small roles at the Met. At the beginning of this year, I noticed that she is engaged again at the Met. She will be covering Brünnhilde for the new *Ring* cycle. In the almost ten years she lived in Europe, Nina has tackled all of the big dramatic soprano roles. It's been an extraordinary career.

It is not my goal to hang out in their dressing rooms with these singers and interview them. I don't want to do that kind of reporting. I'm more interested in what a season is like from the audience's point of view, from my point of view. I have written to all of the singers to inform them what I'm planning to write about. They've been supportive of the idea, although if I don't know what I'm likely to find and write about over the next few months, we're essentially in the dark together.

Snagging a ticket to opening night at the Metropolitan Opera isn't as easy as I thought it would be. I learn right away that one of the barriers to enjoying opera is gaining entrance to the opera house in the first place. I can imagine that for many people who are curious about seeing their first opera, the hunting and gathering skills required to get tickets are a significant deterrent. If I were to walk up to the box office an hour before any given performance, the chances that there would be a ticket available would be slim. They same could be said a week before the performance, a month, or even several months.

Tickets at the Met begin to be sold in the spring for the season that will commence the following September. Subscribers get first pick. They choose subscription series in packages of three to seven operas. This year, the Met is mounting 26 operas; seven of them are new productions. For a patron who wishes to catch a performance by a favorite singer or conductor, or who wants to

see a specific opera on a specific date, the best option is to subscribe to a basket of operas rather than risk a "sold out" sign. Individual tickets go on sale about one month before opening night.
By then, subscribers will have had the first shot, and the individual ticket buyer gets the leftovers.

I have never subscribed to the Met, although I've used other
people's subscription seats here and there. The bottom line is that
it's a lot of dough for a subscription. The advertising brochures
tout that subscribing is a value tactic, and they guarantee sav-
ings over single ticket prices. But there's always something on
the full subscription series that isn't really a first choice offering.
People who are really into opera and have amble funds for their
habit commonly subscribe to multiple series, even when they include operas they don't intend to see, in order to catch the performances they want the most. There are subscription packages
for a specific day of the week package—a Monday-night series,
for example, or Saturday matinee series; a package of all seven
new productions; a package of consecutive performances three-
in-a-row, which is great for visitors to the city; and themed packages. Subscribers may also put together a do-it-yourself package
selected from a repertory of favorites. But even this option does
not guarantee the exact night you want.

When you subscribe, you choose an opera rather than an
exact date. Given the way performers move in and out of productions—he sings the first and second performance, leaves for a
while, and comes back for the last one, for example—it's a chal-

lenge to book seats for something that guarantees to be a hot ticket. It's a crapshoot. And then, of course, a subscriber buys a series and the performers cancel, become ill, and so forth. Ticket buying is a gamble.

I'm curious about all of these ticket shenanigans because they seem opaque to me. It's like operagoers have a secret society. Part of my journey during the season is to crack the code of entry. It isn't advertised too heavily, but the Met has a program of sponsorship at the Patron level. For those donating $2,500 a year or more—payable in a lump sum or spread out with four payments, quarterly—individual opera tickets can be purchased beginning in the spring before each season. Other perks of patronage are tickets to attend four dress rehearsals during the year, a subscription to *Opera News* magazine, and entrance into the Belmont Room (which is a private lounge on the Grand Tier level of the house). During intermissions and before the opera begins, patrons can preorder and consume cocktails and light refreshments with other patrons. It's a mini-opera club. Patrons are invited to concerts conducted by James Levine and featuring young Met artists in the Lindemann Artists Development Program. They are invited to Met Talks. These are behind-the-scenes presentations by the management and artists about new productions. Patrons can take backstage tours of the Met, and finally, patrons are assigned ticket service representatives who exchange and secure tickets when last-minute plans play havoc with their schedules. Perk packages are sent out in July to patrons.

This year, by the time the box office opens for the business of individual tickets to the public on August 14th, the majority of seats for the entire season are gone. The first sections of the house to sell out are the extremes: the most expensive and the least expensive. Individual tickets range in price from $25 to $440, unless it is a gala performance. There are four galas this season: opening night's *Anna Bolena*, the New Year's Eve Gala of *The Enchanted Island*, and the premieres of new productions of *Manon*, and *Faust*.

The opera house has six sections. It has a large orchestra (parallel to the stage) and five tiers in semi-circular arcs above the orchestra—from bottom to top: the Parterre, Grand Tier, Dress Circle, Balcony, and finally, the Family Circle. At a regular performance, for $25, one gets a seat on Mondays through Thursdays for the Family Circle sides and rear and the sides of the Balcony below it. At the same performances, a seat in the front of the Balcony is $100. The middle of the Dress Circle is $120, the front row of the Grand Tier is $320, the middle of the Orchestra level is $205, and the most expensive section, the Parterre boxes, is up to $430 for each of the seats.

Each of the Met's six levels is subdivided into additional sections with separate pricing. Friday and Saturday night seats are slightly higher—adding $5 to $10 dollars a seat. And the most expensive time to go to the Met is the Saturday matinee, which cost $5 to $25 more per ticket. Whoever determines the prices must have an elaborate algorithm set up. It feels almost as arbitrary as airline seat purchasing.

Everybody assumes that tickets to the opera are out of reach for the average person, and I wonder if that's true. After I wade through the various levels of pricing, I begin to see that compared to going to a movie, the opera isn't all that rich. At least, for the cheap seats, a night at the opera won't break the bank.

Opening night is another story. It is a gala performance, and the prices reflect the difference. On the ticket stub, the single ticket price is listed on one column and then the "contribution" is next to it. In marketing materials, the Met lists the individual tickets from $85 in the Family Circle to $700 for the sides and mid-to-rear section of the Orchestra. There are also six price levels of the house that are listed as "Please call for Gala ticket pricing." The unadvertised prices are up to $1,400 a seat on opening night. Scalpers may get more than that. On the day of opening night, the Met website lists about 25 seats remaining. If I paid a thousand bucks for an opera ticket, my wife would kill me. I decide to go to plan B.

I arrive at the Met at 7:30 in the morning on the day of the opening night gala. The box office opens at 10:00 AM. In front of the revolving doors, in the corner, an elderly lady sits with a clipboard in her lap. We make eye contact, and she waves for me to come over. She asks my name, writes it down on a simple form that lists name and time of arrival. I am number fifteen to get a standing room ticket. The lady tells me that I can go and get a cup of coffee but that I need to be back at 8:00 AM to line up. This is civilized. I go to a chair under a tree and make a plan on where I want to stand during the performance.

This is my ticket-buying strategy: each person in line for standing room can buy up to two tickets. For opening night, the prices are at a premium. For the orchestra stalls, the price is $40. At the top of the house, behind the Family Circle, tickets are $28. Regularly, a standing room ticket is $22 in the orchestra and $17 upstairs. There are also standing room spaces above the Grand Tier, but these are tickets that performers in the production receive as perks. I've occasionally used these freebies from singer/ friends. The orchestra stalls are on both left and right sides of the house, but they are in several rows, with a considerable overhang of the Parterre above. The stalls have a floor that is slightly raked, which comes in handy if someone in front of you is tall, but it is still difficult to see anything if you're not standing in the front row of the stalls. I calculate for the worst-case scenario. If all fourteen people ahead of me in line take their maximum number of tickets, I will be number 29. I think about these maneuverings and determine that I'm likely to end up on the front line of orchestra section standees. But if for some reason I don't make it, I'd rather stand at the top of the house, inches away from the ceiling, and with great acoustics, than in the cave downstairs. Now, I have two hours to wait. I brought the newspaper, and I can always do the crossword puzzle to kill some time.

There is a monkey wrench in my planning. The box office also sells standing room on the day of performance by phone and online. If the people waiting at the Met are given first shot at tickets, I should be all right; otherwise, it's impossible to know where I might end up, perhaps out of luck altogether. The website also notes that there is an online ordering preference for people who have signed up as Members of the Met, whatever that is. I suspect it's something like the Met's Patron Program, but at a lower contribution level. I figure that, since I live five blocks away from the opera house, and it's 75 degrees and sunny outside, I might as well take my chances in line rather than online.

There has been a big publicity run-up to the season opening. Anna Netrebko's face rides on the tops of taxis throughout the city and peers at people on sidewalks from billboards overhead and wraps around those who use the city's telephone booths. She is glamorously photographed in costumes from *Anna Bolena* and a previous production of *La traviata*. But all the advertisements feature a quizzical line of copy, "At any moment a *Great Moment*." These added capitalizations and italics are as odd as the slogan itself. What does it mean? I can't figure out what it even intends to convey. At any time during a three- or four-hour opera, be ready, because a great moment might jump out and surprise you. Is that it? Or, opera is so great and full of great moments that any one of them is better than what you were planning to do at home.

I'm following the Met closely in order to figure out its various maneuverings, but anybody in town with a newspaper subscription can't avoid the season-opening hype. In *The New York Times*, there are long articles about Netrebko, James Levine, who has recently been ill, Levine's primary replacement Fabio Luisi, and the season itself. The institution of the Met makes opening night newsworthy, which is a challenge because most of the time, however great its moments are, it's just another night at the opera. For journalists, it must be an odd assignment to cover the ramp-up. There is no news. The players are more or less familiar. They have performed these roles before. The production may or may not be new, but these preview articles aren't reviews, so the journalists are left talking to the creative staff about intent. This tactic can backfire because it raises expectations or sends a message that conflicts with a colleague's take on the production.

This year, the pre-opening night article is an interview with Netrebko. It is called, "Diva, Defined," and it's just plain weird. It starts with her complaints that the lights at her dress rehearsal are blinding. The *Times'* Zachary Woolfe tries to equate that anxiety with the critical spotlights that are on the soprano. But the "diva" seems utterly un-anxious about the upcoming performance. Her language is casual, her approach businesslike. In the old sense of a diva, she doesn't strike me as temperamental and capricious; she's just a pro. But Netrebko doesn't do herself any favors in the interview. She says that now that she has a husband and toddler, she is working too hard. The interview quotes her from a couple of years ago, "I can tell you honestly, I'm not that passionate anymore about singing and all this stuff, you know. Once I have a family and a kid, I'm so happy to have a family, and I'm not that enthusiastic anymore."[1] But the article quotes her from two weeks earlier, "I think I'm still doing way too much. Life is not just about singing." I question whether this attitude—which I sort of admire—is doing the box office any favors.

Opening night curtain is at 6:30 PM. The opera is listed as three and a half hours long, including one intermission. I can probably manage to stand for that long if I wear running shoes. According to the opera's website, which is named metoperafamily.com for reasons I can't readily explain, the performance is not sold out, although the Sunday *Times* advertisement the day before opening said it was. The people ahead of me in the standing room buyers line are a mix of youngish students, middle aged, and retirement age. 80 percent are men. I wonder if they know each other. Some are already chatting, as people do in lines like these. The doors going into the opera house are open, and people come and go delivering flowers and packages. At 8:00, the woman with the clipboard calls the standees' names, we line up in order, and we walk into the lobby of the Met. There are only 20 people, so the velvet ropes that keep people in line are less necessary than they might be otherwise. Will more people arrive closer to 10:00? It's as quiet as a library in here. People read, peruse the calendar of upcoming performances, sip coffee. I sit on the floor. Luckily, I'm toward the front of the line, so I can lean against the white marble wall for back support.

The last time I bought standing room tickets was about fifteen years ago. My wife worked at the Metropolitan Opera House after we first married. She was a waiter at the Grand Tier Restaurant at night and taught English at a private high school during the day. We lived in Brooklyn back then, and on Saturday mornings, we would wake up before 5:00 AM, cook a casserole lunch and put it in a thermos jar, board the F train, and ride into Manhattan. We would arrive at the opera house at 6:30 or so, get our names on the list, and then go off somewhere warm until we had to be back, about 8:30, to line up. On those often freezing mornings in the dark, we would walk towards McDonalds, pick up a newspaper along the way—hopefully find a newsstand selling the sections of the Sunday edition that subscribers receive on Saturdays—buy one Egg McMuffin to share, read the paper, and talk. That was our weekly routine. In those days, the Met sold standing room tickets for the entire week on Saturday mornings. There were hundreds of people in line to buy them, and anyone arriving past 8:00 or so risked disappointment. People could buy two tickets per person for any opera playing that week. They could see as many operas as they could stand, so to speak.

We attended the opera together on nights Marcia didn't have to work and when I didn't have classes, and sometimes I went alone when she was at the restaurant, and we'd meet up afterwards. Our pattern of operagoing continued for ten years or so. In that decade starting 1986, we saw, more or less, everything of importance that happened in opera in New York, and a lot happened—old works, premieres, young singers and old, debuts and farewells too. Even after we moved into Manhattan from Brooklyn, close to Lincoln Center, as luck would have it, we went to the opera often, sometimes once or twice a week. Since a standing room ticket cost less than a movie ticket in those days, it seemed to us an excellent use of our entertainment budget. The lady who managed the standing room operation at the Met—her name was Helen—lived in our building. She was a crusty, acerbic tyrant. Anyone trying to sneak ahead in line never attempted it twice.

Our habit of going to the opera via standing room ended when our first child was born. Afterwards, money and time were spent elsewhere, except when friends were performing or something unmissable was staged. I found it harder and harder to justify going to *Tosca* for what, the tenth time? Or *La bohème*, again? But in our last burst of standing, we were rewarded. At least, Marcia was. When she was pregnant, ticket holders always gave her their seat if they left early or let her have their extra tickets if a guest didn't show up. I think she started to get used to great seats, and by then I had a boss with a subscription of orchestra seats that she never used. We became jaded and spoiled, and that made the ordeal of standing room tickets less fun in comparison.

Tonight, I am going to opening night alone. We have teenagers now, and they have to get homework done. My wife has a work event, so I'm on my own. By 9:30, a few more buyers have arrived. Theres's a total of 30. Not very impressive, really. We once stood in line for opening night tickets for *Otello* starring Placido Domingo, Renee Fleming, and James Morris. There were about 400 people waiting, half of whom had no realistic chance of getting in. When we got up to the box office window, we realized that the ticket price was more expensive than we had planned, since it was a gala performance. We didn't have enough money. Only one of us could go. Both of us wanted to see it although we'd seen the same production three times already and so we walked away and left the ticket for someone else to buy.

A video loop of opera highlights previewing the season plays on lobby monitors. The audio behind it is a Queen of the Night aria from *The Magic Flute*. When I note that *Magic Flute* isn't in the repertory this season, it strikes me that it's the kind of detail only an opera nut would care about. It's like the Yankees advertising their season by showing clips of MVP Hideki Matsui, whom the team traded within a few days after giving him the MVP award.

Am I an opera nerd? I'm not sure exactly what that means. I do know that I've been exposed to a lot of opera throughout my life and that I like it. At the same time, I'm aware that years can go by without seeing any opera at all and I don't miss it. The strange thing about this experiment of opera rebaptism is an awareness that there is a built-in silliness to the endeavor, and yet I find myself feeling nostalgic for opera. I'm surprised to note how many significant memories in my life have opera-connected associations.

The lobby has changed a little since I last hung out here. There used to be two banks of box office windows on the north and south ends of the building. The south end was used for the ballet in the spring and summer, but it hadn't really been used for a long time. It's now an art gallery space dedicated to leading contemporary artists who are invited to create work inspired by the operas of the Met season.

Tour groups walk through the lobby, two dozen people in each, with cameras around their necks and wrists. Both of these groups are German-speaking. They can't go into the house itself, so they stand at the foot of the grand staircase, shooting pictures through the metal gate of large, overlapping circles. They stare at us, sprawled out over the floor and leaning against the marble walls incised with donors' names.

The plaza is set up for a simultaneous broadcast. Thousands of brushed silver and orange metal stacking chairs sit in banks facing the house—no folding chairs at the Met, thank you very much. An enormous screen approximately 25x40 feet is mounted to the center columns of the house, with a pair of tall speakers on each side in front of two stories of glass and the balcony that is normally open at intermissions for patrons to go outside. A high-resolution projector has been placed at the top of a scaffold that covers the Lincoln Center fountain. For now, it is under heavy tarps. The seats are arranged precisely in rows, three banks of 20, 30, and 20 seats with two aisles. There are 32 rows, then the fountain and projector, and 24 more rows behind. If my math is right, there are 3,920 seats outside. That's 100 more than inside the Met. They were set up on Saturday. Tickets were distributed free on Sunday, but they are required; theoretically, you can't just walk in and take a seat tonight. The opening night broadcast will also be shown live in Times Square, on two jumbo screens. Hundreds more will sit there, first come, first served. There is also standing room in Times Square, according to the Met. I think we call them sidewalks. I thought about going to the opera outside. But the early curtain means that the sun would be in my eyes, or worse, there might not be sun. The forecast is for thunderstorms.

During the previous weeks, Lincoln Center hosted fashion week, or rather, Mercedes Benz Fashion Week. An enormous tent was set up to the immediate south of the Met. Parts of the white tent are being taken down now; meanwhile, a strip of red carpet and a white tent leading into the south entrance of the opera house are being put in place.

I discover that Lincoln Center has free Wi-Fi. I check to see the stock market opening, and it's up a little, enough to pay for today's ticket. 10 more ticket buyers arrive. Now there are 40 of us. Sometimes there is an air of competition in standing room lines, some jostling with an anxiety that there may not be enough tickets for everyone. It can turn primal, which sounds odd, but it's true—*The Lord of the Flies*, the opera version. Today though, there's none of that. There will be food for all.

Anna Bolena is the first of seven new productions this season. It is billed as a Metropolitan Opera premiere, which means that the 181-year old opera by Gaetano Donizetti, more famous for *Lucia di Lammermoor*, *The Daughter of the Regiment*, and *The*

Elixir of Love, has never been staged here before. Of the seven new productions, three of them are to be conducted by Levine. He has officially pulled out of the *Don Giovanni* that starts October 13. He's still listed as the conductor for Wagner, but a lot could go wrong. Vegas odd-makers could make a bundle placing bets on that.

At ten to 10:00, we stand up and get in place before heading to the box office windows. Those who went to sit in more comfortable places elsewhere in the lobby come and squeeze back into spaces they were assigned. At the front of the line, a little white shopping bag is looped over the metal barrier. The word "donations" is written in capital letters in black marker. At ten, another clump of people arrive and ask if this is the line for "standup tickets." Years ago in the Pavarotti-Domingo days, lines for standing room routinely started forming at 5:30 AM every week that they performed. By 10:00, the line was over three hundred people long. I wonder if a singer today has that kind of star power at the box office. Two windows open at precisely 10:00. The line moves quickly. I drop a little money into the tip bag. I ask the box office man for one standing room ticket in the orchestra. I pay my $40. It's 10:05, and I'm done. Tonight I am number 29.

I haven't heard *Anna Bolena* before. I haven't seen a live production or a video, and I don't own a recording, not of the full opera, or, I think, even an excerpt. The sensation of this opera ignorance is embarrassing to me, just a little bit, although I can't count the number of times over the years that people have sat down next to me at the Met and said to their companion, "So, what are we seeing tonight?"

I do a bit of homework. Online, there are multiple scenes from the opera and the full libretto and score. I go to YouTube and watch the *Anna Bolena* mad scene, "Coppia iniqua" (Wicked couple) sung by Maria Callas first, then Joan Sutherland, then Beverly Sills. I stumble across a compilation video of a dozen singers performing the aria. The performances span a period of about 50 years. What an odd range of ability! The video's purpose is to show that some sopranos sang the score as written, and others interpolated a high D at the end instead. It's painful when singers almost hit high notes. It's something like an Olympic weightlifter who can clean and jerk the record weight above his head but quickly realizes that he can't hold it there long enough for it to matter. The dueling Annas likewise struggle, and most crash and burn, frankly.

Of the lot, Sutherland sounds incredible to me. The clarity and richness of her singing is like the creaminess of the world's best gelato. As the high note approaches, her body language is utterly relaxed, as if to say, *Are you kidding? I could sing this and eat a meatball sub sandwich at the same time.* She is a champion powerlifter, to be sure. In another video, Callas acts the heck out of the aria. Had I been in the front row during the 1957 performance on screen, I'd have been scared of flying daggers. But my favorite of the video clips is Sills, who really acts up a storm. Regal, unhinged, betrayed, shocked—it's all in her voice, and it's simply extraordinary—so bright and supple. When she gets to the end, she blasts the high D over the orchestra, and for all I know, through the back wall and into the next county.

I make the mistake of clicking on a YouTube video of Anna Netrebko's "Coppia iniqua". It's puzzling and deflating. I suddenly feel ticket-buyer's remorse. It was a novice's mistake to click the play button. It's definitely a disservice to listen to the other sopranos and then jump to Netrebko. There's a tentative quality to the singing. When she gets to low notes, it's like she's hiding out. But they're clear. The high notes, when she has to sing full voice to carry over the orchestra, sound strained and not particularly pretty. On the other hand, the video comes from her first performance of *Anna Bolena* and that was only five months ago at the Vienna State Opera. I'll give her a chance.

Netrebko is known for her sex appeal. She's beautiful and photogenic. The Met is committed to her career, and the General Manager, Peter Gelb, has said that she is opera's future. There's a lot riding on her performance as Anna. Recently, she's been inching her way into the bel canto repertoire. This music is technically tough. You can't fake trills, arpeggios and all those exposed high notes. Whether she can pull it off is a big question mark. The criticism of her performance in Vienna, which was also recorded and broadcast throughout Europe, was that she was much stronger than everyone else around her. Reviews said that nobody else was acting.

The press leading up to the opening night appears to be straight from Netrebko's publicist. It's all about her personality. It doesn't get any more revealing than a confession that she likes *The Tudors,* the hyper-sexy, royal family TV soap opera. Articles also discuss the production which features costumes and sets based on Holbein paintings. This strikes me as being a nice choice, given that Holbein was a painter at Henry VIII's court. The director said he wanted a production that changed scenes without the curtain coming down. I'm expecting something fluid and cinematic.

My main concern, however, is Netrebko's voice. Operagoers are likely to carry more baggage with them into the theater than other types of spectators. Sure, a baseball fan has memories of a perfect triple play, a grand slam, or a clutch strike-out, but I don't think that baseball fans judge current players by historic standards in the same way opera fans do. Opera fans carry iTunes folders brimming with the greatest moments ever. Many of these sonic memories were generated by studio recordings that are manipulated and scrubbed to implausible levels of clarity and precision. What live performance can match that? You can't splice a high note into a live performance, after all.

Theoretically, an opera nut could listen to tonight's Netrebko with one ear and have Callas piped into the other through ear buds. Why anybody would do that is beyond me, but it's the kind of problem that probably drives singers crazy with anxiety. If all the great operas have been recorded and taped and are perpetually available on mobile devices, why bother staging productions? The answer is because the operas are more than a mere sonic playback or an athletic pursuit. Something happens in performance that can't be easily described. It's about the music, but at a certain point in a terrific performance—the Met would call it a "great moment"—the effect is almost outside of music.

That's the feeling that keeps me connected to opera, and more specifically, to live performance. I pity the people who haven't seen dance, theater and opera live. Video broadcasts are mere proxies. I have friends who are hockey fans. They say roughly the same thing. The camera just doesn't get it.

Opera video technicians consider the audience to be noise, and they do their best to eliminate it. Videos can't capture the sensation of being in a theater seat and having people around you react to what is happening. Baseball on TV, actually, is much better at including the fans in a broadcast than the performing arts are. In a stadium broadcast, you hear fans and see them constantly. In an opera, an audience holds its breath together, cries together, laughs, mocks, and groans together. It is a cumulative power of thousands of spontaneous reactions of people, more immediate than Twitter. But those sensations are recorded rarely. Aside from the limitations of the technology to capture the full experience in audio and video, recordings completely fail to document the sensation of the audience's participation in what is happening onstage. It fails to record rapture. The audience is relegated to darkness. Participation is what the audience adds; this and much more, and a camera focused on the stage misses it. The performers can feel it, but the cameras don't. It misses the emotion and only accounts for the trigger of the emotion.

With about an hour to go before the curtain rises, I stand at home in front of my meager selection of suits in the closet and try to decide what to wear. There will be tuxedos tonight. There will also be blue jeans. Down in the orchestra section though, everyone will be dressed up, so I go with a black silk and linen Nehru jacket, Japanese crinkled grey shirt, black slacks and... sneakers. I'm a bit embarrassed about the shoes, but I give myself permission to be comfortable.

The only other opening night I've attended was at the Chicago Lyric Opera, and there the patrons seemed to put on every expensive piece of jewelry they owned, a bling-a-thon as vast as the open prairie. I faintly remember going to the inaugural season of the Utah Opera Company as a teenager. I somehow convinced my music teacher to rent a yellow school bus and drive six hundred miles with me and her choir of high school students. The performance was *Otello,* and the tenor Glade Peterson mostly got through the performance whole. He was wearing dark makeup, obviously, to look like a Moor, but in a moment of spontaneity, he ripped open his shirt to bare his chest. Unfortunately, he had forgotten to put makeup on his chest. Ah, tenors.

By the time I arrive at the Met, the red carpet parade has ended. It's just as well. New York doesn't really know how to do them very convincingly. It's a Hollywood thing. At the Met, the celebrities are hedge fund managers, society matrons, and artists—none of whom is particularly lens-friendly—and few of them are recognizable to the public. It disintegrates quickly to a fashion show of old people. Nothing wrong with that, of course, but it ain't the Oscars. People are starting to take their seats, both inside the theater and in the plaza. The chairs outside are sparsely filled. This is disappointing. Two entire sections of stacking chairs have been removed to avoid further embarrassment.

Earlier in the day, I checked online to see what tickets remained. There were still about 20 left, mostly in the orchestra. The most expensive, $1,400 seats, were gone. As I enter and find my place, I don't see any empty seats at all. I look out over the crowd and see a few famous faces. Martha Stewart is a few rows ahead of me. She is really lovely in person, regal almost. There's Barbara Walters strolling down the aisle.

As everyone finds their seat, I look around and see high definition video cameras. There are two at the back of the orchestra section, in the center. They are large and mounted on stands. I feel sorry for the people whose views are blocked by them. Additional cameras are visible at the very front of the house, on both sides, and in the orchestra pit. I assume there are also cameras in the levels above me that I can't see. The front cameras are smaller, particularly the one inches away from where the conductor will stand. I suppose we're not supposed to be distracted by such things, but it is a bit bothersome, like an odd anachronism thrust into proceedings at the king's court. In October, the

Met's HD network will kick off a season of video transmissions with over 50 countries watching *Anna Bolena* in movie theaters. We are not yet to the point where the opera is being performed for the camera alone, but we're inching closer to it.

We peruse our programs. There's a booklet insert for opening night. It recognizes the Opening Night Gala Committee—a shout out to Mercedes and Sid Bass, whose generous gift made the production possible, to The Agnes Varis Trust for the fall ad campaign, Deutsche Bank for underwriting the gala (for the 11th consecutive season, it notes), Manhattan Jaguar for additional funding, and Bloomberg (the corporation, not the mayor, necessarily) for the dough to transmit the broadcast to the plaza and to Times Square. The insert lists the gala committee, and it reads like a who's who of New York money: individuals, families, couples of men and women and men and men, foundations, corporations, and a few listed as "anonymous." I smile reading the divisions of donations into chairman, co-chairman, corporate chairman, corporate vice chairman, vice chairmen, principal benefactors, benefactors, principal sponsors, prime sponsors, sponsors, and committee members. I am a mere ticket buyer, and I don't even have a seat. On the totem pole of social importance tonight, I know exactly where I stand.

I examine the opera program, pausing at the striking cover photo featuring Netrebko with hands poised in front of her lips in coy supplication, Two acts with one intermission. That's good. The program even predicts the time of intermission: 8:00 PM.

It's time to review the synopsis. I'm aware that the stories of operas strike many people as implausible, laughable, and lame. Friends of mine who read lots of novels, see all the Oscar-nominated movies, and attend plenty of theater can hardly get past the clunkiness of opera plots. I think of it differently. Opera stories unfurl in slow motion. Anything sung takes more time than it would if it were spoken. (I could tell the tale covered in the "Star Spangled Banner" in ten seconds, for example.) But music has its own timetable. What it lacks in brevity it makes up for in richness.

There are consequences for the (lack of) narrative speed of opera. The plots have to compensate for it, and this they do by embracing symbol and metaphor. Hamlet's "To be or not to be" soliloquy might take 15 minutes if it were sung instead of spoken. In a three-hour opera, that would be a problem. Instead, opera characters have to become archetypes, plots turn into fables and settings into symbols. Music makes up for the rest.

I am the kind of person who is receptive to storytelling. As a Christian student of scripture, for example, I am drawn to what people do and say more than any compilation of shoulds. A good parable is worth more to me than a good commandment, I'd say. Part of my curiosity about opera is the way it reflects how I respond to stories. I think of opera plots as fables. And just as I have given up trying to rationalize the quirkiness of some of Jesus's parables, I take the stories of operas, however unrealistic, as a way to explore what we humans are.

I review of the story of *Anna Bolena*. Fortunately, it's not too convulted. The opera's action takes place in 1536 in the court of Henry VIII. The king, finally rid of Catherine of Aragon, his first wife, has married Anne Boleyn and crowned her queen. The rumors at court are that Henry has fallen in love with another woman since, after three years, Anne has been unable to produce a male heir. Jane Seymour is Anne's lady-in-waiting, and she confides to her that she is troubled. Anne asks her young page Mark Smeaton to sing a song to cheer them up. Later, the king professes his love to Jane and promises to make her his new queen. This is known, in opera, as karma.

Meanwhile, Anne's brother Lord Rochefort meets Richard Percy, who was Anne's lover years ago and has been in exile. The king has pardoned him, Percy thinks, because of Anne's intervention. Wrong; it's a trap. Smeaton, who is secretly in love with the queen, steals her portrait in a locket as a memento. Next, Percy meets Anne privately to say he still loves her while Smeaton hides in the room. Anne warns Percy of danger, and he draws his sword. This causes Smeaton to emerge with his sword drawn too, and then Rochefort enters to say that the king is coming. All four are caught. Smeaton's stolen locket gives the king all the evidence he needs to arrest them all. (The logic is thin here, but there you have Act I.)

In the second act, Anne is under house arrest. Jane urges Anne to confess to infidelity so the king can divorce her. Anne refuses and curses the other woman. Jane admits that it is she.

Anne forgives Jane and blames Henry. Under torture, Smeaton falsely testifies that he has been Anne's lover, thinking it will save her life. (This makes little sense, but moving along....) Anne tells the king she's ready to die. Percy jumps in and claims that he and Anne were married before she married the king. (Again, not a persuasive legal argument.) Jane pleads for Anne's life. Anne and the men are sentenced to death. In the final scene, Anne recalls happier days and drifts in and out, mentally. Smeaton acknowledges that he caused Anne's troubles, and Anne embraces her brother and Percy. They hear the royal cannons that signal Henry has married Jane Seymour. Anne comes out of her delirium (sings quite a lot, presumably), and then she goes off to her execution.

The lights begin to dim but just a bit. There is a drum roll and "The Star Spangled Banner" begins. The audience isn't singing very loudly. Maybe they're intimidated by the setting. There are critics in the house, after all. By the time we arrive at "the rocket's red glare", momentum is building in our participation, and the volume increases steadily. The man standing next to me, at about six foot six, has a big, deep voice. He's an opera guy for sure.

I wonder if some show-offs in the crowd will try to scoop up to a high note when they get to the "land of the free-eee", but the conductor is not in an indulgent mood. There's no fermata. A few sopranos try to get up high only to discover that the rest of us have moved on to "the home of the brave." We applaud ourselves, the Swarovski chandeliers rise up to the ceiling, the house lights dim except for the blue glow around all of the video cameras, and the curtain rises.

Holy cow! That's a beautiful set. It's an interior room of the castle. The design approach is realistic. Natural, hand-crafted materials predominate—wood, stone, glass—and detailed, wood paneled walls rise up majestically, and somewhat oppressively to the ceiling. There is a bank of windows on stage right, and the light coming through them is absolutely Vermeerian. Dozens of women appear in richly draped costumes, dark, austere, with white silken touches above the bodice. Funky little hat-helmets. On the floor, there are some large pillows and Persian rugs. When Anne enters, there is applause. That's weird. Usually audiences don't like to break the music with clapping like that. I know that Netrebko is opera's it-girl of the moment, but it feels a tiny bit vulgar to me.

Still, she looks incredible. Costume designers must love making clothes for extravagant royal characters. Bolena's costume is like the other women at court, only richer and sexier. Her plunging neckline scoops very low and very wide. And by "very," I mean *very*. Pearls are draped and sewn all about. Netrebko is lovely. The audience has perked up. The man standing next to me holds his breath as she sings her opening notes. My first thought is that if she can sing even half of the score, the audience is going to fall at her feet.

But I am here to see Tamara Mumford. She is performing the role of Mark Smeaton. In opera-land, we call it a pants role when women, usually mezzo-sopranos, portray male characters. The reverse doesn't really happen, men playing women's roles, unless it's a comic, drag thing, although countertenors sound like women because they sing in falsetto voice, so there's that. The problem with a pants role is the question of believability. Usually the characters are young, passionate men. When the woman singing a role like this looks boyish enough, then the audience just goes with it. My experience in the past with pants roles has been uniformly positive.

Audiences new to opera probably wonder why the roles were written for women in the first place. It's not a gender issue; it's about a fullness of sound. When multiple characters sing together the high voices of the soprano and tenor, and the low voices of the baritones and basses are missing a richness in the middle. As tenors get higher, they lose that fullness, and a woman singing in midrange offers much-needed power and balance.

Smeaton enters in white tunic, light grey tights and shirt. It's a stark contrast to everyone else on stage in their dark velvets. He has a sword at his waist. His dark hair is cropped short. I'm buying it. In the first scene of the opera, Bolena is troubled and asks Smeaton to sing a song to cheer her up. I love moments in opera like this when characters are called upon to read poetry or letters, to sing a song, or to pray. It gives the composer a break from the narrative drive in order to create a concert-within-an-opera. These opportunities are little self-contained song recitals. There's a purity to them, a chance to be all about the music. Within seconds of Mumford opening her mouth, I'm assured that she's going to rock it. Her aria, "Deh! non voler costringere a finta gioia il viso" (When your spirit sighs with grief, never pretend to smile) is a reminiscence of better days. She is holding a lute and she plays as she sings (although the accompaniment in the orchestra is a harp). It's a lovely tune, and Mumford's voice is strong, agile, florid. She dashes off some very cool ornamental flourishes. This is brilliant, assured singing. She is the real deal.

Unfortunately, the director of the opera has decided that during the second half of the aria, a couple of court dancers should also perform for the queen. This reduces Mumford's performance to background music. The choice undermines the psychological importance of the song—it's a harbinger of what's to come and it connects the queen to her past. Smeaton isn't a starring role, but much of the action hinges on him, and the dancing diminishes the audience's involvement in his story. The director's upstaging decision is distracting and disappointing because he doesn't trust the singers and the score of the opera enough to leave it alone. The end of the aria is abrupt; the queen interrupts Smeaton, and the plot continues.

We are introduced to Jane Seymour and King Henry VIII. I'm particularly impressed with the king, who gives off a Mephistophelian vibe. He's a bass, and sometimes low male voices have a hard time being both loud enough to carry in an opera house and agile enough to sing this style of music. The singer's name is Ildar Abdrazakov. He's also tall, thin, and strong. Impressive. Kingly. I'm also liking the set changes in the middle of scenes. Walls glide to shrink or expand the spaces. It's elegantly done, and it keeps the tension going in the opera. In performances of operas, whenever the curtain drops down or the lights go to black for a set change, my interest wavers. But this is a very smoothly accomplished trick. For the next scene, the setting changes from interior to exterior. Again, the shift is deftly handled.

It's almost like the Met is showing off. These folks have stage-craft machinations down pat. The physical stage facilities in this house are incredible. If a designer and director choose to have the entire stage rise or lower or spin or tilt in full audience view, no problem. The full breadth of the stage has a hydraulic base. Entire sets can be preplaced below, to the right, left, or behind the stage, and they can be whisked into position. The Met used to have a Franco Zeffirelli production of *Tosca* that I saw a few times. At the end of the opera, as the tenor goes from his lonely jail cell and climbs the stairs to the rooftop, the set gradually lowered to reveal an entire rooftop with parapets from which Tosca jumped. The tenor climbed the stairs, essentially staying in place at center stage. Unfortunately, Luciano Pavarotti, as he got older, had bad knees, and he couldn't climb the stairs anymore. So he just walked offstage as the prison disappeared and then magically reappeared to get shot.

I think of such production excesses in *Anna Bolena*'s second scene, when the king's hunting party arrives outside the castle. The stage is full of men and weaponry. Then, two enormous Irish wolfhounds are led onstage in a grand arc toward the orchestra. I feel like the audience wants to applaud for their entrance too, but they show restraint. And just as suddenly, the dogs are led off. Did the Met just hire exotic dogs the size of ponies for a one-minute appearance? Of course they did. It's the Met. (Surely, there is a director somewhere planning for a production of *Aida* and wondering how they can get African elephants through the Met's stage door.)

A more rewarding surprise is the singing of tenor Stephen Costello in the role of Lord Richard Percy (Anne's former lover). He is awesome. I think to myself, *who is this guy?* Tenor roles in Donizetti operas are very high and very exposed. There's no place to hide. Tenors with high voices tend to have light voices. If they are called upon to sing repertoire like this with all its ornamentation, it's rare to find someone who can hit the notes and sound big enough to fill a hall like the Met. Costello really impresses me.

The dogs come back, center stage, just behind the queen. The scene ends with a glorious quintet. This is wonderful music. Many people know the sextet from *Lucia*, but I'm enjoying this even more. It's more rhythmically complex and it breathes like winds in a sail. One voice will be prominent and then another blossoms over it, and then another, passing the melody back and forth across the stage. Essentially, the plot has stopped. The main

Anna Bolena

characters are simply repeating what they've already declared, and so this is all about the music. And it is beautiful. One of the dogs disagrees. It doesn't howl, thank goodness, but it plops down on its side, during the climax of the quintet. It is directly behind Netrebko. That's what we call upstaging.

The third scene of the first act has many entanglements, betrayals, accusations and arrests. I'm eager to hear Smeaton's second aria as he steals the queen's locket and reveals his love for her. To my mind, Mumford's performance of it is a little tentative. Perfectly acceptable, but shy of amazing. There are some high notes at the end that come off a bit dry. The audience does not applaud at the end of it.

And what about Netrebko's singing? This is certainly a production built around her, and the conductor, Marco Armiliato, is very supportive. When she sings anything softly, the orchestra pulls way back, to almost nothing. That's a tough thing for an orchestra to do without being anemic, and I admire the sound of it. She is always heard. Netrebko has a spectacular vocal trick, particularly when she is singing something wistfully or longingly— she jumps up to the ultra high note, pianissimo. It floats out over the audience like a spritz of perfume, and the effect is terrific. Time feels suspended, like those slow motion movie shots of particles in air gently spinning. To the audience's ears, it is as if this fragile high note is a miracle that couldn't happen and may never happen again. People around me whisper, under their breath, "Wow."

As beautiful as these high notes are, I'm equally impressed with her lower notes. This role is punishing. The exuberant arias ask the soprano to be all over the place, and in other recordings I've heard the low notes are sacrificed for the glamour of the showier high notes. Netrebko, instead, gives those rich, chesty, earthy sounds full value and weight. In turn, they make the high notes seem even more incredible. And, by the way, she's acting this role to pieces, so far. It's nuanced, detailed, dramatic, expressive. It doesn't feel clichéd to me. She's regal and vulnerable both. Good for her. And I mentioned that she's beautiful, didn't I?

There's a downside in her performance, however, and it's major. When Netrebko is called upon to sing big, loud, and high, the sound can turn scary rather quickly. I'm surprised how much power she has in her voice, actually. It's a big instrument, and even more unexpected because of the ethereal quality of the high, pianissimo singing. When the drama builds and the orchestra gets loud, she can carry over the top of it all. She isn't straining either. If it gets too high, though, pitch goes awry and the beauty of the voice disappears. To be fair, only a handful of sopranos have ever been able to pull this off, let alone be heard over a huge orchestra in a cavernous theater like the Met. At the end of the first act, just as the king has condemned her, everything builds in a crescendo of power with a sextet and a five-part chorus underneath. Finally, Bolena wails over it all, resigned to her fate, "Assoluta appien saro!" (I will be absolved one day). Netrebko goes for the D natural above high C (although the score calls for the D an octave lower). The score also has all voices cutting off together, but Netrebko performs it as everybody else does in recordings I've heard, by holding out the last note a few extra measures, alone. The note itself is loud and long. Tonight, sadly, it's also flat and painful. It's not secure. She struggles to hold it like a trooper, and she sustains it until the cutoff, which feels to me like watching a train wreck. The note isn't ugly, exactly, but had it been as wonderful as the rest of her singing and acting have been, the audience would have ripped up their programs into confetti and tossed them over the balconies in celebration. Up until her last note, the singing had been that good.

And she has a mannerism that I find funny. Right before a final high note of an aria or an ensemble—and Donizetti telegraphs that these climaxes are coming a mile away—Netrebko turns her back to the audience, takes a huge breath, waits, and then whips back front just in time to deliver the big note. Think of Maria and the opening shot in *The Sound of Music*; the camera zooms in, Julie Andrews twirls and lets it fly, "The hills are alive...." Well, this is like that. It is a cool effect the first time Netrebko does it in Act I. It feels like she is spontaneous and completely in the moment. Oddly, it happens every time there's a high, loud, dramatic note. What is she doing as she faces upstage, anyway? Is she peeking at the last word of each aria, scribbled on her palm?

At intermission I find a place to sit down, I make a few notes in my program, and then I wander around looking at people.

Parading up and down the helix of a staircase are bejeweled women and slightly bored-looking men. A man in a tank top and jeans is waiting at the elevator and looks terribly out of place. There is a tall woman whose dress is backless, nearly backside-less, and she is wearing bigger diamonds that I've ever seen outside a Smithsonian jewel exhibition. I hardly know where to look. Rattled, I turn to go another way. On the lower level, opposite the bar, is a long wall completely covered with black and white headshots. It is a photographic history of Met singers. Waves of memories and sounds come back to me as I look at these pictures. I've spent so many hours in this building. Many of the faces conjure a specific reminiscence. I crane my head to see Ariel Bybee, the most renowned of the LDS singers at the Met. The photographs are arranged in alphabetical order. Ariel is between Henry Butler and Monserrat Caballe.

When the lobby chimes ring, ticketholders meander back to their seats. I make conversation with the people standing around me. The woman at my right lives in the neighborhood. Her friend asked her to get standing room tickets for the two of them. She confesses that she doesn't like opera all that much and prefers to watch it on the "big screen" outside in the plaza. When I ask her why, she says that the sound is much better through the broadcast speakers. I don't know how to respond to that. A battle brews between the ushers and a male standee who tries to get out of the stalls to find an empty seat down front—so not gonna happen! The lights dim, everyone settles down, and Act II begins.

This production of *Anna Bolena* is directed by David McVicar, a forty-five year old Scottish opera and theater man with many, many productions under his belt. In 2009, he directed Verdi's *Il Trovatore* at the Met, that was deemed a success if for no other reason than it broke a curse of terrible productions of that opera. The Met's previous two stagings were laughably bad and universally detested. McVicar's 2009 production was simply a transplanted design he had done in Chicago, but it swept the old productions out. I happened to see the worst Met *Trovatore*, in 1987. The entire set was made of gleaming black stairs, rows and rows of them. And they were loud stairs that echoed the clanks and clangs of every foot of the hundreds of singers onstage. Audiences hated it.

Opera audiences don't merely like or dislike things; they love or hate. My performance featured Pavarotti (love) and a new mezzo-soprano from Nevada named Dolora Zajick, who absolutely raised the roof (love). The Met tried to soften the production later (hate), but you can't cover mirrored black stairs very easily. Carpet? What these had to do with gypsies and the switched-at-birth plot of *Il Trovatore* was never clear to me in the first place, but on the other hand, Verdi's story was never clear to me either.

McVicar's *Anna Bolena* is the first of three new Donizetti opera productions to be unveiled in successive seasons. They will form a trilogy of "Tudor operas," *Anna Bolena, Maria Stuarda,* and *Roberto Devereux*. Ticket buyers love trilogies. Donizetti himself probably wouldn't like the idea of a Tudor trilogy, particularly since there's another Donizetti opera, *Il castello di Kenilworth* about Queen Elizabeth. I don't know it. But with Donizetti, I cut myself some slack. He wrote about 75 operas, depending on how you tally revisions and tweaking of earlier operas, sketches, and incomplete and lost works.

Gaetano Donizetti was born in Italy, in 1797, and into poverty. His family wasn't musical—his father ran the local pawnshop—but young Gaetano was a scholarship choirboy, and that led to musical studies and finally to composition. He had written over thirty operas before he composed *Anna Bolena* in 1830. It became his first international success, and it made him famous. Over the next ten years he wrote a succession of works that remain in the operatic repertoire today in varying degrees: *L'elisir d'amore* (1832), *Lucrezia Borgia* (1833), *Lucia di Lammermoor* (1835), *Maria Stuarda* (1835), *Roberto Devereux* (1837), *Poliuto* (1838), *Le fille du régiment* (1840), and *La favorite* (1840). During that decade, he also wrote twenty-one other operas that nobody today has ever heard of.

I'm aware that scholars are dismissive of Donizetti and consider him lightweight—boy meets girl, boy loses girl, girl feels betrayed, goes mad, and stabs somebody—but I think all of the madness is a wonderful dramatic invention. It presents so many sonic possibilities. What's more, I can't help think, when I'm listening to a Donizetti soprano losing her marbles, of Donizetti's own sad end. All three of his children die, his wife dies of cholera within a year of his parent's deaths, and he is institutionalized. He wastes away, insane, and dies in 1848 at the age of 51. I am 51.

To say that the second act is all downhill is merely to go along with the plot of the opera. It is regret piled upon regret—lost loves, betrayals, corruption, seductions, lies, misguided sacrifices. Anne acknowledges repeatedly that her sin was to seek the crown. It is all familiar territory. To my mind, this sinking sensation of inevitability is also the problem of the opera, its music, this production, and my reaction to it. The newness of the first act starts to wear away. The sets that felt noble originally begin to look cheap and flat the more closely I look at them. The mannerisms of the singers wear thin, and their vocal weaknesses appear. Ears start to take even great singing for granted. I find the repetitive vamping of the orchestra, a sort of Italianate, 4/4 oomp-pah-pah-pah, wearisome, even grating. I feel guilty about that reaction, and I know it's laziness on my part, but compared to the psychological dramas that will appear 100 years after Donizetti, this feels shallow.

The drama of *Anna Bolena* grows more dire but not more interesting. Is it a crisis of fate or of creative lethargy? Act II plays out more or less as Anne predicted it would at the end of Act I. The only surprise occurs when Anne falls into a trance of madness. Smeaton confesses that he has lied to the king, which only gives the ruler more ammunition to destroy them. Anne then asks Smeaton why he isn't playing his harp anymore. She wonders if someone has cut the harp's strings. She has lost her mind. And here, finally, is some glorious imagination to go with beautiful music.

Netrebko is astonishing. The stage is covered (littered, even) with characters and chorus. They are squeezed onto the front edge of the stage, practically tipping over into the orchestra pit. Bolena is oblivious to them all as she wanders about and sings of harp strings and the broken strings of her heart. As a performer, Netrebko is expressive, volatile, and, when she floats those insanely high notes out of nothing, mesmerizing. Wow, this woman is an extraordinary singer and actor. It's a privilege to have been able to see this performance.

A cannon sounds, signaling the marriage of the king and Jane Seymour, his new bride. The blast brings Bolena out of her delirium. Soldiers arrive to take her to her death. She turns and gives the big aria, "Coppia iniqua" one of the treasures of the bel canto repertoire. It is not an indictment of betrayal; rather, she goes out of her way not to call down heaven's wrath on them. She says she will go to her grave with pardon on her lips. She asks that the couple someday will obtain mercy in the presence of God.

At the end of the aria, Anne is joined by Smeaton, Percy, Rochefort, and a sizable chorus for a swift finale. The crowd parts, and Netrebko grabs her long brown hair with one hand, lifts and twists it like a rope to reveal her neck, ready for the beheading. It's a great moment, as promised in the Met advertisements. She is completely vulnerable but absolutely defiant at the same time. The music is big and full. Her final words are a reiteration that she will not curse the king and his new queen.

For her last note, Donizetti wrote for Bolena to sing a big B flat, everyone cuts off, and then Anne drops down to an E flat, singing "No!" Netrebko, however, turns away from the audience, gasps, turns back, hits the B flat square on, and then blasts fortissimo a ridiculously high E flat above high C while marching off to her death. By now, she is walking away from the audience, upstage, and her strident sound is quickly overpowered by the blare of the orchestra. For those not actually listening, the drama is tremendous. But it isn't entirely successful because of the strained singing of its star. The moment is defeated, it seems to me, by unsupported ambition. Netrebko, like King Henry's Bolena, has reached too high. The opera thunders to a close only eleven measures later.

And the crowd goes wild.

Galas attract happy audiences, and this one is showing a lot of love and joy. The opera production is new, and so in addition to the cast's curtain calls, the team of designers walks onstage to the cheers of the audience, which by now is on its feet. The conductor gets a wave of cheers, and, no surprise here, Netrebko receives an enormous ovation. Earlier tonight after a beautiful aria, the audience roared especially loudly, and Netrebko looked surprised, broke character, and grinned. Now, there is an even louder response. There is no gratuitous milking of applause. She takes a few solo bows, graciously and swiftly, and the lights come up.

By the time I get outside, the outdoor audience is starting to disperse. Then, suddenly on the big screen, the cameras catch Anna Netrebko walking through the lobby with the conductor. What is going on? Then spotlights hit her. She and the conductor are coming outside onto the balcony in front of the opera house. People are cheering, yelling "thank you", and blowing kisses. There is a look on her face of gratitude. I find it touching. Again, not overstaying her welcome, she is gracious, and she turns away. The lights go off her, and she is gone. For all I know, she is getting into a cab to drive to Times Square to thank more operagoers for their attendance. I am impressed.

Who knows how many people listened to the performance? In addition to those at Lincoln Center, in the Met and on the plaza, there are people at the Times Square transmission. There are also people listening to Met Opera Radio on SiriusXM satellite radio and on the Met's website live audio streaming. Both audio broadcasts are membership-based. SiriusXM channel 74 is dedicated to the Met. For a $119 annual fee, subscribers can listen in on three live performances weekly. These include interviews with musicians, artists, conductors, and directors. The Met's archives also play on the station, which is commercial-free. The historic Saturday matinee broadcasts go all the way back to 1936. They have been restored and remastered for digital transmission. On Sunday nights, Met Opera Radio plays a full-length studio-recorded opera, and on the first Sunday of the month, a program uninventively titled, "This Month at the Met" guides listeners through behind-the-scenes preparations for upcoming productions, often led by General Manager, Peter Gelb. There are also Opera Quizzes because every fan is also a trivia throwdown contestant-in-waiting.

The reviews appear the following morning. The early curtain time of opening night has a dual benefit—patrons can attend a gala party after the performance, and critics can send reviews to their editors in time to make the next morning's papers. Anthony Tommasini, the chief classical music critic of the *Times* praises Netrebko with gentle complaints aimed at the director and conductor for not taking bigger risks. Tommasini calls Netrebko's singing lustrous, warm, and achingly vulnerable. He writes,

> At 40, Ms. Netrebko may be in her vocal prime. Her sound is meltingly rich yet focused. Sustained tones have body and depth. Her contained vibrato exposed every slight slip from the center of a pitch, especially in midrange, but I'm not complaining. This remains a major voice, with resplendent colorings and built-in expressivity.[2]

He notes the fine singing of the cast, particularly the tenor Stephen Costello. Of Tamara Mumford, he writes, "Her singing was sometimes shaky but always honest and ardent." He concludes his review by returning to the theme of danger for the Met's artistic mission, "Anna Bolena represented a different sort of risk. To make a case for this great, overlooked opera, a company must have a stellar soprano in the title role. Ms. Netrebko is that artist."

The *Times* is the principal paper for opera reviews, but several city papers cover the Met in detail. The *New York Post* headline reads, "Netrebko makes 'Anna'-xtraordinary queen." (You've got to love the *Post*'s front page story lines. My favorite of all time, "Headless man found in topless bar" almost fits *Anna Bolena*.) The first sentence of the review by James Jorden, opera critic at the *New York Post* is simply this: "Queen Anna is dead—long live Queen Anna!"[3] About Mumford, Jorden writes, "Tamara Mumford unfurled a warm, wide-ranging contralto." The *New York Daily News* review title is: "Metropolitan Oprera (sic) "Anna Bolena star Anna Netrebko has a voice to die for". The theater critic, Joe Dziemianowicz, also writes, "Mezzo Tamara Mumford's big, plummy voice gets showcased as Smeaton, the youthful page whose real infatuation with Anna is, ironically, what seals her death sentence."[4] *The Wall Street Journal* is more tentative in its reaction and particularly to Netrebko, "With her dark, voluptuous vocal timbre, Ms. Netrebko has the power and range that the role requires, but she hasn't captured the soul of Donizetti's beleaguered queen." It's a lukewarm review. It grudgingly applauds what might have been. The opera critic Heidi Waleson notes that Netrebko is better than she used to be. I'm not sure that this is actually journalism. It is cocktail party chatter in print. I find that kind of remark snarky. Of Mumford, she reports the performer was "boyishly ardent in her singing and body language." Ultimately, the review is deflating, "...there were moments of fierce excitement, but the sustaining, overall tension that makes an evening transcendent was missing."[5]

On October 10, Netrebko, tenor Peter Costello, and Met General Manager Peter Gelb appear on Charlie Rose's PBS talk show. Rose begins the interview with a clip from the opening night, the finale of Act I. After it is over, Rose asks Netrebko about her reaction to watching the excerpt. Anna says, "The one who was shouting, it was me. And I say that, take out the last note, it didn't really count well. It was a premiere. But it's okay," she says, starting to giggle, "I can correct next performance." That critics' opinions vary is the nature of the business of criticism. I find it interesting and refreshing that Netrebko, who is perfectly comfortable with self-congratulations, is also humble enough to be constantly on the hunt for ways to improve.

To my mind, the best music critic today is Alex Ross. He writes for *The New Yorker*, and his award-winning book on contemporary music, *The Rest Is Noise: Listening to the Twentieth Century*, is the most exciting and engaging book on music I've read in a long time. He tends not to suffer fools gladly in his magazine columns, but he doesn't seem to get caught in the traps of critical dishiness or academic posturing. He writes from a position of advocacy rather than a clubby, insider seat of judgment. His review of *Anna Bolena* appears in the October 11 issue of *The New Yorker*. The essay is titled "Resurfacing," and most of it is devoted, not to Anna Bolena at all, but to the conductor and harpsichordist William Christie's production of Jean-Baptiste Lully's 1676 opera *Atys* at the Brooklyn Academy of Music. The critic makes a case for this rare Baroque work. He bemoans the commercial marketplace that keeps such music out of sight, and he praises the production and its company, "confirming its reputation as a semi-miraculous feat of theatrical resurrection." He moves on to discuss the Donizetti opera—"arguably his masterpiece"—as "another victim of the repertory of convenience." This critic cares a bit more about the music than the performers who are making music. That's a distinction I'm comfortable endorsing. Composers come first. And yet he realizes that Netrebko is the news story here. He calls her, "unquestionably a star", but he adds a caveat, "In the final scene, I marveled at the beauty of her voice without believing for a moment that she was a queen going mad." He ends the review with serious reservations, not about the performance of *Anna Bolena*, or even the choice to produce it for opening night, but about the institution itself and the role of James Levine, its Music Director,

Perhaps not coincidentally, this was the first opening in many years without James Levine. Beset by medical problems, the maestro had already scaled back his schedule, and a few weeks ago he cancelled his fall appearances.... The need to address the vacuum in artistic leadership is urgent. It is time for Levine to step aside, receiving due veneration for his legacy, and for Gelb and the Met board to decide on a long-term musical leader—and not one included to rubber-stamp dubious ideas. Otherwise, the Met will devolve into business as usual:

familiar repertory in perpetual rotation.[6]

Whether or not Ross's call for Levine to step aside is influential inside the halls of the opera house at Lincoln Center, I notice over the few weeks after opening night an escalation of reporting on Levine's health troubles. A *Times* reporter on September 24 writes about the dilemma of Peter Gelb, who has to juggle conductors continually such as Principal Conductor, Fabio Luisi to replace Levine. The general director of the San Francisco Opera, David Gockley, responds to the Met's pressure by saying of Levine, "He is no ordinary music director. He's a god. And gods get to make their own decisions on their own time." The article uses the word "firing" and indirectly quotes Gelb, "...a timely decision about the remainder of the season was only fair to Mr. Luisi, whose recent cancellations in Europe in order to step in at the Met have caused some irritation."[7] Levine is 68 years old, reports the paper, and he has already been forced to leave his directorship at the Boston Symphony Orchestra after repeated cancellations on short notice. Understandably, the *Times* gives credit to Levine for the Met's artistic and financial health. It states the Met's budget is $300 million, which is larger than the next eight largest American opera companies combined. The only company in the world that is larger is the Vienna State Opera, the article says. That's another way of saying a lot is at stake with Levine's health. On October 4, Levine officially withdraws from the January premiere of the new production of Wagner's *Götterdämmerung*. He will be replaced by Fabio Luisi, who will also conduct the Met Orchestra at Carnegie Hall on January 15. The statement from the Met appears in the *Times,* but says Levine will still conduct three full *Ring* cycles in the spring.

The Metropolitan Opera appears in the newspapers in various places. As a brand, it is omnipresent. There are reviews, of course, in the papers' Arts sections. The Met advertises heavily, too. Financial news about the Met might be in the Business sections or, depending upon its relevance to a wider audience, writing about the Met may appear in the International or National sections. The writers of these pieces are likewise scattered throughout the departments of the publication. This is helpful, I suppose, with the awkwardness of a paper such as the *Times* printing a negative review of a performance while on the same page printing an expensive advertisement paid for by the Met.

Publications draw a line in the sand between editorial and advertising, and the critics who work in editorial sometimes over-criticize performances to prove their independence. In the Met's case, various newspapers are also donors to the Met, which clouds things even further. The New York Times Company is a founding patron of Lincoln Center, of which the Met is one of ten constituents (along with The Chamber Music Society of Lincoln Center, The Film Society of Lincoln Center, Jazz at Lincoln Center, New York City Ballet, New York Philharmonic, The School of American Ballet, and Lincoln Center for the Performing Arts). Both The New York Times and The Wall Street Journal companies contribute more than $250,000 annually, the highest level of corporate donation, to the Lincoln Center Corporate Fund. Other media companies contribute lesser amounts—Crain's New York Business, The Walt Disney Company, News Corporation, Thomson Reuters, A&E Television Networks, and Viacom. This makes all of them stakeholders in the success of the Met, and they also make money on the Met's success, given that advertising budgets hinge on the performance entity's financial health. In addition to these corporate donors, individuals of influence, including executives and board members, have overlapping duties at Lincoln Center. These include the donations of Samuel I. Newhouse Foundation (the founder of the Condé Nast empire); the city's mayor and richest citizen, Michael Bloomberg (founder of the Bloomberg business media empire); and various individuals from the world of media who donate monies and lend expertise. There is a lot of gray area in these relationships. It nearly borders on conflict of interest. But this is the reality of the performing fine arts without national subsidy.

The *Times*, the same day that *The New Yorker* calls for Levine to step aside, prints a lengthy, front page article titled, "A Metropolitan Opera High Note, as Donations Hit $182 Million"[8] There is no way to read the article without seeing it as a powerful endorsement of Peter Gelb, who stepped into the role of General Manager, took big risks, and expanded the reach of the Met through high definition broadcasts into 1,600 theaters in 54 countries—all against the background of a global financial recession. The donations have risen in tandem with the Met's visibility. Its HD audience is growing. Three million people saw a Met performance in a movie theater last year, versus 800,000 who watched a performance inside the opera house. If Levine's ship is sinking, Gelb's is ascendant.

The Met makes a lots of money, and it spends a lot of money. Budgets are up 50% over the past five years, according to the article in the *Times*, and it has $41 million in debt. Its pension accounts are said to be underfunded, and for the past seven years it has been operating at a deficit. By spending money though, Gelb has raised the profile of the institution and the checks are pouring in. $182 million in donations (this is apart from ticket sales, remember) is a very large amount, indeed. To give some context, in 2003, donations were $68 million. It has a luxurious endowment, $253 million, down from a high in 2007 of $336 million, but it withdrew 8.6% of it two years ago when the economy went south. Last year, it spent 7.1% of the endowment, says the *Times*. The Met disputes that number.

$182 million worth of donations is quite extraordinary. The money came from 49,100 donors—although the big donations come from a small pool, the 1% as it were, or more likely, the .001%, roughly half were in cash. Gelb sounds both hopeful and cautious, "If anything, donors who give large gifts become accustomed to giving larger gifts going forward. We're not in the business of making iPads. We're making opera." And finally, "We're not miracle workers here. We're trying to use intelligent business practices on behalf of an art form that is not businesslike."

CHAPTER 2

THE EARLY WEEKS INTO THE SEASON PASS, and if the Met's bank accounts look healthy, the same can't be said of the performers. Every operagoer knows all too well that singers get sick. Voices are temperamental musical instruments after all, and New York is a city of millions of people brushing against each other. In winter, most of them seem to have colds. If anything, it's more of a mystery that singers aren't sick even more often. Not infrequently, then, at the Met, a stage manager will walk out in front of the curtain, holding a microphone. These interruptions happen between acts and sometimes at the beginning of a performance. The audience knows what's coming, and a collective groan is heard. So and so is ill and begs your indulgence, the bearer of bad news will sometimes say, if the singer intends to keep going. To which the audience responds with a unified, uplift of support because it means that they'll get to hear the singer anyway, even if it might be less that optimal. I've grown a little cynical about the begging of indulgences as a manipulation of expectation, a lowering of the bar, but the fact is that I don't really know who is sick and how sick they are, do I? When the manager announces that a singer has had to withdraw because of illness—being "indisposed" is the term they like to use—the audience groans audibly, and I imagine the replacement singer backstage listening to the chilly reception. Of course, the theater is known for tales of its understudies getting their big break on such occasions. For every *42nd Street* or *All About Eve* fiction, there is a real-life counterpart. Nobody wants to see a cover at the opera, but on the other hand, operagoers love to discover new talent.

Any recounting of Mormon opera singers at the Met has to include the tenor, Stanford Olsen. He made his Met debut opposite Joan Sutherland on December 18, 1986 in a production of *I Puritani* staged to celebrate Sutherland's 25th anniversary with the company. Singing alongside Sutherland had its own kind of pressure. Critic Donal Henahan, reviewing the opening night of the opera a month earlier, describes the fanatic reception for the 60-year old soprano,

> This is the kind of night it was: when Joan Sutherland made her first entrance in *I Puritani*, the Metropolitan Opera House resounded with such a prolonged stomping, screaming ovation that the performance came to a dead halt. La Stupenda, as opera history will know her, finally gave up, left the stage and returned to start over, allowed at last by her happy fans to take on the persona of Bellini's famously unstable heroine, the on-again, off-again madwoman Elvira.[1]

A month later, in December, the production's tenor Rockwell Blake became ill mid-performance, and Stanford Olsen, the LDS, Salt Lake City native, in his first season on the Met roster, walked on stage for the last act of *I Puritani*, sang the opera's biggest tenor aria, which traditionally includes a truly crazy high note, an F above high C, and made a huge name for himself. I have friends who were in the audience that night. When the announcement was made that Olsen would be taking over, the audience groaned, but my friends cheered because they knew Stanford already. They stood up and told people next to them, "Don't worry, he's terrific." Olsen had been one of 11 Metropolitan Opera National Council Winners the previous April. In 1989 he won first prize in the William W. Naumburg Competition. Later, he won an Eleanor Steber foundation award, and the Richard Tucker grant, the highest award given to an American singer.

Olsen, by the way, is still singing, particularly in the concert repertoire of oratorios and symphonic works. By the time he retired from singing at the Met, he had sung more than 150 performances. He has had an astounding career, really, with opera performances at the Met, La Scala, and many other notable houses. To my mind, even more impressive has been his work with great conductors and symphonies. These include—to be economical—more or less everyone and everywhere that matter in classical music, from early music's Christopher Hogwood to modernism's bad boy, Pierre Boulez, to Broadway's Stephen Sondheim.

So there are worse things that could happen than an opera singer getting sick. In this season at the Met, though, it is like some kind of curse has befallen the singers. On October 10, the Polish baritone, Mariusz Kwiecien, star of a new production of

Mozart's *Don Giovanni*, hurts himself during the first scene of the opera in the dress rehearsal. He is rushed to the hospital by paramedics. Then, two weeks later, after having surgery for a herniated disk (or as the *Times* writes, "a herniated desk"), Kwiecien announces he'll be back in *Don Giovanni* starting October 15. The Met manages expectations, since the operation took place only four days earlier, saying that the baritone will do all of the stage action except in the opening scene when the character is supposed to climb down a ladder. Met, ladders, history: wise decision.

On October 21, Gary Lehman, the tenor and star of the new production of Wagner's *Siegfried* pulls out of the fall performances citing an "energy-sapping virus." In the *Times*, Lehman's manager explains that the tenor—and Siegfried isn't the easiest role in the world to replace, just so you know—"caught the virus after eating seafood while on tour in October 2010 and could not shake the ailment."[2] Apparently, it was bad enough that he stopped singing early last spring but tried to muscle his way through rehearsals at the Met. The decision to step away from the role, says the *Times*, was "mutual."

The following day, on October 22, Anna Netrebko cancels her Carnegie Hall recital debut four days before it is scheduled to take place. She says that her doctor has ordered her to rest her voice after seven taxing performances of *Anna Bolena*. In 2006, Netrebko cancelled her New York recital debut. Then, she said she wasn't "artistically ready." I'm not going to analyze that one.

Her publicist tries to smooth the waters by saying that she booked the 2011 Carnegie Hall recital before she learned the role of Anna Bolena—a role that Netrebko told Charlie Rose she had never studied and selected of the three Donizetti Tudor Queens offered to her purely by intuition. The publicist also says the soprano didn't realize how tired she would be. The notice in the paper ends with a quote from Netrebko, "No one is more disappointed and frustrated than me that I won't be able to perform for New York audiences next week."[3]

Meanwhile, at the Met, the cast of *Anna Bolena* has changed. Angela Meade has taken over for Netrebko and the Jane Seymour role has suffered a replacement because of illness. Sometimes the newspapers return to performances of an opera when leading cast members change. In this case, Zachary Woolfe of the *Times* writes about Meade and her performance on October 23. He ends his review with this comment, "As throughout the run, the under-the-radar star was the mezzo-soprano Tamara Mumford, a fascinatingly unsettled, impassioned Smeaton."[4]

The last-minute replacements cause headaches at the Met, but they start a chain-reaction with other opera companies around the world, too. This occurs when Levine withdraws, but with leading singers, too. For example, the fallen Siegfried, Gary Lehman, was himself a replacement for Ben Heppner, who decided earlier in the year he didn't want to sing the role. With Lehman suddenly out, the Met found Jay Hunter Morris to replace him, but Morris was engaged to sing in the San Diego production of *Moby Dick* by Jake Heggie, a new opera that had its premiere last year in Dallas. San Diego released Morris to sing at the Met and found a new Ahab in...Ben Heppner. Sometimes things work out.

Even without the juggling of singers' illnesses, casts change throughout the run of performances of a production. Singers are contracted to perform specific dates rather than a complete run of an opera. This accommodates international travel, all of which is scheduled four to five years in advance. A singer does a couple of performances here, then has to fly back to Europe for something, then has a recital somewhere else, then maybe comes back and sings the last performance at the Met. The rehearsal process for a Met production must be a complete nightmare. With all of this jet-setting, it is a wonder that singers even know what to do on stage. It is one thing to have an understudy walk into a role in a crisis, but surely this kind of who's-on-first casting undermines the ability of the singers to perform. I can't imagine a production of a Broadway play with all of the leading characters flying in and out that way. In my experience, singers today really want to be convincing actors. Very few adopt a style of "park and bark" performing, where they land center stage, obvious to everyone else around them, and give a recital. The by-product of all of this upheaval is that a singer who can adapt quickly is more likely to rise to the top.

Finally, on December 10, the Met and Levine announce in a joint statement that Levine, who has already pulled out of conducting performances throughout the fall, including both new productions, *Don Giovanni* and *Siegfried*, will not perform in the spring either, including the final installment of the *Ring* cycle and the four Wagner operas in multiple cycles. This means that he will not perform during the current season at all. For the first time since 1971 there will be no Levine in a Met orchestra pit. And, in an even more troubling declaration, he withdraws from the entire 2012-13 season as well. This leaves the company without its musical center. The Metropolitan Opera has no "strong artistic leader," says the *Times*.[5]

Levine suffers from spinal stenosis, a painful condition of an abnormal narrowing of the spinal canal. His brother, Tom, posts in the *Times* "Arts Beat" that Maestro Levine has been suffering excruciating back pain for years.[6] After three surgeries, he seemed to be on the mend, but he fell in Vermont over the summer. The papers report he is currently in a rehabilitation center where he has been for three months. That number jumps out at me. Three months? I take that to mean that the Met has been toying with these announcements of withdrawals from performances, giving them out piecemeal in the hopes that Levine would miraculously improve. It means that they continued to sell tickets and kept some pretty important and discouraging news to themselves. Or maybe it means that Levine has held out every hope of conducting until it simply became obvious that he couldn't do it, the realities of his situation finally overwhelming him and succumbing to the opera house's need to have an actual body standing in front of the orchestra. I assume that all parties concerned are feeling a lot of pressure. Ultimately, Levine states, "We have come to the conclusion that it would be profoundly unfair to the public and the Met company to announce a conducting schedule for me that may have to be altered at a later date." He adds, "I have reluctantly decided not to schedule performances until I am certain I can fulfill such obligations."

I don't want to portray this as a power struggle between Levine and Gelb. I have no information that such is the case. To a great extent, they're all simply trying to get through the day. Gelb does hint at a shift in artistic balance, however. In his interview about Levine's condition, Gelb says, "The Met is a very large institution with many moving parts, and the artistic stewardship of the company really rests with my position."[7] I would have thought the artistic stewardship would rest with the Music Director. Who currently chooses the operas and the performers? I'd like to know that. Gelb makes it sound like Levine is some freelancer who just walks in and conducts operas. That's like saying the city's mayor only works when he's giving a press conference. The waters are muddy. Gelb adds that "the Met was still not ready to ask Mr. Levine to relinquish the title of Music Director, at least as long as there was the chance he might return to the pit." I can't imagine that all of this is going to end well. The article, "Levine to Stay Off Podium at Met Through 2012-13" concludes by saying that Levine, after he returns home, will take up duties as best as he can that don't require him to conduct.

These include planning, coaching, and leading the Lindemann Young Artists Development Program.

Meanwhile, performances of operas continue in rotation. By November 3, thirty-six performances have taken place in the new season: *Nabucco* (Verdi, eight performances), *Il barbiere di Siviglia* (Rossini, nine), *Don Giovanni* (Mozart, seven), and *Siegfried* (Wagner, two). *Anna Bolena* has seen ten performances with two more to come in February. Except for Sundays, when there are no performances of operas (only an occasional recital or rented event), the Met puts on a show every day of the week and twice on Saturdays from late September to mid-May. And then they sometimes go on tour.

This Met practice of works playing in repertory requires a constant atmosphere of change. Most opera houses don't work like that, with so many productions rehearsing and performing simultaneously. At the Royal Opera House in London (Covent Garden), the Bolshoi in Moscow, and the Paris Opera (Bastille), for example, the opera and ballet companies share the house. One night, an opera plays, and the next night, it's ballet's turn. The companies alternate that way, occasionally with two different operas playing back to back evenings, but logistically that's nothing like the Met, which has four operas in repertory every week (and five operas, including a new premiere, the last week of 2011). In addition to the number of operas being performed at night, other operas (and their full sets and costumes) are also using the same stage for rehearsals during the day.

Regional opera companies in the U.S. have more modest repertory challenges. The number of operas that smaller companies present in a season is reduced, and many of those productions are shared with other opera companies in the U.S. and abroad, thereby keeping down costs and making production simpler. In some ways it appears that the Met tries as hard as they can to make its work difficult and complicated. The Met's 2011-12 season contains twenty-six operas, the Lyric Opera of Chicago will present eight works (one of which is the musical *Showboat*), the L.A. Opera six, San Francisco ten, Houston Grand Opera six, Washington National Opera five, Dallas Opera six (one of which is a one-act opera for children), Utah Opera four, Seattle Opera five. Then there are festival opera companies that pack a relatively large number of works into a few weeks: Santa Fe five, Utah Festival Opera four (two of which are musicals). The New York City Opera has four productions this season, a painfully dramatic cutback from its ordinary ten to twelve. But that is another story too, and one that affects the Met financially now that the New York City Opera has abandoned its Lincoln Center home.

Of course, the Metropolitan Opera isn't the only opera game in town. The exact number of companies presenting opera in the city is difficult to pin down. A Stanford University report of opera companies lists 14 companies in New York City, but in addition to those companies that put on a number of full productions every year for ticket buyers—all five boroughs of the city have multiple opera companies, and the cities nearby also have companies— there are numerous schools such as Juilliard, Columbia, NYU, Mannes, and Manhattan School of Music that mount full productions of operas with their students, many of them rare or new works that the Met has never produced. In addition to the performing arts schools, other universities with a music department will sometimes stage a production of an opera. If universities were added to the number of opera companies in the city, the list would double in size, at the very least. Then there are the classical music venues that produce concert-versions of operas from time to time. These appear at big institutions like Avery Fisher Hall, Brooklyn Academy of Music, Carnegie Hall, Symphony Space, the 92nd Street Y, as well as at more cutting edge venues such as La Mama downtown. Broadway will also occasionally produce opera too. *The Gershwins' Porgy and Bess* is currently in previews at the Richard Rogers Theater near Times Square. For that matter, some people consider the musicals that are continuously sung-through to be operas, and new music venues and even rock venues produce shows they label as "opera."

Additionally, pop-up opera companies exist under the radar. These are entities that file non-profit status, rent a small Off-Broadway space and put on shows under restricted Equity Union rules. Their budgets for advertising are small, and as a consequence, productions arrive and depart without widespread knowledge. Only rarely do these seat-of-your-pants groups continue for more than a few years, so they tend not to create the kinds of governance that traditional companies amass. Still, these are marvelous endeavors because they bring a strong point of view and can tackle riskier projects than a large institution can attempt. They have shoestring budgets and often severely limited numbers of accompanying musicians, but on the other hand, they present big voices in small spaces with works that can't be heard elsewhere, and that has a thrill of its own.

In part, I am viewing the Metropolitan opera season through my experience as an opera librettist as well as an opera fan. I had an opera produced by a small company in New York almost twenty years ago and have completed two more operas since then. In 1993, I wrote the libretto for *The Dead*, based on the James Joyce short story. The composer, Murray Boren, was approached by the Hell's Kitchen Opera about a commission. His wife, Susan Alexander had sung a Monteverdi opera, *The Coronation of Poppea*, that they produced, and the two-person founders of the young company asked us to write a new opera for them. It was produced around Halloween, in 1993, at the Vineyard Theater.

I sat in on auditions and rehearsals with wide-eyed amazement at everybody's dedication to the work. I found it all very flattering. These were generously talented musicians. Well, that's not entirely true. The lead of the opera, the baritone who sang the role of Gabriel, was chosen, it seemed to me, because he was really handsome and the producers had a crush on him. Ultimately, they had to teach him the score by recording every note and drilling it into his memory. As it turns out, he didn't read music. Not unheard of, I've since discovered, but singers of contemporary music are typically spectacular sight-readers. At any rate, it all turned out fine and even I had to concede that Gabriel (looked and) sounded pretty good. Our one-act opera was paired with *The Wise Woman* by Carl Orff in a performance double bill. The theater had under 100 seats. Happily, most of them were filled for the performances, spread over two weeks.

After a couple of years of productions, the Hell's Kitchen Opera disbanded, and its artists moved on. The director of The Dead, Linda Lehr, is now Principal Stage Director at the Regina Opera Company, a Brooklyn entity that is currently in its 42nd year of existence. The experience of having an opera produced in New York revealed to me a glimpse of available talent in the city apart from professionals. It is an ocean of competent musicianship. If our little show, which didn't pay the singers anything for weeks and weeks of rehearsals (learning very challenging new music), could attract interest as broadly as it did, the musical resources in New York could easily sustain all the opera that the public can stand.

As valuable as the small opera companies are—and I consider them to be indispensible—they are not rivals with the Met. But there are occasionally opera events in the city that out-Met the Met musically. I'm thinking of classical music organizations such as the New York Philharmonic and visiting orchestras at

Carnegie Hall that produce concert recital or semi-staged performances of opera in symphony hall spaces. Set free from playing in a covered pit, the orchestras put the music front and center, often with spectacular results. Years ago, most of these concert hall operas consisted of a row of stools at the edge of the stage with singers dressed in tuxedos and evening gowns. More recently, these performances tend to be semi-staged events with lighting, costumes, movement and selected props. Audiences flock to see them in repertoire choices that they would be unlikely to visit at the Met and that, furthermore, would be unfeasible for the Met to stage. Each production in the opera house is a long-term investment. Its sets and costumes are designed to make repeated returns in the repertory, year after year, to gradually amortize its costs. In this difference, symphony orchestras have an enormous advantage with a concert performance of opera. They can hire the best singers, produce a work that creates a lot of attention for a week, and then forget about it. It is a passionate love affair without long-term commitment.

To my point of view, the Metropolitan Opera isn't in competition with other opera companies or performance groups in the city. Or elsewhere in the country, to be frank. It doesn't really compete with them for ticket buyers' attention or donor's contributions. The Met just does what it wants to do and hopes that it can keep up its reputation and ambitions without buckling under its own weight. But when the New York City Opera and the Met were operating a few yards from each other, there seemed to be a certain unease to their relationship; yet each focused on its strengths and ceded things to the other. Their repertoire choices were mostly distinct. They carved out audience niches and expectations. The houses' singers jumped from one to the other. Many young singers got their first break at the City Opera and then moved up, so to speak, to the Met. Midcareer singers took jobs at both houses, particularly if the City Opera offered them something they would not otherwise be engaged to do next door. Retired singers with substantial Met experience occasionally reappeared at City Opera with other responsibilities. The most notable of these was Beverly Sills, who became General Director of the New York City Opera in 1979 after being its star early in her career. She retired from singing in 1980. In 1994, she became chairwoman of Lincoln Center itself, and then from 2002-05 chairwoman of the Metropolitan Opera.

In early October, I receive a mailing from Gotham Chamber Opera and Music-Theater Group. The postcard catches my eye and I can't quite describe the reason at first. It is a picture of a woman looking back over her shoulder at the viewer. It is her hairstyle that I recognize. It is pulled up away from her face and piled atop her head, like the women I used to see as a child, growing up near a polygamist's compound in Southern Utah. In the bust-length picture, the woman's shoulder is toward me. She appears to be wearing a prairie dress, one of the nightgown-like fashions that continue to be the style of many Fundamentalist women. The picture's medium is red sand, the exact color of the hills of Southern Utah. It is as if the artist found a pale, flat rock and loosely brushed sand over it to create a delicate portrait. The advertisement says simply "Dark Sisters", music by Nico Muhly and libretto by Stephen Karam. This work is going to premiere on November 9, 2011 at John Jay College, which is two blocks away from my apartment and halfway between me and the Met. I suppose I will be able to call it a "Mormon opera." I contact the box office and purchase a ticket for Thursday, November 17.

Both Nico Muhly and Stephen Karam have ballooning reputations. They're the kind of artists that magazines like to label "ones to watch." Karam has a hit play running Off-Broadway now. It's called *Sons of the Prophet*, and there is growing speculation in the press that after it closes its limited run before Christmas it will transfer to a Broadway stage. It is likely to be on the short list for the Pulitzer Prize. The play was produced by Roundabout Theatre. They also produced his first play, *Speech & Debate*, in 2007. It has since had more than 100 separate productions in the U.S. The new play is a dramatic comedy about suffering and family. The prophet of the title is Kahlil Gibran, the Lebanese writer (Karam is half-Lebanese) whose perennial-selling book *The Prophet* becomes a talisman for the characters of the play trying to keep a family together as wave upon wave of misfortune hit them. Muhly composed the incidental music of the play.

Nico Muhly's music seems to be everywhere suddenly. His

work has been premiered by the New York Philharmonic, the Chicago Symphony, and the American Symphony Orchestra. He's written ballet scores for American Ballet Theater, Paris Opera Ballet, and Dutch National Ballet, as well as choral work, and chamber work, and Hollywood film scores, and music for pop singers and classical artists. All of this, and he is only thirty years old. The Metropolitan Opera co-commissioned an opera from him with the English National Opera titled *Two Boys*. It arrives at the Met in 2013-14. Among many projects, he is writing a quintuple piano concerto commissioned by the LDS artists the Five Browns.

The chamber opera, *Dark Sisters*, was a joint commission of the Gotham Chamber Opera, Music-Theater Group and the Opera Company of Philadelphia. It is to premiere in New York and then travel to Philadelphia in June of 2012. Muhly received the commission and then looked for a librettist. He was introduced to Karam because of his successes as a breakout playwright. As they talked, according to an interview that Karam gave to the *Times*, they discovered a shared interest in American polygamists. "I had spent four months in Cedar City, Utah, right after graduation, as an intern at the Utah Shakespearean Festival. It's a town that has many people living the polygamous lifestyle," Karam said.[8] This statement strikes me as a bit off for several reasons, since I was born and raised in Cedar City, but it also makes me curious to discover what an opera about contemporary polygamists would be like, written by artists as young as these men.

As the date approaches for me to see *Dark Sisters*, I determine not to learn too much about. I do want to know whether I'll be bombarded with half-truths, however, so I am tentatively encouraged as I peruse the opera companies' websites and their descriptions of the work:

> The opera follows one woman's dangerous attempt to escape her life as a member of the FLDS Church (Fundamentalist Church of Jesus Christ of Latter Day Saints), a sect that split from mainstream Mormonism in the early 20th Century. Set against a red-earthed landscape filled with revelations, dark prophets and white temples stretching towards heaven, *Dark Sisters* charts one woman's quest for self-discovery in a world where personal identity is forbidden.[9]

My seat is in the balcony for the performance at the Gerald W. Lynch Theater, a jewel of a performance space. The theater is occasionally used by Lincoln Center and other nearby organizations, and it's a place that feels perfect for chamber opera, which is simply opera with a reduced orchestra. The theater has 415 seats in the orchestra section, and another 180 seats in the balcony. By the time I get my ticket, all of the orchestra seats are gone. I end up on the second to the last row of the balcony, against the wall. The balcony is a short climb from the street level. The crowd is typical for events like this; it differs from a Metropolitan Opera crowd in appearance. There's a sort of adventurousness visible in the audience. It is less luxurious, certainly, but in its own way, more stylish. It is a studied bohemian-ism as calculated in its way as the Met's opening night opulence. I am tempted to describe it as a downtown crowd, but the theater is in the middle of John Jay College of Criminal Justice on the Upper West Side of Manhattan. There are hipper neighborhoods in Manhattan than this.

The printed program has a synopsis of its two acts, but be-cause the performance is in English and is in such a small room, I don't predict I'll have trouble following the action onstage. I skip the synopsis and move on to the essay in the program by Ken Verdoia, titled, "The Faith and Fear of Polygamy." Verdoia is the director of production at the University of Utah, and he has been tapped as a talking head in recent television documentaries about Mormonism. He is listed in the program as a consultant. The opera essay is a gloss on the history of polygamy in the U.S. It attempts to clarify, particularly as it gets closer to contempo-rary history, the forces that combined to push Mormon polygamy underground, and later, to separate its believers from its mother church to form the Fundamentalist Church of Jesus Christ of Latter-day Saints.

The opera will be about a police raid of a Fundamentalist com-munity and its aftermath. Verdoia sets up the action this way:

In a curious mixture of publicity and isolation, plural marriage communities have survived police raids through the 1930s, 1940s, 1950s, and the first decade of the twenty-first century. Talk to the polygamist veteran of a raid, and they wear the event as a badge of honor. A mortal price they were willing to pay, a test faced in the name of their religion. They have returned to the fold hardened in their beliefs.[10]

I have visited the community that is going to be depicted in the opera, the twin towns of Hilldale, Utah and Colorado City, Arizona. The towns straddle the border between the states at the base of the breathtaking Vermillion Cliffs of the Colorado Plateau. My parents used to tell me stories about the people of Short Creek, as Colorado City was named until 1963. I have always been curious about them and how they live. I found the cities to be sleepy, almost lonely in their desolation. I saw very large houses scattered about on ill-kept roads without sidewalks or green public spaces. Many of the homes seemed to be in various states of dilapidation and abandonment, which seemed curious to me, because a lot of the community's money comes from the construction business.

On the other hand, I grew up on a sheep farm, in a house that rarely saw a fresh coat of paint and with wooden post fences all around us connected haphazardly with bailing wire. In Hilldale and Colorado City, I don't remember seeing any people. It has been three decades since my visits there. From photographs and blog posts from recent visitors, I gather that much has changed, particularly in nearby Centennial Park, where the polygamist residents adopt more contemporary clothing styles and are more integrated into the lifestyle of the greater region of the South-west. While I lived in Southern Utah, I became friendly with some female members of the faith as we attended some classes in college together, and they were also co-workers with me at a local store. They kept to themselves, mostly, but my own experiences have humanized this group in my mind. I'm unwilling to accept a portrayal of them as caricatures.

The opera begins, and five sister wives stand, dressed in white prairie dresses—long-sleeved, gathered at the wrist and across the yoke and neck, and cascading loosely to the ground. The stage floor is the rich color of reddish umber. From where I'm sitting, I can't tell if the floor's surface is loose pigment or simply a painted texture, but it holds the light in the most magnificent way. The costumes are white, but as they near the floor, slightly below their knees, the fabric has been dyed in ombre shades to match the ground's color. The effect is that when the women stand upright, they meld with the landscape. The background is a changing projection of sky during a lunar eclipse. The arresting stage is otherwise bare.

The women mourn the removal of their children from their homes by the police. They are in a state of shock and don't know how to proceed. The text of the opera is set to music in a really interesting way. One character will sing a line and then another will repeat a snippet of it and continue; other characters will latch on to some other phrase and start there. It is a continuous canon of overlapping discourse. The ensemble becomes like a tumbleweed that gathers debris as it rolls along. Their husband, called the prophet, appears and tells them that he has received a revelation and is to go into the desert for further guidance. Before leaving, he tells the women to "keep sweet." It is a refrain that recurs throughout the scene. If they keep sweet, they are promised that all will be well.

The action moves inside, and across the back of the stage are projected large portraits of former prophets. The first three I recognize as Joseph Smith, Jr., Brigham Young, and John Taylor. After that, the faces are unknown to me. The main female character of the opera is Eliza, the prophet's fourth wife. Her only daughter, a teenager named Lucinda, is one of the children taken by the police. In a flashback, Lucinda appears and sings to Eliza these lines, plaintively, "Mother dear, I love you so, your happy, smiling face is such a joy to look at...."

It is a strange sensation to be in an audience of operagoers in Manhattan and hear an aria onstage from the LDS Primary Children's Songbook. It's a song I sang for the first time in a tiny white room in Enoch, Utah, sitting on carved, white wooden pew with a purple banner hung in front, "Be Reverent", and with a parlor organ in the corner, the organist pumping with her feet to generate its reedy sounds to accompany a chorus of perhaps a dozen of us children. In the opera, the orchestration of the children's song begins recognizably and then spins into its own harmonic world. I have chills. I presume that no one else in the audience is reacting this way, but I find it difficult to breathe for fear of missing a single note of this music.

Equally beautiful is an extended aria of Eliza recalling the night of her marriage, at age 16, to the prophet. She sings of the stars in an endless sky and her unwillingness to marry. A chamber orchestra doesn't have very many musicians. There are only thirteen listed in the program, but the composer is employing his resources in the most extraordinary and inventive ways. Musicians are playing multiple instruments. As Eliza describes stars, a xylophone sound shimmers faintly and then disappears. A flute trills the song of a bird and fades away. A horn glows in an expansive breath as the horizon is evoked. It all has such economy, such creativity. The orchestration has a shimmering texture, like a veil of music. There is a thinness to it rather than the heft of a big opera orchestration, but to me it feels full and lush.

The night passes in the scene. Eliza does not want her daughter to be married as early as she was, but she discovers a letter that says Lucinda is to be married soon to a man who is almost sixty years old. She determines that she and her daughter must leave the community before that can happen.

The other wives jostle for social rank. Their petty maneuverings about who is the best cook and who is the best seamstress fall flat to my ears. It is supposed to be a comedic break, but in my opinion it collapses into stereotypes and clichés. The undercurrent of it all is merely this: who gets to have sex with the prophet next? The scene doesn't really get laughs from the audience. This misstep makes me more aware of other problems in the text. They are small things, each one, but they point to a laziness of scholarship or a creative hubris. A Fundamentalist would spot them a mile away: the angels who bring revelations are described as having wings; the women call their husband Father; FLDS scriptures are quoted but they're slightly off; the angel Moroni tells the woman to leave her wicked man. I can't imagine a Fundamentalist Mormon buying it.

I'm not sure how much I should bother with such inaccuracies, and how much I should let them bother me. When my opera *The Dead* was produced, critics came to review it. One of the critics was covering the premiere for the *James Joyce Quarterly*. I was in a panic about authenticity. I had cobbled together the libretto with slavish obeisance to the original story. After all was said and done, I wanted people to like the music and to love Joyce. So when the critic approached me on opening night, I was hyper-aware of any comments about faithfulness to the original text. He commented that some of the lines weren't Joycean enough (in point of fact, they were directly lifted from the original story), but that other great lines could only have been written by Joyce (actually, I wrote those myself, but I didn't say so). I was feeling more Joycean than Joyce until he said that the big problem, "of course," was that in the dinner scene, we had the characters eating mashed potatoes when the story clearly describes three, boiled, whole potatoes. The critic walked away smugly. I didn't chase after him to say that we had tried whole potatoes, but they kept rolling off the set and into the audience's laps. Sometimes in the opera house, the truest detail isn't the most true. I keep that in mind as I listen to *Dark Sisters*. My own experience and prejudices color how I view it, but it's also interesting to see what other artists make of this material.

I may have quibbles with the text, but I certainly have no reservations about the singers. What beautiful voices are in this ensemble! Nearly all of these young vocalists have sung at the Met in small roles and with the major companies throughout the country. The lead role was offered to one of the young LDS sopranos at the Met, but she turned it down. These singers are all bursting onto the classical performance scene. It's a pleasure to hear them early in their careers in such an intimate setting. I won't say they all look comfortable in these unflattering costumes, but are they committed to this soaring, contemporary music? Oh yeah.

When the prophet returns from the desert, Eliza manages to get him to spend the night with her. It is a scene of seduction in order to set him up for betrayal. The first act ends with the couple alone while the other wives fume in separate beds. For the first time in the opera, the action leaves the small community as the second act opens in a news studio interview. The wives, including Eliza who has maneuvered her way onto the panel of wives, answer questions by a national news personality. He asks the kinds of leading questions that were asked to the real women of Eldorado, Texas in 2008 after their children were taken from their homes on the Yearning for Zion ranch compound. Newsreel footage introduces the interview segment. The photographs used in the opera production are from the Texas raids.

Cautiously, the women stay on message as they answer questions. Ruth, one of the wives whose two young children died tragically some time ago, has a mental breakdown and leaves the set. This becomes the catalyst for Eliza to gather her courage and reveal that she was an underage bride, forced to marry. As the cameras roll, she sings directly to Lucinda through the camera lens, "Say goodbye to men who encourage silent suffering—only a false Prophet would ask such things of you. Don't be afraid of what lies beyond the sharp cliffs, the red earth—blaze a trail beyond the canyons, past the forests and gorges. This is my hope for you, Sisters of Zion! Hope and pray! I promise you, kind hearts beat for all of us in the outside world!"

The most visually arresting scene of the opera comes next. The distraught Ruth wanders atop a red rock mesa. She prays for her lost children, to be relieved of her own pain, and to be reunited with them in heaven. Finally, she leaps to her death. This is accomplished onstage by a concealed, raised platform that slowly lowers Ruth in the dark until the lights come up and we see that Ruth is prostrate in her grave. The sister wives circle about her. Their children have been returned to them now. The community crisis is over, although Eliza's personal crisis is just beginning. The wives and the prophet join in outdoor funeral proceedings. They sing, "Abide with me, fast falls the eventide." It is hauntingly and unforgettably beautiful. The music has layer upon layer of material I know very well. Again the tune, familiar to any Latter-day Saint, is retained, but the orchestration and later the disentangling of vocal harmonies is refreshingly new. The moment accomplishes something that I think is the essence of transformative art experiences: it gives me something slightly familiar but it is presented it in a way that makes me see it, and myself differently.

Eliza is now an outcast. Suddenly, her daughter appears. Eliza is relieved that they are to be reunited. But instead, Lucinda confronts her mother angrily about her loss of faith. She fears for her mother's soul, she says, and adds that she would prefer her mother to have died rather than betray her beliefs. Ironically, the mourners sing "Love at Home", another Mormon hymn favorite, while Eliza realizes that she has no home. She leaves the compound in search of a new life. The opera ends.

This opera company is one of those indispensible arts organizations in the city. Its own marketing literature proclaims it to be the "nation's foremost opera company dedicated to producing rarely-performed chamber operas from the Baroque era to the present." Since its founding in 2000, the company has presented seven U.S. premieres by such composers as Mozart, Handel, Martinů, Haydn, and Milhaud. It routinely works with interesting directors and choreographers such as Mark Morris, David Parsons, and Karole Armitage. It's well funded. Many of the names on its donors and board members lists overlap those at the Met. I also notice in the program that its opera next April, Mozart's *Il sogno di Scipione*, will feature soprano Rachel Willis-Sørensen, an LDS singer who makes her Covent Garden debut in February 2012 singing the Countess in *The Marriage of Figaro*. Not bad for somebody who graduated from BYU only three years ago.

I am moved by *Dark Sisters*, and I'm eager to talk to somebody about it. Lucinda's jarring indictment to her mother still rings in my ears. Maybe it's because my late father said something very similar to me. I was boarding a plane to serve a two-year assignment as a full-time Mormon missionary in Costa Rica at the age of 19. I was saying goodbye to a few of my family members who had traveled three hundred miles to the closest international airport. My father drew me in close to him and whispered in my ear, "Remember this: I'd rather see you come home in a pine box than dishonor me." And then I walked onto the plane.

After the opera, I imagine that I'll say to the people next to me that my great-grandparents were polygamists in the desert west too, and that it ended almost as badly for them as for the characters in the opera. But the people in the rows near me are clearly uninterested in discussing the content of the performance. In fact, they didn't particularly respond to it. They weren't engaged by it. They didn't applaud much at the curtain call or find it topical. As soon as the lights were up, they were talking about anything but polygamy and faith. I don't hear anybody talking about the opera, its creators, or its performers.

That's disappointing to me, obviously, and I start to wonder why the show didn't grab them more. As I walk home, I conclude that the emotional disconnect is not between experience and understanding, rather it is a lack of sympathy for the characters. I am tempted to say that the Arts don't do a particularly good job of portraying religious devotion generally, but then I start to rattle off in my mind the best nights I've had at the opera. Several of the operas that I consider to have been the most meaningful to me have centered on religious fervor—the nuns walking to their executions at the end of Poulenc's *Dialogues of the Carmelites*, the Old Believers of Mussorgsky's *Khovanshchina* singing "God Will Save Me" as their hermitage is set afire with them in it, Britten's Billy Budd (a Christ-symbol if ever there was one), singing about his impending, unfair hanging at sea, "I'll stay strong, and that's all, and that's enough," and any number of operas that contain some element of betrayal or martyrdom.

Dark Sisters fails, it seems to me, because it can't bear to portray belief as a viable option. The only characters that are sympathetically drawn are those who force themselves to break away from religion. The others are shown as fools and pawns. Maybe they are fools (maybe I'm one too), but isn't there some way to dramatize why they are so devoted? That must be a theatrical possibility as well. I would think that rapture, however misguided, is inherently emotional and cries out for musical treatment. The libretto for *Dark Sisters* was at its weakest when it attempted to depict the women and their husband's motivation for being. Why do they marry this man? Why do they follow him? The outsider's obsessive curiosity about polygamy has always been the bedroom, the prophet's harem. For the women of polygamy though, is that what it's all about? Is there something beside coercion that connects them to their faith? Unsurprisingly, character development disappears without such a basic investigation.

Many an opera has a strong element of wanting to break free and discover the "world so wide" as Copland's heroine sings to open *The Tender Land*. Muhly stated in interviews that Copland was one of his touchstones in writing *Dark Sisters*. This yearning to see the world is a perfect idea to explore in this opera too. Still, I come to think that however much I loved Muhly's music, the opera hits a wall that it constructs for itself because of a failure to engage the audience and have them care about the women as anything more than zealous freaks.

I hadn't read reviews of the opera, but after seeing it, I look them up online. The *Times* critic, Anthony Tommasini opens his comments this way,

> Sometimes a new opera that seems not to be cohering as a musical and dramatic whole leaves you feeling disengaged. *Dark Sisters*, a chamber opera by Nico Muhly that had its premiere on Wednesday night at the Gerald W. Lynch Theater of John Jay College, is a sensitive and unusual work. But, for me, it did not finally come together.[11]

He continues by saying that he was "rooting for the piece" but that he thought it came up short musically. "Though there is much to admire," he writes, "about *Dark Sisters*, the score seems not yet finished. Mr. Muhly may be spreading himself too thin." The review praises all of the singers and also does something I've never seen before in a *Times* review, it quotes the composer's "engaging" blog and provides a link to it.

I go to the composer's blog and read about the rehearsal process from his point of view. Muhly writes about going to the opening night performance and his helplessness as the subtitles go dark momentarily and then a strange light projection appears where it doesn't belong. Realizing that he can't do anything to fix it, he sits back...,

> so instead I grabbed the librettist's thigh and assumed the brace position. But then it went away; we are talking about a (maybe) two-second apparition here. But then something kind of miraculous happened, that hasn't happened to me before: the singers were so on top of their game, and the conductor and orchestra so in sync with them, that I floated back into my body and actually watched the piece for the first time. Details I had forgotten about became clear, theretofore buried vocal nuances became precise, and the giant rhythmic footprint of the piece started to become visible. In a sense, it felt like a heightened moment of clarity after a near-accident or after one of those vertiginous shocks just before properly falling asleep. Very exciting! Everybody come see this thing![12]

I've seen a lot of opera premieres, and I've never seen a review of one of them that praised it unconditionally. Something is always lacking, they will say, some caveat that stops the critic short of calling it a masterpiece. This brings to mind all the reviews of now-universally-loved music that critics of the time it was written hated. Contemporary composers, I hope, find some kind of solace in that.

I went to *Dark Sisters* as part of a search for Mormon opera. It's a meaningless phrase, really. I don't even know what it means. Is it an opera written by a Mormon? An opera about Mormonism? An opera with Mormon performers? In an interview about his play *Sons of the Prophet* in *Out* magazine, Stephen Karam was asked if he consider it to be a "gay play". The playwright responded,

> I guess an argument that doesn't interest me is, 'Is this a gay play?' I mean, look, I'm a gay writer and I wrote a play with three gay characters in it. If you think that's a gay play then...there's a part of me that goes, 'Yeah, that's a gay play.' But I don't think of plays with straight people as heterosexual plays. I don't walk away from *Death of a Salesman* thinking of it as a straight play. I find it uninteresting because I don't care...that's not the reason to see this play.[13]

By some metrics, I guess, *Dark Sisters* is a Mormon opera. Do FLDS members call themselves Mormons, anyway? I don't know. But I respond to what Karam said, and I decide to put away the forced labels regarding it all. I am curious about the beautiful, emotional responses I had to the opera however, and I wonder if other operas with Mormon characters, Mormon tunes embedded in them, or operas written by Mormon artists will have similar power for me, if they will strike a chord, as it were. There have been several Mormon singers at the Metropolitan Opera, but have there been any Mormon composers at the Met? I decide to find out.

CHAPTER 3

AS IT HAPPENS, a Mormon composer named John Laurence Seymour had an opera that premiered at the Metropolitan Opera in 1935. The name of it is *In the Pasha's Garden*, and it was a gigantic, critical disaster. *Time* magazine reported, "...it had its premiere at the Metropolitan last week and established an all-time record for dullness and ineptitude."[1]

The one-act opera had been accepted by the Metropolitan a year earlier. It was originally titled *The Eunuch*. At the time, very few had ever heard of the Californian Seymour. An article by Talbot Lake in 1934 lays the groundwork of the local public expectation,

> Some men have greatness thrust upon them, but most have to work long and hard before achieving it. John Laurence Seymour, of Sacramento, Cal., probably thought Dame Fortune was treating him pretty shabbily, but now everything is top hole, for the Metropolitan Opera Company has accepted his opera, *In a Pasha's Garden*, [sic] for production this season. Until now Mr. Seymour has been virtually unknown to the public generally, and even among musicians his fame had failed to penetrate. Yet he has written ten operas, besides various instrumental works, during more than half his 41 years.[2]

The New York papers had a champion of American opera in

the music critic for the *Times*, Olin Downes. More importantly, the music director of the Met wanted to champion them too. His name was Giulio Gatti-Casazza. The Met had a lamentable history of neglecting new operas by American composers in its early days. "In the quarter of a century of the Metropolitan's existence, from 1883 to 1908, before Mr. Gatti-Casazza's arrival, not a single American work had been performed."[3] The *Times* took every opportunity to remind its readers of the potential of American, "native" operas. It created goodwill that was rewarded, by the time Seymour came along, of acceptance and excitement for new works that operagoers could call their own.

By 1934, under Gatti-Casazza's guidance, the Met's record of premieres had shifted, somewhat gradually, from all-European fare to an out and out embrace of American music.[4] *In the Pasha's Garden* would be the last new opera premiered under Gatti-Casazza's tenure. He retired in 1935 and died five years later in Italy. With his departure, world premieres of American operas dropped off sharply at the Met. (In the span between Gatti-Casazza's retirement and the arrival of James Levine as Music Director in 1976, the Met only premiered six works, and there were zero between 1967 and 1991.) That is to say that in the 1930s, there was a rare momentum for American opera in the house.

In June of 1934, *The New York Times* announced the premiere opera by Seymour, scheduled for the following January, "A new American opera, *The Eunuch*, by John Laurence Seymour, a composer comparatively unknown until now, has been selected for performance next season by the Metropolitan Opera Association. It will be the sixteenth native work given at New York's ranking opera house, all American productions having been presented by Giulio Gatti-Casazza, who enters his twenty-seventh year as general manager of the Metropolitan next season."[5]

Newspaper articles around the country announced Seymour's opera and printed photographs of the composer. These notices generally included brief interviews with Seymour and a plot summary of the opera. The initial articles were reprinted by city papers across the country—by large city dailies, but also smaller community papers: *La Crosse Tribune and Leader-Press* (Wisconsin), *Ogden Standard-Examiner* (Utah), *San Mateo Times* (California) *Salt Lake Tribune* (Utah), and *The Daily Mail* (Maryland), for example. The articles heralded the new composer with headlines like this one from the *Huntingdon Daily News* in Pennsylvania, "John Laurence Seymour Achieves Fame When Metropolitan Opera Accepts His New Work."[6]

The announcement in North Adams, Massachusetts printed this quotation by Seymour, "I am delighted and gratified. It is a testimony to the sincerity of the Metropolitan to promote genuine native American music."[7] Journalists began to use Seymour as proof that the tide of prejudice against American music was shifting. They wrote about music by U.S. composers with Emersonian pride.

An unattributed newspaper article in *The New York Times* to announce Seymour's premiere, presumably written by Downes, beat the drum for American works,

> One of Mr. Gatti's first acts on assuming the manager-
> ship was to start a contest for a new American work, with
> a prize of $10,000 to go to the winner. Mr. Seymour is in
> California. His music has not been performed in New York
> before, according to available records. The Metropolitan
> receives many compositions of native origin from com-
> posers who have not been commissioned to write them,
> and The Eunuch was one of these....[8]

Some speculation as to why Seymour's work was selected
hung over the announcement of the premiere from the beginning.
It appears to have been primarily unsettling to New York journalists. Time magazine mockingly imagines the scene,

> An obscure California schoolteacher sat down at his desk
> one day last week, flicked on his pince-nez and proudly
> put his name to a contract which soon was advertised all
> over the U.S. In Manhattan, a slender Irish girl of 20 bub-
> bled to reporters: "I'm thrilled to the ears." From his
> murky backstage office at the Metropolitan Opera, big,
> bearded Giulio Gatti-Casazza had just announced his
> plans for next season.[9]

The innuendo was of behind-the-scenes machinations. For the
rest of the country, the presumption was simply that Seymour
was American and talented.

Time's piece is a strangely hateful, gossipy article that heaps
skepticism on the unknown composer by attacking him personally:

The California schoolteacher was John Laurence Seymour, 41, a soft-spoken, nervous little man who lives with his mother in Sacramento, teaches dramatics at the State Junior College, wears gloves to keep his hands from sunburn, and composes operas. With little hope he submitted his latest effort to the Metropolitan. It was called *The Eunuch*. Henry Chester Tracy, a Los Angeles author, had written the libretto from a short story by Harrison Griswold Dwight ("Stamboul Nights"). The Metropolitan picked John Seymour's opera for its next U.S. production and promptly renamed it *In the Pasha's Garden*. Gossip was that the Metropolitan judges, pessimistic about discovering a great U.S. opera, had stacked the best of the proffered scores and drawn lots. More likely, John Seymour's opera was chosen because it is brief, inexpensive to produce. It requires only one act for a pasha's wife to philander with a tenor, hide him in a chest which, thanks to a tattling eunuch, the husband orders to be buried.[10]

Of those speculations, the jab about the Met's finances rings truest. The Old Met was located at 1411 Broadway, between 39th and 40th streets, just below Times Square. It certainly had money troubles. In those days, wealthy New York families owned the theater's most expensive boxes outright. When the Old Met was new in the 1880s, seventy subscribers purchased boxes for about $15,000 each, which provided the company with over a million dollars. But by the 1930s, the situation, and the building, had deteriorated. The condition of the house, which the papers referred to as shabby, to great extent depended upon the united initiative of these box-holders.

In 1934, the holders announced a plan to mortgage the Met for $600,000 in order to modernize and restore it. However beautiful the auditorium was, the Old Met had a notoriously antiquated backstage. The same article that taunted Seymour announced, "Electrical engineers from New York's new Fire Prevention Bureau had found the ancient lighting system so dangerous that they threatened to withdraw the building's permit unless repairs were made. News of the heavy mortgage stilled all talk of a new Metropolitan Opera House."[11] And as it turned out, the new house at Lincoln Center would not be built until 1966. The Old Met was torn down in 1967, unable to obtain the landmark status necessary to preserve it.

The conjecture in the press about Seymour's opera did not include that fact that the composer and the great American baritone, Lawrence Tibbett, who would sing the title role of the Pasha, and to whom the published score is dedicated—"To Lawrence Tibbett in admiration and gratitude"—grew up together. They both attended Polytechnic High in California. "Tibbett was two years older than Seymour. They didn't know each other then, but Seymour writes in his autobiographical papers that while Tibbett was performing *Pelleas et Melisande* in San Francisco, Seymour met with him after the performance and interested him in his opera score, *The Eunuch*. At the time, Tibbett was one of the leading voices of his generation, and he had taken a starring role in nearly all of the American opera premieres in the Gatti-Casazza era. Following his debut at the Met in 1923, Tibbett had already sung 395 performances at the Met before taking the role of Pasha. He was one of its biggest stars. Tibbett was interested in Seymour's one-act opera. In short order, the Met promptly accepted it, and the score was published by Tin Pan Alley.

The anticipation for Seymour's opera vacillated between a public that rooted for anything new and American, and a more skeptical, even insular, critical press in New York. Seymour was not exactly the naif that he appeared to be. Although his music had not been produced before, he had written nine operas—seven before *Pasha* and two after it. He graduated from Berkeley with a degree in languages, and then went abroad to study music composition with Ildebrando Pizzetti and Vincent d'Indy in Italy and France, respectively.

As the date of the premiere approached, Seymour seemed to be in high spirits and conducted interviews that gave no indication of troubles. He told the United Press that he, "was perfectly charmed with preparations for the premiere of his one act opera at the Metropolitan next Thursday." After describing the action of the story to the reporter, he said, "It's tough on the lover, but the motto in writing opera is: 'Get the tenor.'"[12]

The world premiere of *In the Pasha's Garden* took place on Thursday, January 24, 1935. It boasted Lawrence Tibbett as the

Pasha and the debut of a 20-year old soprano, Helen Jepson, a soprano popular in her day because of her performances with the Paul Whiteman Orchestra. As an opera star, she would have a rather distinguished career as well, but this was her first appearance at the Met. Another notable debut was the scenic designer, Frederick J. Kiesler, who would become an influential force in modernism in the U.S. He was a Viennese architect, and articles in the press leading up to the premiere called his concept of projections and abstracted scenic elements revolutionary. Ettore Panizza conducted the orchestra. With only one exception, the entire cast of singers was American. This fact was another source of pride commented on in the press.

The premiere performance was a benefit matinee, an annual fundraiser for the Southern Woman's Educational Alliance, an organization that aided rural young women with educational and vocational resources. The 50-minute opera was advertised as a double bill with Puccini's familiar *La bohème*, which followed it. According to the *Times* report, the benefit raised $4,000 for the Society and had an "exceptionally large audience." All told, Seymour's opera was performed three times. First, paired with *La bohème* on January 24, next with *Pagliacci* on January 28, and finally partnered with both *Cavalleria Rusticana* and *Pagliacci* on February 13 (with Lawrence Tibbett and Helen Jepson singing roles in both *Pasha* and *Pagliacci*).[13]

The curtain rose on *In the Pasha's Garden* to reveal a series of curved ramps, stairs, a low wall, and a circular platform with a canopy hanging over it. Behind the set—a large chest was its only furnishing—hung a screen 70 feet wide and 40 feet high. Onto the screen was projected three large black and white leaves. The set designer described the intended effects to one of the many publications that reported on the premiere,

> They overhang the action vastly and seem to brood above it. Those leaves are threatening, sinister, watchful. But…it is not a static decorative setting. They whole movement of the plot is carried on in the movement of the background, the fading out of the microscopic sections of two leaves, the lighter moments of the lovers' happiness, to their dark retraction during the moments of the Pasha's vengeance.[14]

Kiesler's design was calculated to focus on perpetual movement—a spiral always spinning, relationships between objects (and between characters) that are constantly evolving.

The opera is a betrayal story which was represented with an enormous moon that grew in brightness and size as the story unfolded until it was some 20 feet in diameter, according to the *Cleveland Plain Dealer*.[15] The abstract design represented a rise in the garden of a Turkish Pasha. Many in the opera house were confused by it.

> An angular, ascending ramp led up to it, and underneath was an object reminiscent of a back-yard tool shed. But it was the sky that kept the audience bewildered. On

the left was a stereopticon effect in black and white, like cabbage leaves being devoured by a log of wood. On the right was a similar effect, apparently the microscopic photo of a leaf, or an X-ray of the venous system of a frog. All was very modern.[16]

The action begins with Hélène, the young French wife of the Pasha, inviting the attentions of a young male countryman, Étienne, in the garden at sunset. She flirts, "April's a gracious month. What do you think? Does not the day itself stand on the brink of some avowal?" He presses her to romance, but she keeps him at a distance, "Well, don't be vexed but, tell me, after April, what comes next?" Étienne replies, "A bliss is flawed, when once the end of it's foreseen." And she counters, "Flawed? Yes; and how could I forget that, truly, when shadows haunt us here, lest, quite unruly, we seize a happiness too great?" She is about to send him away when they hear others approaching. The lovers are nearly discovered by the eunuch, Zümbül Agha. Étienne hides inside a chest in the garden kiosk, but the eunuch hears voices and refuses to leave until the Pasha can arrive and be told of his suspicions. The eunuch threatens Hélène, "You can't deny that...you cannot! You would have your Christian friends, and so by Allah, this is where it ends!" Hélène commands him to be silent.

The eunuch, without telling the Pasha what is inside the chest, suggests they open it, "Now if this chest be opened, more, I think, might be confessed than I should care to speak; and it shall show who's faithful in this house, if you would know." The

Pasha angrily threatens to put him back on the street and into poverty. The eunuch starts to leave as dinner arrives. Seeing that there is no table, the eunuch suggests they place their food upon the locked chest.

Hélène asks her husband about the kiosk in which they're sitting. The Pasha replies that it was built for a beautiful Greek woman, "My grandfather, the Vizier, he'd charm the hours for that fair slave of his...Pomegranate, he called her." The garden is decorated with the fruit and the Pasha notes how happy she was here. He asks if Hélène is happy. She replies, "I cannot say."

Hélène tells him the story of Pandora. "Zeus, in the myth, is angry, and he seeks Revenge, because the Titan stole his fire for men; and so he panders to desire and gives this girl, who's full of ev'ry charm but brings him sorrow; ev'ry sort of harm and woe is hidden in a certain chest which, woman-like, she opens; and the rest the world knows—trouble sprang like wind from it and seeded all the earth; behind was left but one small waif." The Pasha asks who would that be, and she replies, "Hope was its name. When she had clapped the lid, it stayed. We never see it, but it's hid deep down; we cannot lose it, we cannot lose it, while we live."

The Pasha decides to leave the chest closed. Hélène retires for the night, but before leaving, she gives her husband the key to the chest. She calls to the eunuch who has been hiding to join the Pasha and says to him, "Who loses burdock heads must throw them far... 'Tis well: one bears with dignity the things that are."

She leaves without knowing the fate of Étienne. The eunuch asks to have the key and take care of what he finds. Instead, the Pasha dismisses him and calls for a more trusted servant. Alone, he holds the key in his hand and walks to the chest. He listens to it and considers what to do. Shaban, his servant, arrives with a pistol. Instead, the Pasha asks him to go and get a shovel. They will bury the chest. As they dig a pit, the Pasha says, "Until this night, I have not cared to do the work of slaves; but now I think I will not shirk the weight of this. I see that all are slaves to something bigger; diggers, too, of graves." They hoist the chest and deposit it in the hole. The Pasha blows out the garden's candles. The sole illumination is a gigantic moon. He bows down to listen for sounds from the chest. He hears nothing but the nightingale's song in the distance. He buries the chest and flings its key into a distant pool. The curtain falls.

The audience reaction to the opera is difficult to gauge. It certainly did not go off without a hitch. The modernist set surprised the audience. The costumes were also updated (the character of Hélène wore a flowing, white gown with a bejeweled chiffon cape created by a Fifth Avenue couturière; Étienne donned a blue coat and white flannels, and the Pasha wore a dinner jacket topped with a crimson fez.) Laurence Tibbett struggled, at one point, to light a cigarette onstage. He tried three times, his hand snapping more vigorously each time, until finally, a couple of weak sparks emerged. That is, I suppose, an apt metaphor for the opera's reception in the opera house.

One newspaper wrote about the muted audience response, "At its conclusion, the audience for the most part sat silently for a minute or so. Then came a long round of curtain calls..."[17] The audience applauded and gave numerous curtain calls to performers, conductor, and composer. Seymour was presented onstage with the Bispham Memorial Medal Award. Presented by the American Opera Society of Chicago, the medal was given annually, beginning in 1921, for operas written in English. It was named after David Bispham, a Wagnerian baritone from Pennsylvania at the turn of the twentieth century who championed the performance of operas in English. Upon receiving the medal, Seymour said, onstage,

I thank first Mr. Gatti-Casazza for his sympathetic support and fine production, and Maestro Panizza for his preparation and reading of my music. If I single out one among the artists, it is not because I am ungrateful to all the others who graced my little work. To Lawrence Tibbett I am grateful especially, since I believe him to be the foremost exponent of American opera active in its behalf at the present time. And last of all, let me thank the Metropolitan audience, because we folk who choose to labor in the theatre do it all in the hope of pleasing you. Thank you![18]

Seymour must have been pleased at the amount of attention the opera gathered. The premiere was covered across the country. The *Times*, for example, wrote nine separate articles about the opera in the month of January 1935 alone. After opening night, papers printed follow-up reviews for each of the performances of the opera. After the January 28th performances, the *Times* noted that the opera was "warmly received" and that the composer joined in one of the curtain calls. It published a letter from Seymour to Gatti-Casazza,

> Permit me to thank you cordially for having produced my little opera (too little, it must be admitted, for your vast stage) at the Metropolitan. The adventure of this production has introduced me to the great public which seemed to be well disposed toward *In the Pasha's Garden*. I venture to predict that this little work will win the sympathy of the public more and more this season. But whether it does or not, please accept the assurance of my sincere gratitude.[19]

After the final performance of the opera on February 13, the *Times* ran the last of its articles leading up to and reviewing the work. For the first time, it added a modifier to the opera, calling it, "...Seymour's modernistic episode of the Near East."

Although the audiences responded warmly for the most part, as the critics' reviews appeared in print, it was clear that the critical reaction was unambiguously negative to the point of hatefulness. The set design earned mocking analogies, particularly the projections of the leaves. "Just plain silly",[20] "A Magnified clam...uncooked tripe",[21] "A slightly mildewed butterfly climbing a twig the size of a liner's smokestack."[22] *Time* magazine wrote, "The kiosk resembled the turret of a battleship topped by an old-

fashioned lampshade. To suggest the garden a lighting arrangement projected on the backdrop a horizontal stem and four big
embryonic leaves. A moon was suspended in the sky like a
bruised alligator pear."[23]

And the music? Here, it gets especially nasty. About the
opera, *Time* wrote:

> (It) had its premiere at the Metropolitan last week and
> established an all-time record for dullness and inepti-
> tude.... Composer Seymour had said that the orchestra
> described the characters' true feelings in contrast to the
> words they sang. Perhaps this scheme was too subtle for
> the literal-minded. The music was never unpleasant, but
> for 50 minutes it ambled along like a monotonous intro-
> duction to something which never began. Unfortunately
> for the libretto, the Pasha was played by Lawrence Tib-
> bett whose diction is so clear that the audience under-
> stood every word he sang. And fortunately for John
> Laurence Seymour a Manhattan audience will applaud
> any new opera. For the occasion the delighted composer
> had been granted leave of absence from the California
> State Junior College where he teaches dramatics. His cur-
> tain calls sent thrills down his spine. He has written nine
> operas and the only other one to be produced was a comic
> thing called The Farmerettes, put on by the Hollywood
> High School in 1933.[24]

The New York Times review is even more damning, if possible, because the tone eschews mockery and simply renders a painful judgment. It begins by citing again Gatti-Casazza's goodwill toward American composers,

> ...which he has shown year in and year out, by his production of their works. It would be particularly pleasant, under these circumstances, to agree with complimentary remarks made on the stage by Dr. Henry Hadley to Mr. Seymour after the performance, but it is quite impossible to do so. This work impresses the writer as not one of the best but one of the worst American operas produced hereabouts in years. *In the Pasha's Garden* is tedious and inept to a degree. It lasts only fifty-five minutes, but that becomes a very long time.

The *Times* review continues by adding something that the other critics ignore: the reasons why it didn't work.

> One listens, hoping to find something eloquent, distinctive, worthy of remark. The conclusion is forced that the work has little or no virtue for the stage, or as a musical score. It is dramatically ineffective. The music says nothing, either as melody without relation to the stage, or as means of characterizing the dramatis personae, or publishing their emotions. The style is post-Debussy with admixture of various influences. The writing for the voices is uneventful, monotonously rhymed, oblivious of laws of prosody or accentuation where treatment of the English language is concerned.[25]

Thoroughly humiliated, John Laurence Seymour returned home to Sacramento and stopped composing.

I once met Seymour, briefly. I had a job as an English tutor in the library at Southern Utah State College when I was a student. I saw an old man in the library from time to time coming and going from an office in an isolated corner of the building. He was a frequent subject of wild stories of his eccentricities and history. At the time, I was more curious about his collections of things than his musical exploits. It was rumored that he had thousands and thousands of seashells that he gathered from his travels around the world. For those of us raised on farms in close proximity to the college, Seymour's tales of travel and accomplishment were tantalizing peeks at the possible. Somehow, he had ended up in Cedar City, Utah and had set up a special collections department in the college library in honor of his mother. I was told that he had had an opera performed many years earlier at the Metropolitan Opera. When I eventually spoke to Seymour, I found him to be gentle and a little more than a bit peculiar. I never broached the subject of opera with him. He didn't bring it up, either.

I had forgotten about John Laurence Seymour. It is only by chance that I come across his name on the Metropolitan Opera database. Next, I begin to put the pieces together. I discover that Seymour moved to Utah after placing a lucky bet on the Las Vegas real estate boom in mid-century, which left him and his mother well off for the first time in their lives. They had happened upon the small town of Cedar City and its 15,000 residents on a drive to the region's National Parks. There they settled. Seymour converted to Mormonism, and he began to form relationships with colleges in the state of Utah that would later perform his old compositions and premiere new works, including some with Mormon themes. In gratitude, he later endowed the libraries in Cedar City, now known as Southern Utah University, and at Brigham Young University in Provo.

I see in the library database at BYU a listing for the piano/vocal score of *In the Pasha's Garden*, and I become curious about it. Was the music really that bad? The score was commercially published in 1934 by Harms Inc., New York. That name rings a bell, too. T.B. Harms was one of the largest publishers of sheet music in Tin Pan Alley. The company discovered and promoted Jerome Kern, George Gershwin, Richard Rodgers, Cole Porter, and others. They had a stranglehold on Broadway show tune sheet music, as high as a 90% monopoly. In 1929, Max Dreyfus, who had bought out Harms but retained the name, sold the company to Warner Brothers. At any rate, Seymour's opera must have been considered valuable enough to publish in 1934. I wonder what they saw in the score that the critics didn't?

My search for a copy of the score takes me to Columbia University. I discover that they have a copy, but it is non-circulating. I write to a friend who teaches at Columbia, and within the week, a book bound in a hard, green library cover arrives on loan, courtesy of Claudia. The score is 97 pages long. On the title page, the one-act opera is listed as opus 17. On the dedication page is a photograph of Seymour—young, handsome, with dark hair combed back away from an oval face, his dark eyes behind pince-nez spectacles (old-fashioned, wire framed glasses that sit on the bridge of the nose rather than wrap over and behind ears). He looks slightly away from the camera, unsmiling. He reminds me of a young Robert Downey, Jr. He is wearing a dark suit and with a high-collared white shirt. The volume lists characters of the opera, gives the setting and the time ("Early Twentieth Century"), and gives a brief synopsis which is called "The Argument."

I play the piano well enough to give a vague approximation of the score. It's beyond my abilities to sight-read the piano accompaniment and sing at the same time, but I spend a few hours slowly making my way through the opera at my piano. Seymour doesn't make the sight-reading easy. The score is mostly in the key of B major, with five sharps. That's a lot of black keys for my fingers to negotiate, and there are plenty of accidentals, too. This key lends itself to an exotic sound, I think. There are plenty of ornamented figures in the score, also trills, runs, turns, slurs, triplets, and interesting rhythms. Occasionally, the composer has indicated an instrument playing—a flute, for example, piccolos, or a violin—and as I play I try to imagine the opera's orchestration. The texture of the music is not thick. There is a shimmering transparency to it, like a harp's glide that colors the music without burdening it unnecessarily with too many layers of sound.

The music itself feels modern to me. The chords are surprising, the colors of them constantly shifting around underneath a base of melody. It reminds me of Debussy more than any other composer. It is filigreed music and creates an atmosphere right away of orientalism and exoticism. I am certainly intrigued by it. At the same time, there is a melodramatic quality in the score. This is less subtle. Bass notes bound upwards in octaves as if to proclaim something dramatic is about to happen. When the voice parts arrive, their melodies are not doubled in the score. That aspect feels modern to me too.

Having read the plot already, I am aware of what is going to happen in the story. I keep looking for these narrative signposts, but I find them difficult to locate. I've imagined that I'll encounter an aria by Hélène or a duet between the lovers. These never arrive. Instead, it is all a sort of musicalized banter. It rolls along without a particular cadence to it. This strikes me as odd, because the text itself is sing-songily rhymed to a fault. The libretto is printed in the score with uppercase letters to designate what would be the start of a line of poetry if it were printed in stanzas. For example:

How should I venture or how dare

To utter all—and yet, how could I care

To say the lesser, when I would confess

The greater things that on my spirit press?

The iambic pattern of syllables—unstressed/stressed—is really obvious when it's written out poetically, but in the score, Seymour mellows it out and doesn't set it so routinely. The story of the opera is supposed to be in the twentieth century, but the style of the libretto is old school, and I don't mean that as flattery. The composer wisely, I think, emphasizes the syllables that suggest something rather than mechanically following the librettist's archaic rhyme scheme and rhythms. Words in the score are set stretched out in time and others are clustered together. The sense of the text isn't lost, but the musicality of the libretto, however predictable, doesn't seem to inspire the composer to follow suit. To me, the result is an artistic struggle that is at cross-purposes.

I think the plot of the opera is kind of cool. There's a mystery about it that I respond to, and I admire that the libretto isn't obvious. Does Hélène love Étienne? Is Hélène betraying Étienne or her husband, by leaving the key behind? If not, she's quite a gambler. Anyway, I'm happy about the choices made that give the audience something to think about. In fact, very little is on the page. I'm left to guess about motivations and consequences, and I find that more satisfying that being presented with a melodrama of heroes and villains. By the end, is the Pasha a good guy or a bad guy? I like the fact that initially, I can't say.

About halfway through the score, it starts to bother me that there haven't been any big moments yet for the singers to shine. It's all polite background music. All the same tempo, and mostly the same dynamic level of mezzo forte. Maybe the collaborators were going for subtle, but ultimately, it comes off as passive. I do like the story of—I wish I could call it an aria, but it feels nearly shapeless to me—Pandora's box sung by Hélène. It's a good conceit, but as the drama moves toward the end of the opera, I'm finding it all not particularly dramatic. The musical sound has stayed consistent. It's almost entirely in the same key with a brief excursion to C major that my brain and fingers enjoy, like a vacation from rarer climes.

Finally, the Pasha hears a sound in the locked chest, and the action turns murderous. That's a problem though, because the sound isn't represented in the score. At that moment and later on as well, including the scene in which dirt is heard falling against the buried chest, the stage directions indicate that the Pasha hears something, but the audience doesn't get to hear it musically. Another lost opportunity, it seems to me. And by the way, if I were a composer writing an opera that I knew Lawrence Tibbett was going to premiere at the Metropolitan Opera, I'd be sure to write him something dazzling to sing, something that showed off his voice and gave him a spotlight to wow the audience. Even if I had composed an opera before he was attached to its production, I'd rewrite moments to give his role some extra zing. I sing through his final pages of the score, which are almost entirely devoid of emotion in the vocal parts, and I am left scratching my head. No big notes, nothing held out, or loud, or high, or—I should just say it—of interest. There is a lot of emotionality in the accompaniment, however. Still, it's the characters that audiences relate to, and I am left wondering if the character cares at all about his wife's indiscretion. And as a result, I imagine that Seymour's audience didn't really care, either.

Seymour died in 1986. Before his death he wrote a document about his life titled, "Foreword to a Life Story: Suggestions for a Biography by John Laurence Seymour." He deposited it with a portion of his scores and papers in the Harold B. Lee Library at Brigham Young University. He placed a restriction on the autobiography. It was to be sealed until 2010.

In early December, I write to some friends employed at BYU to investigate the possibility of getting access to Seymour's papers. They generously open doors for me. My request travels quickly through the necessary channels, and a package arrives at my door from the L. Tom Perry Special Collections of the Harold B. Lee Library about one week later. It is a photocopy of a 65-page document, written out longhand by Seymour, beginning March 28, 1980. That is six years before his death.

The act of reading an account like this is uncomfortable to me. It's an intimate thing looking over a document that is, essentially, a last will and testament, and to some degree a settling of scores. I guess that historians encounter this all the time, but I'm unfamiliar with the rollercoaster of having admittance to a man's final thoughts. As Seymour neared the end of his life, he responded to the urging of friends and librarians who wanted him to tell his life story. He had been a life-long diarist, but he was aware that those documents would be preserved but also reserved for only a few scholars to read. Instead of writing an autobiography, he began to make notes for some future biographer who might want to tell his story to a broader public.

In many ways, his was an ordinary and happy turn-of-the-century childhood. He was an only child to parents who loved him and encouraged him. After he showed early promise, they provided violin lessons for him and exposed him to great music, literature and nature. He was gifted with languages and music. He saw his first opera, *Faust*, in 1907, and he then more and more operas and was deeply affected by them. By 1912, he determined to become an opera composer. He had already started composing an opera in high school, writing in full orchestra score (rather then just the voice and piano accompaniment). Although he abandoned and destroys his first effort, he began what would become his first completed opera, *Antigone*, in 1916. (In old age, he called *Antigone* his masterpiece.) Seymour graduated from the University of California at Berkeley in 1917 with a degree in languages. His father died of pneumonia; he cared for his mother; and he ended up teaching at Sacramento Junior College. All the while, writing music.

The tone of the Seymour document is surprisingly free of bitterness. That said, he noted how closely and repeatedly he came to success, and how things outside of his control often scuttled those ambitions. It was not that he was criticized that bothers him, but the savagery of the antagonism. He was a mild-mannered gentleman, at least that's the sense I get from his recollections. Although he was aware that he was smart and able, Seymour didn't seem to expect the world will open its arms to him. He didn't not feel entitled, I guess I want to say. And I wonder, as I read, whether he was owed to a fairer appraisal of his music than he received. When the *Pasha* score was published, for example, Harms planned to pair it with Gershwin's *Porgy and Bess*. Gershwin used the *Pasha* stars Lawrence Tibbett and Helen Jepson to record *Porgy and Bess* instead of the African-American stars of the original cast. (This became the classic recording made shortly after the Broadway premiere.) The two operas and their stars were intended to be intertwining American opera success stories.

The public interviews and letters written by Seymour at the time of the Metropolitan fiasco show no bitterness at all. I find them to be gracious and self-effacing. He repeatedly had used diminishing language when referring to *Pasha*: "my little opera," "my little work" he said. It is as if he was grateful for any attention afforded him. But in his "autobiography", he tells a fuller tale.

When Seymour arrived in New York in December 1934 for rehearsals, he was immediately told to expect trouble. A colleague on the board of the American Society of Composers and Conductors warned him that certain writers in the New York press were indignant at Seymour because they had submitted works to the Metropolitan and were passed over in favor of an unknown composer from Sacramento. He writes, "...they organized the press in a body to handle the upstart from the 'sticks' in such a manner that he would never get back on Manhattan Island."[26]

It was his naiveté that caused as much trouble for him as the

the score itself. He blundered his way through crucial social gatherings and upset members of high society, handled the press awkwardly, and signed a contract that gave the Met the rights to stage the opera however they wanted. This last problem became especially acute when Seymour discovered to his horror that the design of the opera ignored the stage directions in the score, "…with complete disregard of the requirements of the libretto and with every evidence of a conceit amounting to mental disorder." Seymour's only options were to do nothing or to cancel the production. He was told that the Metropolitan was in bad financial shape and had ceded design to the Juilliard Foundation in order to finance the season. In return, in part, Kiesler would design the production of the new opera. "We rehearsed under a cloud because everyone in the production was disgusted and discouraged."

Then, the reviews came out. Seymour wrote, "The newspapers and musical magazines attacked the opera ferociously. *Musical America* later stated that nothing so violent had ever occurred before in the city's musical history. All of the criticisms were of the most mendacious and inappropriate source." To add a blow upon a bruise, Seymour discovered that his hometown newspaper sent a journalist to cover the premiere who knew nothing about music and failed to get a reaction from the composer. Seymour arrived home to find his reputation destroyed. Other than a glee club performance of his *Two Gentlemen of Verona* in 1937, Seymour's music disappeared from view for the next 30 years. He suffered a mental breakdown, lost his job, and stopped composing.

Why do we treat our creative artists this way? I immediately think of Samuel Barber and his own fiasco at the Met: the premiere of *Antony and Cleopatra*, which opened the new house in Lincoln Center in 1966. After its critical denunciation (again, triggered by the overwhelming set design, this one by Franco Zeffirelli), Barber, who is surely one of the great American composers of the 20th century, fell into depression and alcoholism, and died a broken man at the age of 70.

I am happy to see, as I read his papers, that John Laurence Seymour was luckier than that. He happens onto a real estate deal in Las Vegas and moves to Nevada. There was little anchoring him to his home state. He had left teaching and writing music. He was working at Sears and Roebuck's. His timing was perfect; he sold his parcel of real estate and became, for the first time in his life, able to travel the world and to endow libraries. He also joined the Church of Jesus Christ of Latter-day Saints.

Utah's universities offerred him opportunities to hear his old music performed as well as to write new works. BYU produced his early opera *Ramona* in 1970. He participated in the Mormon Arts Festival at BYU in 1972 with two ballets, *The Maid, the Demon, and the Samurai*, and *The Closed Gate*. He wrote a musical folk play, *The Lure and the Promise* for possible pairing with the Utah Shakespearean Festival in Cedar City. He also wrote an operatic work based on the Book of Mormon, *Nephi, The Tender Bough*, for BYU (although it appears that neither of the later two works was produced). There was a rebirth of his confidence, and he forged additional connections with producers in South America who premiered new operas in Peru. As occasional barriers and disappointments blocked his path, Seymour seemed able to sidestep them and continue on.

Although *Pasha* was a bomb at the Met, Seymour survived it. I wondered, as I read about the *Pasha* debacle, what the performers thought of his music. At the library of Southern Utah University, I discover a story about the *Pasha* soprano Helen Jepson. She later became a champion of his music, and she performed Seymour's song "The Poet's Prayer" on her first concert tour in the U.S. There were 48 performances. When she toured through California, she performed at Stanford Unviersity, close to Seymour's home. At the concert, Jepson called the composer up to the stage to acknowledge applause.

He ended the writing of his truncated autobiography on April 3, 1980 with the following statement of purpose,

> I believe that each of us is here in this imperfectly explained experience to discover for himself and realize a divine mission. All our powers and all our longings and impulses are bestowed upon us in order to realize through what we term externalization the intentions of God, Divine Mind. I am convinced that my mission is to realize my potential—which is God's design and endowment—to be an international composer and educator. If I am correct in this conviction, it is not conceit.[27]

Ultimately, Seymour divides his compositions, papers, and collections between four institutions. His own musical manuscripts end up at Brigham Young University. There are nearly 100 works—for orchestra, chorus, and chamber musicians. Most striking are the operas and theater works. There are 22 of them, not only in a wide range of subjects and styles, but in English, French, Spanish, and German languages.[28]

In 1972, he was interviewed about his conversion to Mormonism. He said, "And long before I decided to join the church, if the church would have me, I made up my mind that I would devote myself to trying to preserve in an artistic way, that would be available to me and according to my talents, some of the interesting aspects of its history and culture."[29]

John Laurence Seymour's body was buried in the Evergreen Cemetery in Los Angeles. His grave is adorned with a large, black granite stone marker. On the back, it reads, "Dr. John L. Seymour, devoted son of Herbert W. Seymour and Rose Anne LaPointe, lifelong educator of drama, music, literature and language, prolific opera composer, international philanthropist, metaphysical practitioner, renaissance man, beloved friend of mankind." On the front, beneath an arch of engraved flowers, appear his name and birth and death dates, "Jan. 18, 1893 and Feb. 2, 1986". A verse from Job 19:25 is given, "I know that my redeemer liveth", some musical notes are shown on a scroll, and at the bottom sits a farewell in German, "Alles liebe." At the top of the stone is engraved his name, which is misspelled.

CHAPTER 4

AS CHRISTMAS APPROACHES in New York City, an enormous tree decorated with lights, musical instruments, and toys is placed on the outside balcony of the opera house. It features a large toy train that circles its base, tilted up for all to see. It doesn't compare with the Rockefeller Center tree. But in recent years, Lincoln Center has attempted to muscle into the rarified holiday bankability enjoyed by the lighting ceremony of the Rock Center tree, with its live broadcast by NBC featuring performers on the rink and from landscaped terraces of the Art Deco buildings in midtown. Uptown, the neighborhood produces Winter's Eve at Lincoln Square on the first Monday night after Thanksgiving. (The Rockefeller event is usually the first Wednesday in December.) A tree is lighted on the little triangle of a sidewalk and grass opposite of Lincoln Center, Dante Park. Local government officials and minor celebrities participate. Local stores attempt to lure shoppers inside with one-night-only promotions. This year, an estimated 20,000 people attended.

One of the major supporters for Winter's Eve at Lincoln Square is the American Folk Museum, which is next door to the LDS church. The church building on the corner of 65th Street and Columbus Avenue, diagonally across the street from Lincoln Center's Avery Fisher Hall, sporadically participates as well. Before the building was renovated to include a temple, the larger lobby was home to a live nativity display, and for Winter's Eve, members of the church's congregations took turns in costume as Mary, Joseph, and assorted others. Parents of infants volunteered to stand watch over the manger in half-hour increments. Visitors on their way to Lincoln Center stopped by the windows and peered in. When the Manhattan New York Temple was dedicated in 2004, the size of the lobby was reduced, the painted set no longer fit, and the tradition faded away.

Although Lincoln Center presents unrivaled holiday shows— is there anything that signals the arrival of the Christmas season more reliably than the swirling snowstorm and growing Christmas tree of Balanchine's *The Nutcracker* at New York City Ballet?—as a whole, Lincoln Center has been unable to solidify its reputation with the public as anything more than a critical mass of performing institutions. When the City Opera finally decided to leave Lincoln Center, the announcement was met with a sad shrug of inevitability. Still, the conglomerate of buildings' reputation was particularly affected.

For the constituents of Lincoln Center, business goes on as usual during the holidays. At the Met this year, that means more instability. On December 18, mezzo-soprano Wendy White is injured during a performance of *Faust* and is taken to a local hospital for treatment. I speak to a friend who was in the theater that night. She relates that in the third act, White disappeared while walking on a platform above Mephistopheles played by the German bass, René Pape. A crash is heard; Pape senses that something has happened. He stops the performance. A hinge has given way that connects a wooden platform to a stairway. White isn't seriously injured, but she is taken to St. Luke's-Roosevelt Hospital around the corner from my house, for tests. The article in the *Times* on the accident—papers love to report on accidents at the Met—ends with the following:

> Such mishaps are rare on the opera stage but do occasionally happen. Fears of stage accidents at the Met lately have centered more on its new production of Wagner's 'Ring' cycle, which involves a giant 45-ton mechanized set. It has malfunctioned several times, but with no reported injuries."[1]

The following day, the papers update the story with news that White has been discharged from the hospital and is recovering at home. The fall, they report, occurred 8 feet above the stage. The singer sustained bruises, but the performance continued with an understudy after a 30-minute break.

Sadder to me is the news on December 14 that Anthony Amato is dead at age 91. Tony was the founder of the Amato Opera Theater, one of the most delightful places for opera anywhere in New York City. Founded in 1948, it finally dissolved in 2009. It was the un-Met. The theater on the Lower East Side of Manhattan, in the Bowery, had only 107 seats (an orchestra level and a miniscule mezzanine). At the beginning of every performance, as a bow to the grander company at Lincoln Center, a tiny chandelier was raised as the lights dimmed. The stage itself was only 18 feet wide. Initially, the orchestra pit had room enough for a piano or a pianist, but not both, according to the obituary in the *Times*. By the time I started going to performances to see friends who aspired to operatic careers, the orchestra consisted of an electronic keyboard and a couple of woodwinds, and, of course, Tony—who was the conductor, director, and understudy for all the male roles. Tony's wife, Sally, greeted patrons at the door of the Amato Opera Theater. She took tickets, baked and sold cookies at the concession stand, made costumes, ran the lights, and in her younger days, sang the female roles.

The results of grand opera shrunk down to size were sometimes absurd, but it never became a parody. When a friend, Cynthia Pannell, was engaged to sing the role of Aida at Amato, we went down to the opening night. I couldn't imagine how they would stage such a gigantic opera. What would they do during the triumphal march, for example? How could the cast of six or seven singers manage it? Well, this is what they did. The nearly-nonexistent wings of the theater led to a stage door behind the theater. There was an empty lot next door. Actors walked offstage, exited the back door, ran around to the front of the building, entered the lobby, came down the aisle, climbed up on stage, set down a trinket or two, and then raced offstage to do it, again and again. And then, again, and again.

For a number of years, I attended performances of opera in the Bowery. At intermission at Amato, I would walk outside and rub shoulders with the concertgoers from next door, the legendary Punk and New Wave club, CBGB. I always imagined I could hear their music during opera performances (although I couldn't), and I wondered if they could hear the Amato.

The press loved Amato. I never remember seeing a cruel review. The company had a repertory of about 60 operas, some of them works that were not to be heard elsewhere. Singers from Amato went on to sing at the Met, including Neil Shicoff, Mignon Dunn, and George Shirley. Small did not mean bad at Amato. It just meant small. The ticket prices started out a $1.80 when the company began. By the time I started going there, admission mirrored movie ticket's prices. Singers were paid in meatballs at first, cooked by Mrs. Amato and eaten family style with the cast. In later years, singers got subway fare and sometimes a small stipend of $10 a performance.

What singers really received, however, was stage experience, and at Amato, one never knew what might happen onstage. I was there one night when a character bumped into my friend and sent her wig spinning around backwards on her head. She kept singing, with her head atilt so the wig wouldn't fall off. Finally, she looked up, reached her hands up, and yanked that thing back in place. The audience smiled and went right back to concentrating on the music. "Costumes were rehabilitated until they fell to dust; many a wig began life as a mop. And if that wig became entangled with the scenery, the show went on. Onstage, snowstorms were accomplished with cascades of raw oatmeal, to the great satisfaction of the theater's resident mice."[2]

Most of the performers I heard at the Amato never went on to have careers as professional singers. That might have been sad news to them, but for the audience, the experience wasn't about discovering stars. I really liked the idea that these waiters, students, attorneys, salespeople, etc., could do something they loved in front of an appreciative public. There was so much love in that place. It all started with the Amatos—how appropriate that their name means "loved" in Italian. I went to see Mozart's *Don Giovanni* at Amato Opera once, and the tenor, who was not a competent actor, didn't look very appealing, seemed almost unbearably awkward, and could hardly make eye contact with anyone, opened his mouth to sing "Dalla sua pace" (Upon your peace, my peace depends). Out came the most beautiful, pure sounds I expect that I'll ever hear.

At Christmastime, Dance has the *Nutcracker*, Choral Music has the Messiah, but Grand Opera doesn't have much of anything. Menotti's *Amahl and the Night Visitors* is a staple with a few regional companies and universities, but its scale is too small for the Met and has never been produced there. The Met has mostly given up on the idea of a Christmas opera. They have tried to produce family-friendly works and package them as holiday offerings. Recent examples include Julie Taymor's puppet-packed take on Mozart's *The Magic Flute*, sung in English and cut down to 110 minutes; mixed bills of short operas with fanciful designs from modern art masters; and *Hansel and Gretel*, which is sort of long and scary when it comes right down to it.

The Met has taken a page from the symphonic orchestra business in making New Year's Eve an opportunity to celebrate instead. When the Met stages the operetta *Die Fledermaus*, or as my local radio broadcaster in Utah used to mispronounce it, "Die! Fle-DER-muss", it marks the occasion with a parade of surprise performers outside of the world of opera who make a guest appearance at Prince Orlofsky's ball in Act II and give a concert within a concert. The most recent New Year's Eve *Fledermaus*, in 2005, made a gala out of it and featured singers performing Gershwin, Kern, and Traditional Spirituals.

This year, the Met has something new up its sleeve. I hear about it from Nicholas Pallesen, a young LDS baritone who has been engaged to sing the cover role of Lysander in the new opera, *The Enchanted Island*. The world premiere is to be on New Year's Eve. The first thing about the production that grabs my attention, other than the fact that I don't know what *The Enchanted Island* is, is the very cool cast. I also look at the list of composers: Handel, Vivaldi, Rameau, Purcell, and others. For an author's credit, Jeremy Sams is listed as having written and "devised" the work. Hmm? I think. This could be fun. I make plans to go to see it because I hope that Pallesen will end up performing, but as I read more about the work, I become increasingly curious about it.

The Enchanted Island is described as a pastiche of Baroque music cut and pasted to make an opera with a new story. I'm not entirely familiar with the tradition, common in Handel's day, that allows composers to recycle music written for old operas to make new ones. I read on the Met's website about the production, which has been in the works for two years. The plot of the opera comes from Shakespeare. The two young married couples from *A Midsummer Night's Dream* end up on Prospero's island from *The Tempest*. Ariel mixes up the couples again, as Puck does in *Midsummer*, but with Ferdinand, Miranda, Caliban, and his mother Sycorax added to the chaotic brew. Placido Domingo is listed as the role of Neptune, although I have no idea how a sea god fits into things.

I mention to my fifteen-year old daughter Kate that I'll be going to see a Shakespeare mash-up opera. She loves Shakespeare and asks to come along. I wouldn't say that Kate loves opera, but she doesn't hate it. When I try to play some operatic music around the house, she will roll her eyes, sometimes leave the room, but she won't rush to the iPod and hit the shuffle button. I am aware that my enjoyment of opera has seeped into her consciousness. I used to carry her around in a sling when she was an infant. To get her to sleep, I'd sing songs, and not surprisingly, some of them were from opera. One day, when she was a toddler, I was singing a bit around the house, from Britten's *Billy Budd*, "Aye, aye, all is up…." Then I was distracted by something, and little Kate sang the rest of the line, "…and I must up too." And it was in tune.

She's been to the Met a few times already. Her first trip was at the age of eight to see a perfect opera for children, *Salome*.

Well, maybe not perfectly perfect, but it is rather short, it holds the audience's attention, the characters are sort of familiar, and there's dancing. At the time, a friend from our ward at church, Sue Patchell, was covering the role of Salome. She offered us tickets to see her performance. She was a dramatic soprano whose career was mostly in the German repertoire and predominantly sung in Europe. But when she came to the Met and covered a role, the opera house would give her at least one scheduled performance at the end of the run. At the Met, she sang the lead female role in *Tristan und Isolde*, *Der fliegende Holländer*, *Die Frau ohne Schatten*, *Les Troyens*, and *Salome*, between 1999 and 2004.

The production of *Salome* was new, and it was a sensation with the Finnish soprano Karita Matilla, the kind of event that has people who never go to the opera talking about opera. Matilla is a terrific actress, fearless really, and for this role, also unusually physically fit—as the audience discovered at the end of the Dance of the Seven Veils. Anyway, we told Kate a little about what we were going to see. And perched up on her chair, all dressed up in her puffiest Sunday dress, Kate was completely into the opera from the first note to the last. Sue gave a searing account of the love-obsessed teenager. Afterwards, we went backstage to congratulate her. We went into her dressing room, and Kate was the epitome of the sophisticated New York child: gracious, engaged, aware, knowledgeable and friendly.

A few years later, Kate's elementary school went to a student's matinee performance of *The Magic Flute* at the Met. She might have seen that show a couple of times since we all went as a family to a Saturday matinee, too. And then another friend from church, Erin Morley, gave us two tickets to see her in Britten's *Peter Grimes*. It's an opera I love. My wife couldn't go, so I asked Kate. These seats were in the Parterre boxes. I remember that she felt like a princess as the usher unlocked our door and escorted us inside, through a vestibule covered in velvet and rich wood veneer, and out to our seats perched for all the world to see. We had the entire box to ourselves to watch the opera, which is about, well, perhaps another imperfect choice of material for a child. It doesn't matter. Kate fell asleep in Act II.

I'm more confident about the content of *The Enchanted Island*. The marketing materials and interviews leading up to the premiere detail the process of the work's creation. I pick up a copy of *Opera News*, a monthly publication from the Metropolitan Opera Guild. On the cover is Joyce DiDonato, a mezzo-soprano who is one of the stars of *The Enchanted Island*. Inside is an article written by a scholar of Baroque opera from Yale University, Ellen Rosand titled, "Art to Enchant." Rosand explains what pastiche is, the history of it in Baroque opera, and gives a rough timeline of the creation of the new opera.

First came the idea, which was something that Peter Gelb wanted to do to showcase some of the Met's favorite singers in music that is less familiar to its audiences. Gelb commissioned a libretto from Jeremy Sams who is well known as a playwright, translator, stage director and musician: a unique skill-set. Sams came up with a story. Initially he was drawn to *The Tempest*, but he discovered that there isn't enough love in the plot. Baroque music is about love in all its permutations, and frankly, the opera story needed to have more women than *The Tempest* provided. He decided to enlarge the part of Sycorax, the mother of Caliban, whom Shakespeare mentions in the play but never presents. And then Sams hit upon the idea of bringing in the foursome from *A Midsummer Night's Dream*.

Once the rough plot was decided, the hunt began for music. The Met approached Rosand at Yale to identify arias and ensemble music. Gelb wanted music by Baroque composers who are well known, like Handel, but also those who wrote a lot of vocal music that simply isn't performed today, like Vivaldi. The arias themselves were to be, if possible, music that the audience wouldn't already know. Rosand sounds like she had a blast hunting for music:

> Rarely can a scholar feel as free to indulge aesthetic preference and personal critical judgment as I did in this task. Aside from the obvious Handel and Vivaldi recordings, these included works by Caldara, Scarlatti, Telemann, and Keiser. Thanks to the iTunes store, the list could be expanded well beyond collections in any single library.[3]

The scholar and the librettist eventually came up with 100 pieces of music to choose from. The singers had already been engaged for the work. They became part of the music selection process too. They recommended Baroque music that they wanted to sing, they vetoed some of the music suggested for them, and they learned new music. In the same issue of *Opera News*, the star of the opera, David Daniels (Prospero) says that of the four arias that he sings in *The Enchanted Island*, he chose three of them. After all of the music had been nailed down, Sams had the task of rewriting all of the lyrics for the songs. But the opera was not merely a parade of arias. Between the songs are extended scenes of recitative, sung recitations of dialogue to move along the plot. For these, librettist Sams became composer Sams. He adapted the existing recitatives and then created new material as needed, all of which had a goal of flowing seamlessly from one moment to the next.

Sams created a complete score by cobbling together existing music and writing transitional music. Some of the Baroque scores were difficult to find in the first place and had to be transcribed from original sources. All of this musicological digging and publishing was accomplished by the Met library staff. I bet they had a ball doing it. They probably never imagined that one day they'd help compose a new opera for the Met. A workshop followed, a week of getting a few young singers together to rehearse with piano and see if it all fit right. At that point, some of the plot shifted around, arias were added and dropped, and the balance of the characters was adjusted.

The premiere is on New Year's Eve, but I decide to wait until the next performance to get tickets. First I try the Met's rush ticket program. It's pretty great. A couple of very generous donors, Agnes Varis and Karl Leichtman, make possible the selling of 200 tickets for every performance at a steep discount. On weekdays, the Orchestra and Grand Tier seats are only $20; on weekends, $25. This has to be one of the best deals in town. Fifty of the tickets are set aside for anyone 65 years or older. Seniors can purchase them online, at the box office, or by phone. Not bad. For younger buyers, rush tickets are acquired by standing in line, two hours before the performance is to begin. I've never tried it before, but Kate and I walk over one evening at 5:00 or so (for a 7:30 curtain). We're pointed to a line going down the stairs. The line doesn't seem to be too long, and we have a nice chat about high school life as we wait for the windows to open. At 5:30, the line starts moving, but before we can get close enough to get a ticket, a man calls out with the news that all of the rush seats are taken for the night. He kindly informs us that other tickets are available for the evening, starting at $90. We pass.

When I go online to see what went wrong with my strategy and to get advice on how early I need to show up for rush tickets, I notice that the Met also offers student tickets. What's this? The information is not very prominent on the Met's website, but I find out that students with activity cards can present them at the box office, any time the day of the performance, for a discounted seat.

I don't know where the seats will be, but I think it's probably worth it. Kate and I decide to go on Saturday night, January 7. In the afternoon, we stroll over to the Met. At the box office window, I ask a young man behind the glass who appears to be in his twenties if I can get one student ticket and one adult ticket. He explains that we can get two tickets on Kate's dime, as it were. I ask him where the seats are. He smiles and slides two tickets to us, row O in the orchestra. These are $250 seats, ours for $37.50. I officially decide that having teenagers is a good thing. I send a quick note to Nicholas Pallesen to see if, by chance, he'll be performing tonight. I read that his part of Lysander is relatively small, so even if I don't get to hear him now, I'm confident that in future years, there will be plenty of opportunities.

Kate and I dress up a little bit and head over to the opera house for the performance. I don't think that Kate knows very much about Baroque music, so I give her a quick primer: original instruments versus modern instruments, da capo arias, Baroque plot conventions, and so on. For her part, she gives me an overview of the Shakespeare plays. She's recently read *The Tempest*, so it's fresh in her memory. Together we watched about half of Julie Taymor's film version, which was all I could take. I tell her about the singers including Placido Domingo, Joyce DiDonato, and David Daniels, who is a countertenor. She's never heard the term before. Daniels is a friend of friend. I happen to know that he trained as a baritone, but at parties in college he used to do funny impersonations of opera sopranos. Finally, a voice coach heard him and suggested that he consider developing the falsetto singing that is the hallmark of a countertenor voice. To my ears, countertenors sound almost exactly like women, but with a tiny something added in timbre.

The last few years have seen a boom in Baroque operas, and everyone points to David Daniels as one of the primary reasons. No one has had a bigger influence on the changing repertoire of opera houses than he has. There have always been a few countertenors scattered around, but Daniels's voice is different. For one thing, it's big. It's strong enough to carry in a big house like the Met. And he's a terrific singer, period. I've heard him perform a number of times, and I always come away impressed.

So I decide that I should tell Kate a little about countertenors since *The Enchanted Island* has not one but two of them (Prospero and Ferdinand), and their sound can take a bit of getting used to. The conversation includes a little music history lesson including a topic I never thought I'd be discussing with one of my kids: castration. Unfortunately for me, it's not a term she knows— obviously she didn't grow up on a farm like I did and have an Uncle Bud like I did, who castrated our spring lambs with a bowie knife and his front teeth. I suppress that visual image as I talk with Kate. She is slightly appalled, which I think is probably the right reaction.

Our seats really are terrific. There are a few empty seats around us. On the row behind us, a young family sits with two girls. I guess their ages to be 8 and 5. They converse in Spanish. To the side of us are some young people, probably in their early twenties. The chandeliers rise directly overhead, the lights dim, and William Christie, the most laurelled proponent of Baroque opera in the world walks to the podium (to roaring applause from an audience that knows what he means to music like this—he has conducted here only once before, and never Baroque music, which is his specialty). We're on our way. The overture is Handel's *Alcina*. Of the 43 selections that are to come, 26 are from Handel's oratorios, cantatas, and operas.

The stage set is a giant archway of limbs and vines. On stage right is Prospero's part of the island jungle, represented by stairs that climb to a carved doorway cut into a massive tree. The opposite side of the stage has a more modest entrance to Sycorax's dwelling. She lives there with her son Caliban. Prospero once loved Sycorax, but he has abandoned her and banished her to the dark side of the island. Prospero, in his old age, hatches a plan to ensure his daughter Miranda's happiness. He commands Ariel to cause a storm to shipwreck passing royals onto the island. In exchange for this magic, Ariel will be set free from her servitude to Prospero.

The role of Ariel is sung by Danielle de Niese who is super-animated, funny, and agile—both physically and vocally. She's wearing this nutty, golden costume with feathers on her head and wings on her shoulders. She bounces all around the stage. I like her immediately. She sings an aria, "My master, generous master—I can conjure you fire", and as she sings, the stage comes alive with magical special effects. The backdrop of the set is a giant screen. Ariel's fire is projected all over the set in a series of sophisticated animations. It has a Disney-meets-Baroque quality that I really like. Everything about the production so far seems to have one foot in the 18th century—the front of the stage is covered in antique footlights, for example, and the set has a flatness to it, like a painted backdrop. At the same time, it's a high-tech production firmly in the realm of the 21st century. For me the effect isn't anachronistic. I love the push/pull between the styles.

The first resounding ovation of the night comes shortly afterwards. It is for Joyce DiDonato (Sycorax), after her aria, "Maybe soon, maybe now". Hers is an extraordinary vocal instrument. In the aria, the old hag Sycorax asks Caliban to steal a potion from Prospero that will help her regain her powers. I've seen photos of DiDonato before, and it takes a lot of work to make her look this ugly. I suspect a transformation is going to happen.

The texts of the arias are new, and I'm curious to know how much of a rewrite was required of the lyrics. The words are specific to the story, so I know that it's much more than a cut and paste job. They are updated, I guess you'd say, but again there's that tasteful straddling of styles. On the one hand, the lyrics seem to be aimed directly at a contemporary audience—Caliban rhymes "ecstasy" and "next to me", for example—but at the same time, the sounds are so precisely Baroque. They are filigreed, animated, detailed, and extravagant. It's a specific technique of singing, I think. The orchestra is rather large. About 50 instruments, I'd guess. One of the complaints about Baroque music from people weaned on modern instruments is that early music can feel thin. But this certainly isn't skinny music. It fills the hall of the Met easily. The singers are very forward on the stage. So far, they haven't ventured more than ten feet or so away from the pit, and that certainly makes it easier to be heard. I don't think anyone in this house doubts, however, that these powerful singers are going to have any problems being heard tonight.

Ariel's storm is an incredible, multi-layered feat of stage wizardry. The first aspect of it is a projection onto the screen of an ocean. The projection begins to shift; it has become an animation. Then, a ship becomes visible behind the projection. The four lovers (Demetrius and Helena, Lysander and Hermia) sing about their honeymoons. The music is from Handel's opera *Semele*. It's the first time tonight that I'm familiar with the tune in advance of it being sung. In the Handel opera, it's scored for soprano with a choral chaser at the end. Here, the original lyrics "Endless pleasure, endless love" are changed to "Day of pleasure, nights of love." And it has become a quartet. It's an example of how the original texts are tweaked for the production. Cleverly done.

The storm brews. Here, the stage apparatus kicks into gear. There is the ship, animations of the ocean waves crashing in front of it, and then there are board cutouts of waves roiling, like large saw blades that alternately rise and fall. It's all very smart, as if the stage crew is winking at us, *Hey look at what we can do. You*

The Enchanted Island

want Baroque staging, we'll see that bet and raise you....

Aside from the Shakespearean characters, the dialogue from the Bard's plays is employed in the lyrics as well. This is, again, deftly accomplished. After a line of Shakespeare pops out, I marvel at how naturally it all happens. The syllables of words never feel contorted to fit the rhythms of the melody. The craziness of mistaken identities and botched magical spells comes next. The honeymooners land on the island in shattered groupings. Two by two, Ariel messes up the magic and connects Miranda and Demetrius, then Helena and Caliban. It takes a bit of time to set up all of this chaos. Balanchine accomplished roughly the same thing in about ten seconds in his ballet staging of *A Midsummer Night's Dream* by Puck taking one woman's hand and giving it to another and then taking another hand and giving it to someone else. But I'm not complaining. All of this mix-up is funny and further complicated by the presence of Caliban, a trollish figure transformed simply by the attentions of a beautiful woman.

The biggest laugh of the night comes from Demetrius who no longer remembers he's married. He says, "Who the hell is Helena?" The characters are aware that something is wrong, but they can't quite figure it out. Somebody says, "We rhyme, we rhyme." Another: "I conquered the sea for you, what a silly thing to do." It's funnier than the simple, Shakespearean absurdity of crossed loves. The language and music heighten everything because the entire production is a deliciously twisted hash. This writing is so smart.

Ariel continues to cast spells, each a disaster that only further complicates Prospero's designs. Meanwhile, Sycorax gains strength and begins casting spells of her own. At the end of Act I, Neptune appears. Unless I was sleeping when I last saw *The Tempest* and *A Midsummer Night's Dream*, this is an interpolation to Shakespeare. It fits here because Lysander curses the sea god for ruining his life.

The staging of the undersea world is the craziest thing. Neptune, sung by Placido Domingo, sits on top of a giant clamshell throne flanked by a chorus of mermaids and mermen. A few mermaids hang behind him, suspended on wires high above the stage, flapping their arms and fins. A crowd of his subjects is divided into a group at stage level and two banks of people rising up toward the throne. There are tentacles and tridents waving in the air at odd angles, part cardboard cutout, part human. It's like one of those county fair photo ops, a funny man painted on a board with a hole cut for you to stick your face to get a picture taken. Here, the painted elements have arms sticking out, and the chorus's heads stick through the openings. The chorus sings, "Neptune the Great". It's the first time that a big choral sound has appeared in the opera. It has the relative effect of feeling huge.

The casting of Domingo is inspired. He is bearded, with a golden crown on his head and an elaborate gladiatorial costume with Roman breastplates and abounding in metallic armor. He holds a bronze trident, some nine feet tall, and he bellows back, "Who dares to call me?" I don't know how a singer of Domingo's age still has power like this; he sounds incredible to me. Ariel appears (and gets a big laugh) in an old fashioned diving suit with a helmet the size of a pumpkin on her head. She opens the mask of her Captain Nemo helmet to sing. It's very funny. Ariel pleads with Neptune to search the ocean for the lost Ferdinand.

The act ends with Prospero's regrets, "We like to wrestle destiny." David Daniels's Prospero is a perfect combination of power and weariness. His voice is like that, too. A countertenor sound has a brightness to it, and because of the way the voice has to be produced, it is a pushed sound. But the thing about it, which is different from a woman singing the same pitch, is a vulnerability in the artifice. As Daniels wonders aloud, "Chaos, confusion, what have I done?", there is such a pathetic tinge to it all. It reminds me of people at church who are speaking and as they pour out their feelings, their voices break. This edge of an emotionally brittle voice is, for me at least, the big payoff of a countertenor as fine as this one.

During the intermission, Kate and I wander down to the orchestra pit. People are smiling all around, and I overhear bits of conversation. This is a happy crowd. They are loving everything about the opera. I can't get out of my mind the riskiness of this idea. So many things could have gone wrong. This is without precedent in the Met's history, and quality aside, there was certainly no guarantee that an audience would love it. And they do love it. It is familiar and yet fresh; silly and yet touching. I am surprised how resilient the audience is to the convolutions of the plot and the da capo arias that are basically like singing through everything twice. We peer into the pit. The size of the orchestra is a little larger than I imagined. I look at a player's music stand and see that the Met has created an opera score that is complete, as if it were any new premiere. There are stage directions printed in the score, and, at least in the violinist's book that I saw, a fair amount of penciled-in performance notation.

In the corner sits an odd sight. It's a flat, table-like thing with maybe a dozen softballs hanging over it. What? It's about four feet square and low to the ground. The surface is flat like a table and is covered with a skin of some sort, like a drum. There's an armature that crosses over it about two feet or so above the surface. And then there are the softballs. They look like regulation, standard-issue balls that are tied to the crossbars with simple twine. The balls almost but not quite touch the surface of the table. It looks very out of place in this modern orchestra pit. This thing—who know what it's called—is near percussion instruments, timpani and so forth. I can't quite figure out what this mechanism is until I notice that alongside it is an old fashioned wind machine with a crank handle, and I see giant mallets leaning against the thing. This is the thunder maker. The percussionist hits the surface of the table which rumbles up enough to engage the softballs, which bounce around arrhythmically against the drum to produce a random sounding roll of thunder. It's very cool to me, and it epitomizes what this production is all about. Could the timpanist get the same effect from contemporary instruments? Yes and no. I love the whole idea of playing with authenticity like this. However history-bound opera is, performance is a living thing.

Happily for Kate and me, the family that was sitting behind us (and kicking the back of our seats) in Act I, and whose little girl kept saying aloud, "¿Qué pasó?" "¿Qué dijo él?" (What happened? What did he say?) have decided that it is getting late, and they have left. I didn't turn around and glare at them very often in the first act, only because I halfway suspected that they were Domingo's grandchildren, or something. I think we'll have a more restful second act. The woman sitting in front of us has a bit of a distraction of her own. On her finger is a jewel the size, I swear, of a golf ball.

The second act's enchantments and mismatches gradually move toward a reconciliation of all parties. The spells begin to wear off. The clever thing about the *Midsummer + Tempest* concept is the increased number of dreamweavers it provides. In addition to Ariel's spells, Sycorax begins to regain her magic and casts spells. Caliban steals Prospero's magic books and vials of secret ingredients to beguile potential lovers, too. But when the women leave Caliban, he returns to his mother who sings from her own experience, "Hearts that love can all be broken." Caliban causes a harem of women to appear in a dream. The fantasy becomes an extended ballet. It's the one thing in the opera that I don't love—a little long for me. Anyway, Prospero arrives as the dream starts spinning out of control. He scatters the crowd. Ferdinand has been found—well done, Neptune—and Miranda dreams about him. At long last, Ariel gets the lovers sorted out.

Ferdinand, on his boat, sings an aria that is so intensely beautiful, it's like the audience doesn't dare breathe until he is finished, "With no sail and no rudder—Gliding onwards." This countertenor is quite different from Daniels. His name is Anthony Roth Costanzo. He is young. The voice is a sweet and clear. As he sings, it strikes me that as far as beauty goes, this is about as lovely as a voice gets. Then he adds ornament to the musical lines, and the whole thing adds up to a big, impressive moment. He's someone to watch.

In a final scene, Ferdinand lands on the island with the King and pardons Prospero. The honeymooners are properly reconnected. Miranda and Ferdinand fall in love (no spell required). Throughout the opera, every time Sycorax returns to view, her appearance is altered. Her scary costume and makeup have ultimately been replaced by a brilliantly bright gown and glowing, regal countenance. She confronts Prospero and blames him for imprisoning her and Caliban. Neptune arrives to settle the fight. At last, Prospero realizes all that he has done. He gives the island to Sycorax, "Lady, this island is yours." But she cannot forgive him. She demands justice.

It's a pretty great moment. The transformation of Sycorax shifts the balance of power a lot, and vocally, DiDonato is a clarion-voiced tornado of rage. But as Neptune sings, "We gods who watch the ways of man," he tempers her cries for vengeance with an argument for the value of mercy. Prospero is forgiven, Ariel is set free (with a knockout of a lightshow in which the entire set becomes as alive as a firecracker), and all sing "Now a bright new day is dawning", which is a reworking of the "Hallelujah" from Handel's oratorio, *Judas Maccabaeus*. Curtain calls come next. The audience is in the mood to cheer for hanging mermaids and the lead roles in equal measure. Too bad that we didn't get to see Nicholas Pallesen, and I was secretly hoping for a last-minute substitution, but it's hard to complain after an evening this good. The walk home seems to take about ten seconds.

The review in the *Times* is glowing. It starts out, "Forget 'Auld Lang Syne.' The best music to ring in a new year is 'Now a bright new day is dawning,' the joyous chorus that ends 'The Enchanted Island,' the inventive concoction that had its premiere on Saturday night at the Metropolitan Opera."[4] Praise is scattered all around. The only quibble is that it may be a bit too long. Chief music critic Tommasini concludes, "Baroque purists who object should be quieted by the presence on the podium of Mr. Christie, who has done as much as any musician today to champion Baroque opera. I cannot imagine Handel, the Mr. Showbiz of his day, having any problem with 'The Enchanted Island.' His only question would have been whether he would be paid an upfront fee or receive a percentage of the profits."

As the Metropolitan's season rolls along from strength to strength, headlines from the New York City Opera are more ominous. A strike is brewing. Nothing can bring a performing arts organization to a dead stop faster than a strike. They are horrible things for everyone concerned, and I am concerned how it will affect LDS singers who are engaged to sing at the City Opera this year.

On January 9, the papers report that the company has locked out the musicians, the first two of its four operas might be cancelled, and the entire season is in jeopardy. The union talks have broken down. The first scheduled rehearsal of the season, a choral rehearsal for *La traviata*, is cancelled after the unions threaten to strike the performance. Management says it cannot hold rehearsals for a performance with such a cloud hanging over it. There are two unions at the City Opera. Local 802 of the American Federation of Musicians represents the orchestra, and the American Guild of Musical Artists represents the chorus, singers, stage managers, and directors. After the City Opera announced last spring that it was leaving Lincoln Center to save money, negotiations have become increasingly strained. Finally, the parties brought in federal mediation. Now, all parties hope that the company can resolve its problems. Well, that's not really accurate. A resolution of the problem is the City Opera winning the lottery, and that's about as unlikely to happen as me winning it.

Following labor negotiations by reading about them in the newspaper is foolhardy. With all of the posturing and threats and misinformation, it's difficult to know what is truth. I'm never sure what is brinksmanship anyway, once the parties begin to use the media to pressure each other. Is the opera company really considering canceling the season? Are the unions really holding a gun to a dying company's head? In this case, it is not a typical, union-wants-entitlements and management-wants-money-on-the-back-of-its-workers balance. This time, no one is going to end up a winner.

The City Opera, which is essentially homeless, has cut the number of performances down from an average of 100 in years past to a paltry 16 for this season. The four operas are interesting enough—*La traviata*, and the premiere of an opera by Rufus Wainwright, *Prima Donna*, performed at the Brooklyn Academy of Music in mid-February. Then in March, Mozart's *Così fan tutte* at John Jay (in the same space where I saw *Dark Sisters* earlier this season). And finally, Telemann's *Orpheus* performed at El Museum del Barrio, which will feature Nicholas Pallesen as the god Pluto. I've been to all of these spaces, and I think that they're pretty great choices for an enterprise that has always claimed to be the People's Opera company.

I'm aware that an opera company that is only performing 16 times can't afford the same musicians' salaries as in the past. In fact, aside from one act of *La traviata*, is the chorus used at all the entire season? Maybe that was by design, too. I can't imagine trying to determine what is fair in this situation. At issue in the negotiations are sticking points: should the chorus and orchestra be paid for individual rehearsals and performances or be contracted with salaried positions? What about health coverage and, for the first time I've seen this issue raised, the insurance that musicians pay for their instruments? The musicians also want more of a say in the company's management.

There is enough finger-pointing all around to poke out everybody's eyes. The company's general manager and artistic director, George Steel (whom I believe to be among the best programmers of music anywhere, today) has walked into an inherited firestorm. The unions blame him publicly, but I can't believe that in private they don't understand that this situation is bigger than the effectiveness of management. For once, nobody is saying that the unions are greedy. This is not a case of a musician wanting a windfall. The lockout is announced on January 9, the day of the first scheduled chorus rehearsal. For a week, nothing more is announced in the press, but on January 18, the City Opera and its unions announce a tentative agreement. Ratification is still to come, and since the two unions have agreed to stand together, a negative vote could scuttle future talks. In the *Times*, the president of Local 802 is quoted, "I've been in a lot of negotiations, and this is by far one of the most contentious I've ever been involved with."[5]

On Friday, January 20, the City Opera takes out a full-page ad in the *Times*. It is a letter from George Steel. He announces that the company has reached an agreement with the unions. He thanks the "countless" people who have helped the company with its new plans, and he gives special praise to the orchestra and chorus. The photograph behind this open letter is from a musical performed back in 2006, *The Most Happy Fella*. The subliminal message is that everyone is happy now. I doubt it. I don't know how many tickets they've sold for the first half of the season, but it can't be very many. The *Times* ad also announces that two foundations (The Reed Foundation and the Peter Jay Sharp Foundation) have purchased "the remaining seats for all performances" at the Brooklyn Academy of Music, and they will offer them to the public for $25 each. The letter ends with a mission statement, "Earning your applause is, and will always be, our unifying purpose."

The following day, a few specifics of the labor agreement appear in the papers. The orchestra players, who had been previously earning around $40,000 a year, are to receive a guarantee of $7,300, a promise that they will be hired for all productions, and a commitment that their instrument insurance will be paid. The chorus, which had been earning the same as the orchestral musicians, is guaranteed to work 60 hours of rehearsals and four performances a year, about $3,800. Orchestra players will average about $9,600 and chorus singers up to $7,000. The company, whose budget is down by nearly two-thirds to $13 million, agrees to organize a committee to jointly discuss the company's "artistic vision" for the future.[6] However long that lasts.

The Metropolitan has had its own misfires with unions. In a couple of instances, the President of the United States had to get involved to resolve the issues. In 1904, Theodore Roosevelt responded to the American Federation of Musicians' appeal to bar the Met from hiring foreign orchestral players. Roosevelt ordered immigration officials to detain musicians arriving from Europe. The Met abandoned its plan for a European orchestra in the pit. Then in 1961, John F. Kennedy helped arbitrate the dispute between the Met and its musicians, thereby saving the season. Later, after the company moved to Lincoln Center, tensions between management and the unions grew, until in 1969, the musicians were locked out after contentious contract talks broke down completely. Rudolf Bing, the General Manager was not an expert at negotiations, and when the union called for large salary increases—50% for orchestral musicians, 140% for the chorus, and 200% for dancers—Bing pulled the plug. The Met's opening night came and went. The house stood dark. New York City mayor John Lindsay said, "In all my years as a mediator, I have never seen anything so frozen. Each side does have valid points. Neither recognizes that the other has valid points."[7]   Finally, contracts were signed, and the shortened season opened on December 29.

The aftermath of these disputes is more hurtful to a company that most recognize. In the case of the 1969 strike, for example, the Met refunded $2.3 million of tickets. Sales, which had been at 96% of capacity the season before, dropped to 89% and didn't return to their former level for ten years. Deficits grew each year, to $9 million by 1978. For a season, the finances stabilized, but in 1980, the Met management locked out the musicians again. President Jimmy Carter called and offered to help in the mediation. There was no movement on either side. The Met locked its doors. 1,800 employees were out of work. The ensuing months of strikes were covered with rabid interest in the city's papers. It became class warfare: The company founded by robber barons treats everyone like a servant, a violinist said; for its part, management called the musicians "lemmings" who, if they weren't playing, would "probably be out selling ice cream."[8] The smoke eventually cleared, and the opposing sides reached an agreement that finally permitted the season to open on December 10. The deal was brokered in large part by a young man who started working at the Met in the carpentry shop and gradually rose up the ranks to become the Met's General Director: Joseph Volpe.

The brash, blue-collar Sicilian managed a period of growth and peace at the Met. He gained the unions' trust because he was one of them. He got things done, so management liked him. He stood up for the little guys, nowhere more evident than in his firing of the erratic and tyrannical soprano Kathleen Battle. Eventually he won over the blue bloods as well as the blue collars. He knew that the lasting effects of a strike were larger than a fight between two sides in the papers' headlines, "Missing in this and other articles was any mention of the most serious side effect of the class issue: a lot of the 'little' donors whose support had become increasingly crucial to the Met's financial security were turned off by all the bloodletting. Opera is habit-forming, but once the habit is broken, it's easily kicked."[9] During Volpe's tenure, labor issues were handled calmly, long in advance of contract expirations, and to the satisfaction of everybody.

CHAPTER 5

WHEN I OPEN MET PLAYBILLS THIS SEASON, I notice that some of the singers have an asterisk next to their name to indicate that they are current participants or graduates of the Lindemann Young Artists Development Program. Because so many of the Mormon singers have participated in young artist programs here at the Met and elsewhere, I decide to research what the Met's program for young singers is like.

James Levine founded the Met's young artist program in 1980. He had made his debut in 1971 and was named the company's principal conductor in 1973 and Music Director in 1976. There are several programs like it in the United States. These are training centers that run alongside opera houses. To some extent, it is a feeder program mixed with an advanced music degree program. In 1998, George and Frayda Lindemann donated $10 million to the Met endowment to be earmarked for training programs. The Met's young artist program became the Lindemann Young Artist Development Program. (George Lindemann is a telecommunications entrepreneur, one of the 200 richest men in America; Dr. Frayda Lindemann sits on many institutional boards. She is Vice-President on the Board of the Met.) In 2008, the Met and the Juilliard School announced that their institutions would overlap to consolidate the training of young vocal artist at the professional level. Juilliard would continue its undergraduate and graduate vocal degree programs. James Levine was named the artistic director of the Lindemann program and Brian Zeger its executive director.[1]

The Met describes the program on its website this way:

> To meet the individual needs of each young artist, the Program provides specialized training in music, language, dramatic coaching, and movement from the Met's own artistic staff and invited master teachers. Along with an annual stipend for living expenses, the Program also funds private lessons with approved teachers from outside the Met staff. In addition, Program participants have access to rehearsals for all Metropolitan Opera productions.[2]

From reading about the Lindemann Program, I learn that there are approximately a dozen singers and a couple of pianists at any time in the program. The stipend is about $30,000 to $40,000 annually, according to the Times. Aside from the financial assistance and the access to training, what does the program actually do? How does someone get accepted into it?

To learn the nuts and bolts of it, I talk with graduates of the program. First, I want to learn how they get into the program. The Met website has an application process to audition singers, but the people I talk to came to it more directly when someone at the Met invited them to audition. One of the LDS singers to graduate from the program told me that James Levine came to a concert at Juilliard, heard her, asked for an audition, and ten minutes after hearing her, invited her to the Lindemann Program. Others find their way onto the Met's radar through the National Council Auditions. Others are performers at large music schools, and even at regular universities with music departments in them.

I'm told that there are scouts employed by the Met who, like baseball scouts, travel the world and ferret out talent. Mexico, for example, has become a recent hotbed of opera tenors, and China is emerging as another important source of young singers. These talent scouts are constantly on the move, with enormous databases of singers and reactions to their performances. Sometimes opera stars come in contact with young singers as they travel, and they report back to the Met: *You have to hear this guy.* There is a long tradition in classical music of this kind of discovery, mentoring, and sponsorship. Peter Gelb said in an interview in 2008,

> One of my jobs at the Met is to integrate all the different aspects of the company, and our young art program has been less fully integrated than I'd like it to be. We have global talent scouts looking for artists who should be on our stage, and I think they should be looking for young singers who should be in this program as well. We want to attract talents from around the world.[3]

Once in the Lindemann Program, the first year for a singer is something of a test. The work is intense. Essentially, it is like an advanced degree program at a conservatory. There are weekly and bi-weekly classes in languages, acting, movements, and so on.

These group and private classes are in addition to coaching roles and studying music. The Lindemann Program has a general policy that functions at the singer's request; specifically, a singer can ask for extra help in preparation for performances, concerts, auditions, etc. It is on-demand coaching aside from the program's structured classes. The various singers, although all are young, have vastly different academic backgrounds.

Occasionally, there is a singer who can't read music at all, as hard as that may be to believe. If the mentors at the Met have enough confidence in the singer's innate gifts, they will dedicate the time necessary to teach them to read music. All of these classes take place in the Metropolitan Opera house. Although it is not specifically on the curriculum, as it were, the Lindemann Program is an extended exam of how hard a singer is willing to work. Can they stand the constant criticism? Will they show up when they're supposed to? Are they capable of learning fast? How do they perform under pressure? Are they easily intimidated? Are they healthy mentally and physically? Can they juggle life on and off stage? The program is designed to bring these qualities up to a professional standard. That is to say, it aims to develop them as professionals who can function in the world of classical music.

Sometimes, a singer in the program leaves after the first year. Perhaps the singer doesn't need additional development. Frequently, there are immigration issues that come into play. And occasionally, a singer just isn't cut out for it all. Normally, the singers in the program do not get roles at the Met during the first year, although some artists begin tackling small roles in addition to their Lindemann training assignments. After the first year, the program participants can renew their status for up to two more years. Small roles at the Met begin to come their way in the second year, and they begin to cover larger roles too. The development program continues, however. The singing jobs are merely additional tasks to be performed. At this point, stamina becomes a concern. The singers have a number of extra public performances linked to the development program. Levine conducts concerts for Met opera patrons each year; master teachers who are former opera stars come through the program for additional master class situations. Each year the program produces fully-staged operas at the Peter Sharp Theater at Juilliard. For these operas, the Lindemann artists take the leading roles and the other students at Juilliard complete the casting.

It is not all work. One of the aims of the program is to manage the stress and overcome challenges. This happens in multiple ways. For example, the coaches become personal mentors and confidants. The teachers know that sometimes the singer doesn't need a class in movement that day, and they substitute a meditation session instead. A welcome perk is an audience with the biggest opera stars of the day, who pop in to chat with Lindemann artists candidly about whatever they want to discuss—musical or otherwise. For the singers, it is all about access. Imagine being a young singer and having James Levine, four or fives times a year, gather the artists together to sing for him and to be coached by him. There's no price tag that could be placed on such experience.

During the Lindemann years, the Met coaches function as professional managers for the singers—even though some of the performers are finding artistic management to represent them at this point. The coaches look at every contract offer that comes in, and they have the final word on it. If the role is deemed inappropriate for the singer or if it would be too disruptive to the training of the program, it gets nixed. There is no discussion. This becomes important because the Lindemann artists are like shark bait to the world's casting agents.

Frequently—often once a week and occasionally more often than that—opera companies and other producing entities from around the globe request auditions of the Lindemann Program artists. From a logistical point of view, it makes perfect sense. These young singers have more flexible schedules than other professionals whose calendars are booked four and five years into the future. The young singers are willing to learn a new role, even one that they're unlikely ever to perform again, whereas more established singers are less likely to find the time. Younger singers will take more risks and they might be willing to sing for less money than their older peers. New York being New York, it's also a crossroads of the world for classical music, and for global casting, it's almost like one-stop-shopping. As a result, singers in the Lindemann Program might audition thirty times a year or more, in addition to all of the other demands placed upon them.

Is the Lindemann Program worth it? The singers certainly

think so, and recently the Met has begun to tout the graduates of the program too, in a process of branding the Lindemann name. In its playbills, there is a code of asterisks. By the side of the singers' name, one asterisk means "Member of the Lindemann Young Artists Development Program", and two asterisks means, "Graduate of the Lindemann Young Artist Development Program." All of the LDS singers that I see at the Met this year will have asterisks by their names, the exception being Nina Warren, who is a graduate of the Juilliard Opera Center that pre-dated Lindemann. Famous singers who have come through the Met program include many of the house's most valued stars: Stephanie Blythe, Dawn Upshaw, Nathan Gunn, Paul Groves, Dwayne Croft, and many others. The designation of Lindemann is a stamp of approval. As a brand, the Met is reinforcing the Lindemann importance and dedicating resources to make it the best program of its kind.

Tonight I am going to the opera house, and I'm a bit nervous about it. Most of the time, I look forward to spending an evening in the theater, but I'm going to see Wagner's *Götterdämmerung*. It starts at 6:00pm, has two intermissions, and is to end at ten minutes before midnight. Full confession: I've never seen any works from Wagner's *Ring* cycle before. Guilt. Shame. For some reason, I've never committed to sitting down for the duration. It's sort of embarrassing. I feel like a bit of a fraud, an opera fan who is ignorant of a score as famous as this one. I'm not a Wagnerian neophyte completely, I've seen *Parsifal* on Good Friday, endured the glacially slow (and terrific) Robert Wilson staging of *Lohengrin*. I loved *The Flying Dutchman* (with James Morris). I've attended multiple performances of *Tannhäuser* (one of them with the wonderful Bryn Terfel), and *Die Meistersinger* (Ben Heppner and Karita Mattila were especially memorable), and I've come away from each one happy.

Nyctophobia is the fear of the dark. Melophobia is the fear of music. Claustrophobia is a fear of being trapped in confined spaces. Teutophobia is the fear of Germany. Add these together and you get...? Whatever it is, I have it, but hopefully after tonight, I will have faced my demons and triumphed. Wagner, by the way, had triskaidekaphobia, the intense fear of the number 13.

I have a long list of operas that I want to see and hear someday but haven't yet. Most of these are works that I've heard about or read about, but that haven't been staged nearby. Many of the operas on my wish list are either modern works or ancient ones. A few are in languages that less frequently heard in opera houses. These are all rarities, a word that performing arts folks use as a distinction of class, sort of like a pro baseball team versus its minor league club team. The problem with opera rarities is that although some of these works aren't particularly deserving of a big production—maybe they stick around on the fringes of the repertory because they have one spectacular aria in them or because the overture is famous, or perhaps they have casting demands that make a staging unprofitable—many are simply out of fashion, nothing more.

As times change, opera selections change with them. A performer like Maria Callas revived a discarded group of operas because they were showcases for her voice, for example. Or the political climate makes a nation's works popular or unpopular. The best example of that has to be Wagner himself. When the Metropolitan Opera began, it quickly launched an all-German season. Even French and Italian works were sung in German. For a half dozen years, the Met hired the finest European singers of German. The public loved it. As Italian and French language operas reappeared at the turn of the century, the Met had separate choruses for German and Italian operas. And until World War II severely curtailed American interest in Wagner, the Met produced Wagner every single year.

The first complete *Ring* cycle—all four operas, *Das Rheingold, Die Walküre, Siegfried,* and *Götterdämmerung*—to be performed in the western hemisphere occurred on March 4, 1889 at the Metropolitan. It was conducted by Anton Seidl. I'm a little happy to read the review of the first *Götterdämmerung*, which included several musical omissions:

> The drama was subjected to considerable cutting in order to bring it within limits conducive to the comfort of the audience. In addition to the Norn and the Waltraute scenes, which were not given last year, the Alberich scene was also omitted. Moreover, Herr Seidl had cut out many short passages here and there. The work of the orchestra

was admirably done throughout the evening, and it hardly needs to be said that Herr Seidl conducted with fine skill.[4]

After the Met's premiere of the *Ring* cycle in New York—they performed it three times—the *Ring* cycle production hit the road for three months to Philadelphia, Boston, Milwaukee, Chicago, and St. Louis.

When the *Ring* cycle is performed consecutively this spring, it will be the Met's 108th performance of the complete cycle. That tally doesn't include many performances of one or two of the operas as stand-alone works. I've had my chances to hear the *Ring*. The previous production was by Otto Schenk and Günther Schneider-Siemssen. It debuted in the 1988-1989 season and was revived in 1990, 1993, 1997, 2000, 2004, and 2009. But I didn't make it there. *Götterdämmerung* is the final opera to be premiered in the new cycle directed by Robert Lepage. It's the first new production of the *Ring* in more than twenty years. I'm unsure how best to prepare for it. An afternoon nap?

My seat is in row AA of the orchestra. That's behind Z, the 27th row, I suppose. Again, it comes courtesy of the $20 day-of-performance program. It's a bit under the overhang of the Parterre, but a pretty great seat, all things considered. Before the performance begins, the set is already visible. Much of the commentary of the new *Ring* cycle is about the set, the machine, as it's been dubbed by the Met stagehands, so it deserves a bit of description. The Met calls it the most challenging production in the company's history. The floor of the Met had to be reinforced last year with steel girders to withstand the burden of the set off-stage when it is not in performance. Apparently, the main stage of the Met can handle the weight, but the house didn't have a place to put the thing when it wasn't in use.

The 90,000-pound apparatus appears to be somewhat fixed in place. I can't tell whether it's suspended or propped up against something else. The front of the stage itself is raked, but not too steeply, at the front edge. The prompter's box sticks up a bit in the center. Behind the raked front is a flat platform with a hydraulic lift under it. But the most striking feature of the design is the hulking thing itself. The twenty-four connected panels look like giant teeter-totters resting side by side. The set is about 60 feet wide. In height, the planks extend up, about 25 feet. In the middle of the planks, there is a horizontal axis (again, think: teeter-totter) that connects all of the set pieces to a tower on each side of the stage. The axis allows the planks to rotate end over end, 360 degrees. When I first see them, I can't tell what they are. It is as if giant, upright railroad ties are pushed together to form a wall. There is a scrim behind the machine. Onto it is projected a dancing light show that suggests the aurora borealis.

I look around me to see my neighbors for the evening. Some of the people I recognize from our ticket line. The two rows in front of me are sparsely filled. Less than half full. Which is fine with me, particularly since the seats directly ahead of me are empty. When I look at the rest of the orchestra section, however, it looks pretty well full. These are probably difficult seats to sell.

The premiere of this production is something of a warm up for the complete *Ring* cycles that are to come in the spring. I crane my neck to look at the standing room stalls. They are empty. Somebody would have to be in pretty great shape to stand for six hours. It's a Tuesday night. For the working stiffs in the audience, *Götterdämmerung* is quite a commitment. Tomorrow morning's going to come mighty early.

Conductor Fabio Luisi steps onto the podium to a welcoming ovation. I wonder about the extent to which he is seen as a white knight riding in to save this production, if not the entire season, in Levine's absence. It's my sense that there is a lot of goodwill aimed in his direction. Whatever the audience thinks of the set and the production, I don't get the feeling that they are wearing their "show me" coats. I could be wrong, but they seem to want to love this from the first note on. As the lights dim, I notice that nobody's looking at their printed program. I would have thought they'd be boning up on their Nibelungen lore. Maybe they're tried and true Wagnerians.

I've read the synopsis for *Götterdämmerung* and for the other three *Ring* operas. Stepping into the cycle, last opera first, isn't ideal, I know, but on the other hand, the Met is presenting it as a stand-alone work. So if it can't hold up on its own, it's not my fault.

I needn't have worried. *Götterdämmerung* starts with a prologue that might as well be called, "previously on Valhalla...."

Three women who are weaving the destiny of mankind rehearse the story of Wotan and the gods. I'm a little distracted from all of this backstory because the machine is on the move. The 24 segments are rotating, like boards attached to a rotisserie. They are flat on one side and shaped like a V on the other. The angle of the V is about 150 degrees, I estimate, and that must be the place where the axis is hidden within the panels. Each panel can rotate end over end, independently. It doesn't look like the entire set can be raised or lowered, but panels can form a flat surface when rotated to 180 degrees. This becomes a platform about 15 feet above the stage floor. What kind of hydraulics would be required to hoist a 45-ton set?

I still can't tell what the panels are made of. They have imagery on them. How high-tech are they? Has the Met built a giant wall of revolving LCD screen panels that are illuminated independently? I can't imagine what kind of technology would be required for that. I'm looking closely. The patterns on the panels seem to be distinct, and as they rotate, the images look like they are fixed onto the panels. That is, the image seems to be the same whether it is facing the ceiling or facing outward. That's what leads me to believe that the panels are somehow transparent and internally illuminated. But I can't imagine the cost of such a thing. In interviews, Peter Gelb has talked about the extraordinary computerization necessary to make it all work. I don't know exactly what he's referring to, but let me just say this: nobody's calling this *Ring* cheap.

The prologue's history lesson is given by three Norns. As the women weave enormous ropes that hang from the ends of the panels overhead, the ropes start to break. In this production, they don't weave so much as braid the enormous ropes. As the tethers start to break free, each panel spins, seemingly out of control. This is a violent action, not completely chaotic, but unnerving. The panels can flip around pretty fast. And they do have 360 degree movement. Yikes! The women appear to be directly underneath these gargantuan things. The Norns predict the end of the world.

Still in the prologue—why should Wagner limit himself to just one scene in a prologue?—the setting shifts to a rocky mountaintop. It's becoming clearer to me how the set works. If the panels are rotated to a flat position horizontally, they become the ground. They are sturdy enough to walk on. If facing toward the audience alternating flat and v-shaped, it represents rougher terrain. If all the panels are upright, they become a huge back wall, and so forth. This next scene is Brünnhilde's mountain, and the panels are flat in the center and cock-eyed elsewhere to represent rocky crags. The panels are illuminated with natural imagery of green foliage and also harsher surfaces on the rocks. As to the colors themselves, they are richly saturated. In some configurations of the machine, an expanse of sky is visible behind it. Here, a large light radiates from the center outward, sunlike.

Is there singing in this opera? Oh, I guess there is. Brünnhilde and Siegfried sing of their love. She has cast a magic spell on him for protection. He goes off into the world in search of adventure. Before he leaves, Siegfried gives Brünnhilde the golden ring he took from the dragon when he slayed it (more backstory), and she gives to him her horse, Grane. While they're not as cool as the set, the props are fit for the gods. The ring is illuminated somehow. From where I'm sitting, I can't see how big it is, but the thing glows magically. Nice touch. Grane the meister-steed is pretty terrific too. Full-size, plated with armor, it looks like a display from the Arms and Armor displays in the medieval wing of the Metropolitan Museum of Art come to life. To move, it rolls, I suppose; I can't see its feet. The neck is segmented, so its head can bob up and down, quite lifelike. Grane can't compare with the giant horses appearing next door in the Lincoln Center Theater production of *War Horse*, however. Those giant puppets have two people inside the armature and another permanently stationed at the head to wiggle ears, tilt, whinny, and do, well, everything that you'd expect a horse to do. It's just bad luck to be so near for comparison, but Grane is a mighty enough mount. It's just a bit stiff. But there's no stiffness in the voices of Deborah Voigt and Stephen Gould. They sound completely confident, full, rich and heroic. There's no strain whatsoever to be heard over this large, brass-heavy orchestra. Of course, there are still five hours left to go.

Stephen Gould's voice is new to me, but I've heard Voigt a number of times. This is her first Brünnhilde, but I've long been an admirer of her singing. The first few times I heard her sing, I found it almost impossible to believe. It was so big, but also so beautiful. I don't know how best to describe it. The voice had a Mozartean transparency and ease but with a volume control that could blast you out of your seat without any distortion. Voices like hers don't come along very often. All around town, Voigt is on display in advertisements for the Met. In the photographs of the ad campaign, she is not in breastplate-mode. No crazy, horned helmet here; rather, her red hair hangs down over shoulders dressed in soft fabrics. She is holding a flaming torch in some photos. When the first operas of the Ring were premiered a couple of years ago, Voigt was photographed with a beautiful white horse, wearing a silver tunic of small, overlapping metal disks. To me, it looked like a *Vanity Fair* cover shoot. The message was simple: this is a glamorous, beautiful woman; it's not your momma's *Ring*.

Except, well, it sort of is. Apart from all of the high-tech gizmos on display, it's a pretty traditional telling of the story. Wagner's cycle, more than other operas, it seems to me, has attracted directors who make bold, political, radical choices to reinterpret the mythology. That's one of the most attractive aspects of the *Ring*, in a way. It stands up to being upended. Want to set the *Ring* in an asylum? Ok. How about updating the action to the Industrial Revolution? A feminist reading? Set in America? With an environmentalist agenda? All of these have been done. The Met's new *Ring* looks to me like a traditional reading, essentially. There doesn't appear to be any directorial re-thinking of Wagner here. In one production a while back, Brünnhilde doesn't even die at the end; instead, she has Siegfried's baby. With other operas, changing the ending would be heresy—*Never mind Tosca, don't bother jumping off the parapet.* Directors have been given license to manipulate this opera, but they only have it because audiences have come to expect it. The Met's new *Ring* looks to be following Wagner's directions quite closely. When the score says characters sit at a table and drink (and Wagner is nothing if not a control freak regarding what he wanted on stage at any given moment—I am tempted to use the word Nazi, for a host of reasons), this *Ring* obeys. The mountain hideaway of Brünnhilde has pictures of trees and grass all over it. The experience is literal, almost like watching a fractured film.

Act I begins in a great hall along the Rhine, the home of the Gibichungs. Siegfried steps into a contorted family quarrel. Unmarried brother and sister Gunther and Gutrune plot with a half-brother Hagen to get a husband for Gutrune (Siegfried) and a wife for Gunther (Brünnhilde). There are some problems with the plan. Brünnhilde is surrounded by an impenetrable fire that only Siegfried can pass through, and Siegfried has sworn devotion to Brünnhilde.

Gutrune gives Siegfried a love potion, and he instantly forgets Brünnhilde and falls in love with Gutrune instead. Siegfried has been given a magic cloak by Brünnhilde that will transform his appearance into whatever he wants. Siegfried lets Gunther have it, and he and Gunther swear an oath of brotherhood and travel to Brünnhilde to court her. Meanwhile, Brünnhilde is visited by her sister who implores her to give the magic ring back to the Rhinemaidens before it is too late and the world is destroyed. But no go. Brünnhilde is tricked into being Gunther's bride. He tears the ring from her hand.

As I watch the performance, I can't keep my thoughts from going to pop culture references. *The Lord of the Rings* is the most obvious one. I half-expect somebody to start singing about Gandalf and Sméagol. The plots cry out for comparison. There's a haunted, golden ring, illegally acquired, that controls the people of the world; there are competing gods and dwarfs and heroes and monsters; there's a quest or two. Norse mythology comes into play with regularity. It's pretty obvious that J. R. R. Tolkien knew his Wagner. It occasionally feels like an homage to me. Tolkien denied it to his publisher, "Both rings were round, there the resemblance ceases." Right. The *Ring* was part of every British schoolboy's education in Tolkien's time, and his best friend, C. S. Lewis, was an obsessed Wagnerian, deeply immersed in Norse language, mythology and verse.

There are American resonances, too. Some of the characters sound like Disney cartoons to me. Whenever Hagan and Siegfried enter from a distance, they call out with a musical interval. Hagan's "Hoi-ho!" is so much like the Seven Dwarfs' "Hi-ho!" from Snow White, that I find myself smiling whenever Hagan's interval is sung. Walt Disney, you joker.

It's not only old pop culture that *Götterdämmerung* calls to mind. Siegfried's serial dating is straight out of an episode of *The Bachelor*. He'll fall in love with anybody. And these quests are not dissimilar from *The Amazing Race* or any number of reality show quests on television. Siegfried's magic cloak is like Harry Potter's invisibility cloak meets *Transformers*. And Wagner's music, of course, is everywhere in contemporary life. The themes of the *Ring* are featured in more advertisements, films, and television shows that anybody can count. People who have never heard the Valkyries' battle cry from the stage, recognize a good Ho-jo-to-ho! when they hear it.

I suppose it's not really a question of quoting Wagner, although for the purposes of parody, nothing hits the spot like an audio snippet from the *Ring* or a picture of a buxom woman in braids wearing breastplates. Aside from the tomfoolery, these characters and their situations are archetypes. This is part of the reason why audiences respond to the Ring with such devotion. The brilliance of Wagner was to make the mythological characters real enough to be proxies for ourselves but distant enough that they stand as symbols. I don't see myself in Tolkien's *The Lord of the Rings*, but I'm everywhere in Wagner's *Ring*.

Now, I'm enjoying the first of two intermissions. Downstairs, there is an exhibition of photographs from *Ring* cycles past, and I make my way down into the underworld of the Met to check it out. There's a clock above the coat check window. The time is 8:15. I do a double take. Two hours have already passed? Maybe a six-hour opera isn't such a crazy idea after all.

It's really fun seeing these old photos and putting the performance tonight into historical context. The complete *Ring*'s premiere was in the Bavarian town of Bayreuth. Wagner had visited the town in 1870 and thought it would be a good place to design and build his own theater, inaugurate a music festival to honor himself, and premiere his epic cycle of operas. This modest task he accomplished in 1876 with the first performances of the dramas, *Der Ring des Nibelungen.* London performances followed in 1882, and in Italy in 1883 (two months after Wagner died, in Venice). New York caught its first pieces of the *Ring* in 1885 with *Die Walküre* at the Metropolitan Opera; then in 1887 *Siegfried* and *Götterdämmerung.*

The complete cycle was performed for the first time in the western hemisphere, at the Met in 1889. The reception was a lovefest. The public already adored Wagner's music. For the *Ring*, the audience filled the house. The tone of the *Times'* review on the occasion gives some indication of the appetite for Wagner,

> It would be unjust to the memory of the greatest genius that ever revealed itself through music as well, as to the management of the Opera House and the conscientious singers engaged in the work to sum up the merits of last evening's production in the brief time at one's disposal after the performance. Extended comment must, therefore, be deferred, but it may be said that the representation embodied many noble features that made a

deep impression on the audience. In respect of stage apparel it can at once be set down as the most satisfactory achievement of the Metropolitan.[5]

The performances were conducted by Anton Seidl, who had also conducted the premieres in London. Seidl certainly held claim to his assignment. He was a protégé of Wagner, he lived in Wagner's house, and he worked as a copyist on the original scores. The exhibition materials point out the cost of a ticket for the American premiere: 75 cents for the Family Circle, $3 for an orchestra seat, and $60 for a seat in the first tier boxes, which sounds like a lot of money. Maybe it was the price for the entire box. I am surprised to read how warmly the U.S. embraced Wagner's music. The Met performed a lot of Wagner at the turn of the century, starting with *Lohengrin* in 1883.

An unidentified journalist reprinted in the Met archives notes the attention paid by an audience eager to embrace German music immediately after the Met was founded,

> The interest exhibited by the public in the event—unfortunately a Wagner opera is an event with us—was a most gratifying and significant fact. The beautiful opera house was filled by an audience that did not seem to lack more than two hundred persons of being as numerous as the audience that the unique attraction of the [inaugural] night brought within its walls. It was an audience, moreover, that for the greater part seemed filled with a different spirit than the ordinary audience of the house. The

pitch to which interest in the music was raised, and the anxiety to ignore the conventional things of an Italian opera performance which was felt, were attested by the rapt attention with which the music and the play were followed and the impatient emphasis with which outbursts of applause during the progress of a scene were hissed into silence. Other things than high notes engrossed the attention of last night's listeners, and many of the unobtrusive instances of intelligent, artistic effort received prompt recognition and decorously expressed reward. It might be argued from this that the patrons of the opera in New York are ripe for something better and nobler than the sweetmeats of the hurdy-gurdy repertory, and that a winning card to play in the game now going on between the rival managers would be a list, not necessarily large, of the best works of the German and French schools. Certainly, if the difference between last night's audience and eight of the nine audiences that preceded it can be taken as a comparative measure of the interest in the two classes of operas, no manager can keep his eyes closed to the demonstration completed yesterday.[6]

Wagner performances continued in rapid progression in New York after *Lohengrin* (1883): *Tannhäuser* (1884), *Die Walküre* (1885), *Die Meistersinger von Nürnberg* (1886), *Rienzi* (1886), *Tristan und Isolde* (1886, U.S. premiere), *Siegfried* (1887, U.S.

premiere) *Götterdämmerung* (1888, U.S. premiere), *Das Rhein-gold* (1889, U.S. premiere), *Der fliegende Holländer* (1889) and *Parsifal* (1903, U.S. premiere). The operas of Wagner provided the Met with some historic moments. Gustav Mahler conducted *Tristan* for his house debut in 1908, for example.

Audiences embraced Wagner early, but musicians struggled with its demands. Few vocalists were trained to project their voices over such large orchestrations, and in such big auditoriums with the demands of high and loud singing that must have seemed like marathons of vocal endurance.

Here is a glimpse into backstage tumult of the early American Wagnerians. Richard Aldrich wrote, in *The New York Times*:

Very few in the audience who heard Mme. Louise Homer in the part of Fricka in *Das Rheingold* last Thursday evening understood what an astonishing feat she was accomplishing. The notice on the door said that she had learned the part at very short notice: but it did not say how short. The fact was that she began to study it at 2 o'clock that afternoon, after rehearsing *Un ballo in maschera* for two hours at full voice, and after one of the other principal singers of the company had tried to master it and had given it up in despair. Mme. Homer spent the entire afternoon going over the music, which she had never before studied, with Mr. Herz and one of the accompanists of the Opera House. After a brief rest she returned to the task at 7 o'clock—only to find that in her weariness almost all she had learned had dozed from her memory, and a beginning had to be made over again; and even then one phrase vanished as soon as she began to memorize the next. Her rehearsal lasted till 8:30, when the curtain rose on the performance, and was continued when the scene changed to Nibelheim and she was able to leave the stage for half an hour or so, for further study, till she came on again. Her performance under these conditions was a remarkable tour de force. It is difficult enough with plenty of time to master the Wagnerian declamation, which has so little to impress itself definitely upon the memory. Mme. Homer sang with all her beauty of tone and got through the music without noticeable lapses of any kind. For the words she was, of course, almost entirely dependent upon the prompter. Mme. Lehmann once made a record by learning a Wagnerian part in a day; perhaps such a one as Fricka's was never before mastered in an afternoon.[7]

The binge of Wagner consumption in New York came to an abrupt end however. The U.S. entered World War I on Good Friday, April 6, 1917. The performance at the Metropolitan that night was *Parsifal*, Wagner's story of a knight seeking the Holy Grail. It would be three years before a Wagner opera would be heard again at the Met, and even then, only in English. Aside from a 1920 *Parsifal*, no full productions of Wagner operas were performed again in the house until 1922. For an opera house as devoted to a composer as the Met was to Wagner for thirty-four years, this was a monumental change.

Anti-German sentiment had swept the country. And even after the Armistice Day cease-fire ended the Great War in 1918, anti-German persecution continued here. Specifically at the opera house, rumors circulated about German singers and musicians as foreign spies. Legislators drafted laws prohibiting German musicians from performing on stages and in orchestras. Around the country, American-Germans changed their surnames to hide their origins. Schools stopped teaching German to students and radio stations were discouraged from playing music of German composers. Towns, streets, organizations, and buildings with German names were changed. German-language newspapers were forced to close, and the National German-American Alliance (that had tried to block the U.S. involvement in the war) had its charter withdrawn.

The withdrawal of Wagner operas at the Met created something of a pent-up demand, however, and in the mid-1920s, his operas returned, as admired as before. In the exhibition downstairs, the Met notes that the popularity of the *Ring*, particularly with the Danish stars Kirsten Flagstad and Lauritz Melchior, helped save the Met and kept it alive during the Great Depression. For that, at least, I am grateful to Wagner.

But maybe I should just say it: attending the Wagner cycle of operas makes me uncomfortable philosophically. It isn't merely that the composer was a Nazi favorite and that Hitler adored him. It runs deeper than that for me. I can look at art made by repulsive people and still admire it, even be touched by it. I read books that I find confrontational, see movies by directors with whom I would never want to have dinner, and so on, but what are we to do with the hatefulness of Wagner's anti-Semitism? It goes beyond a distasteful case of prejudice. Wagner wrote about the "harmful influence of Jewry on the morality of the nation".[8] He wrote that Jewish music is without expression and is characterized by coldness and indifference, triviality and nonsense and that to admit a Jew into the world of art results in pernicious consequences that poison the public taste in the arts.[9] Wagner—not Hitler—coined the expressions "Jewish problem" and "final solution," which is a call for a holocaust. It's as simple as that.

The intense Teutonic nationalism of *Der Ring des Nibelungen* plays not a small role in the disastrous history of the Third Reich. Hitler's rise to power coincided with the 50th anniversary of Wagner's death. As the event was celebrated at the Bayreuth festival, Hitler latched onto the Ring's themes of the glory of the Germanic race and the recurring emphasis on its purity. The festival itself became a propaganda tool against Jews. Hitler's allegiance to Wagner was long in coming. He wrote in his memoirs that viewing Wagner's *Rienzi* as a teenager made him discover his destiny which was to unite the German Reich. Hitler carried music from *Tristan* in his knapsack during World War I. Wagnerian music was performed at party rallies and functions to animate the masses.

For Hitler's 50th birthday, he requested from the Wagner family original copies of the operas and took them with him into his bunker. Hitler also used Wagner as a benchmark to censure contemporary music and label it as degenerate. But more than that, Hitler loved Wagner's racist philosophies and he looked for ways to bring to pass the composer/philosopher's darkest intentions.

Yes, that was all a long time ago. But it remains an open wound for many people. Israel hasn't heard a Wagner opera performance since Kristallnacht in 1938. Recently, when Zubin Mehta and Daniel Barenboim conducted orchestral music by Wagner as encores in Jerusalem, there were angry protests. The most recent episode took place on August 1, 2001, as Barenboim led the Staatskapelle Berlin orchestra. At the end of the concert, the conductor turned to the audience after the first encore and asked if they wanted to hear Wagner. Thirty minutes of debate followed. A few in the crowd called Barenboim (who is Jewish) a fascist. But most of the audience stayed and gave the performance of the overture to *Tristan und Isolde* an enthusiastic ovation. Still, Barenboim was denounced later by Israeli Prime Minister Ariel Sharon, Jerusalem Mayor Ehud Olmert, and President Moshe Katsav. Olmert called Barenboim, "brazen, arrogant, insensitive and uncivilized."

I don't know what to do with all of this information. On some level, I suppose, my anxiety about a tacit endorsement of Wagner has been the barrier to my attending the *Ring* before now—more than the financial outlay or the time commitment. I understand that *Der Ring des Nibelungen* is viewed by many as a high-water mark of art of the western world, right up there with Shakespeare's tragedies and Michelangelo's Sistine Chapel. I want to know what it's all about. Should I have skipped the *Ring* out of principle? At the same time, I don't feel strongly enough to want to stay away any longer or, for that matter, to try to get others to stay away. Obviously, I haven't sorted it all out in my own head. I go back to my seat for Act II.

I am quickly rewarded. Act II contains some beautiful singing. Hagen's father, Alberich appears in a dream and urges his son to get the ring. Eric Owens, who has been receiving stellar reviews for his portrayal of Alberich in the *Ring*, is magnificent. I've watched his career bloom. That's also part of the fun of operagoing—seeing talent emerge. His singing is rich and powerful. Equally astonishing is the appearance of a chorus of about 100 to welcome Siegfried back to the Gibichungs. Everything about the *Ring* is huge, but this is the only opera of the four that employs a chorus. That's a surprising fact to me. Wagner loves big sounds, and to my ears, a heroic chorus booming over the top of a full orchestra has an effect that can't be matched otherwise, but there isn't much ensemble singing to be found in these operas. Still, the chorus sounds spectacular here. All of the principal characters are together again. Siegfried doesn't recognize Brünnhilde. She is furious that he has her ring, and she promises vengeance. Siegfried swears that he has done nothing wrong. Hagen offers to kill him, but Brünnhilde reveals that she's protected him with a spell. Siegfried's only vulnerability is his back. Brünnhilde knew that he would never turn away from a fight. Gunther and Gutrune join in the conspiracy. A plan is drafted to kill Siegfried on a hunting trip.

This is a battle of teenager emotions. Siegfried is an innocent brute, fearless and gullible. Even before he is drugged by Gunther and Gutrune, he is easily taken in by them. He so desperately wants to be accepted that he fails to look past the surface of their hospitality to their darker motivations. As for Brünnhilde, for all of her talk about holding the wisdom of man, she is petulant and vulnerable to manipulation. As soon as she thinks she has been betrayed, her thoughts turn to murder. At the same time, she refuses to help her family in a crisis that might end their lives, in deference to Siegfried and a promise she made to him. There's a lot of hot-blooded action without thinking in the *Ring*. This is Valhalla High School.

During the second intermission, I determine to figure out how the images are projected onto the stage set. I take a stroll down to the orchestra pit. It's a flexible space and can be reconfigured to accommodate orchestras of various sizes. Mozart requires a considerably smaller battery of musicians than Wagner, for example. I count the empty chairs. The pit is set up for about 100 musicians. There are six harps along the back wall under the prompter's box. I've never seen such a cadre. I get to wondering what the musicians are doing during intermission. Poor things. Unlike the singers who have a scene and then leave for an hour or so, the orchestra has six hours of uninterrupted playing. Are there massage therapists backstage, working on sore muscles? They've been at it for four hours. It's about 10 o'clock, but I still haven't heard the Rhinemaidens yet, one of the reasons I bought a ticket tonight. I would compare it to running a marathon, but this lasts about twice as a long. Whatever these folks get paid isn't enough.

I turn around to face the house, and I see platforms extending out from the base of the Parterre boxes. On top of the structures are light projectors. I have my ah-ha moment. I hadn't been able to figure out the projections. When a character walked in front of the panels onstage, and a spotlight illuminated him or her, a small shadow was cast onto the set, but it didn't obliterate the projected image. I couldn't imagine how the base image was created. If the entire surface of the set was projected as one, single image, like a movie theater, then it would have a flatness to it, and as the set morphed and the panels rotated, there would be quite a bit of visual distortion. There would also be more shadows on it. I wasn't seeing that problem. This explains it. There are six projectors resting on these cantilevered platforms, which are spread out across the distance of the auditorium. I can't be sure, but my guess is that each of the six machines has the same image, but because the sources come from different angles, the resulting image on the panels is color-saturated and also protected from the shadows cast by performers. The projectors would have to be calibrated exactly; otherwise there would be a blur and distortion. Still, this doesn't explain how the panels also seem to be lighted from above, but I'm satisfied enough that I don't have to stare at it and try to solve the technological puzzle any longer. The apocalypse approaches. Valhalla is going down. I return to my seat for Act III.

Here come the Rhinemaidens. The stage panels of the set are practically vertical now. Onto them is projected a moving image of cascading water. Siegfried is separated from his hunting party and he speaks to the Rhinemaidens—Woglinde, Wellgunde, and Flosshilde. The women are costumed like hipster mermaids, in black mesh body stockings, with zany little hats. Immediately they scamper up the side of the steep waterfall, crouch for a moment or two, raise an arm above their head like a 1950s pin-up girl, and then they slide down to the river below, squealing. It's great fun. After all of this ponderous music, the audience is all smiles. They climb up and slide down time and again. It is like a circus act, all the while singing as a beautiful trio. The audience is really eating it up. The *Ring*'s director, Robert Lepage, is from Quebec. He and his design team are veterans of Cirque du Soleil. The acrobatic, high-tech, slightly crazy, immersively other-worldly experience of Cirque is in evidence throughout the production, but nowhere more than on the banks of the Rhine.

I'm smiling as much as anybody because all three Rhinemaidens have a Mormon connection. Woglinde is sung by Erin Morley, a member of my ward, Flosshilde is Tamara Mumford who was so wonderful in *Anna Bolena* at the beginning of the season, and Jennifer Johnson Cano, although not a member of the Church, is married to Chris Cano from our stake who is also an excellent musician, a pianist. These three women are great together. They are sexy women, and their vocal blend is superb. When voices join, the spins of the vibrato are like ice skaters rotating in unison. If the spins were to be out of sync, a wobble would start to happen, a lopsidedness. The extraordinary thing about these Rhinemaidens, who remind me of what the Andrew Sisters would sound like if they were opera singers, is that although one is a coloratura soprano, another a soprano, and third a husky-toned mezzo, it sounds like a single, incredible voice. It's a great blend. As performers, they are charming and in full control.

The Rhinemaidens ask Siegfried to return the ring to them. He dismisses them, and they predict his imminent death. Hagen, Gunther, and the hunters arrive. Imminent indeed. At this point in the *Ring*, I'm at a loss why we need yet more backstory, but Siegfried tells the men of his youth and adventures. Hagen mixes an antidote to the potion Siegfried was given earlier. He suddenly remembers Brünnhilde. As he realizes what he has done, Hagen stabs him in the back with his spear. Siegfried calls out to Brünnhilde and dies.

In *Götterdämmerung*, there are two sections of music that I love. One is the Immolation Scene, when Brünnhilde rides into the flames. I assume that is coming soon. The other is Siegfried's

Funeral March. It is nerve-devouring music. There have been hints of its themes in the orchestra leading up to Siegfried's death, particularly the meandering tune in the woodwinds. The tension builds to the great opening of the March, the double hit of chords like a pounding on a door or the striking of an anvil. In this production, Hagan, with his hands bloodied from killing, climbs up to the side of the waterfall, and as the orchestra begins the March, he extends his hands into the water. The blood on his hands stains the water until it is a river of crimson. With the tragic music playing, it is a beautiful, beautiful moment, a perfect example of what a modern staging brings to a classical work.

Wagner wrote all of these orchestral interludes as set changes. And there are a lot of scenes in a six-hour opera. He wanted the action to be continuous, and he created music that was non-stop. The problem for a modern production is the simple fact that scene changes can happen instantly now. It's a simple evolution of stage technology. So what is an audience to do during these periods of scene changes? Here, finally, is the answer. The river of blood is one of the most powerful moments I've had in the opera house, a devastating few minutes.

For the final scene, we're back in the Gibichungs' hall. Hagen returns and tells Gutrune of Siegfried's death. Siegfried's body is brought in. Brünnhilde accuses Gunther of murder, but he shifts the blame to Hagen. The two men fight for control of the ring. Gunther is killed. As Hagen goes to grab the ring, the dead Siegfried raises his arm, threateningly. Brünnhilde orders a funeral pyre to be built. She curses the gods for their part in the tragedy and promises to make things right by giving the ring back to the Rhinemaidens.

The casting of the *Ring* has a built-in training system. It's something like a farm team in baseball. Young singers that aspire to be lead Wagnerians someday are initially cast in smaller parts. This is true for any opera, really, but in Wagner it works especially well. Take *Götterdämmerung* as an example. First, a soprano will be a Norn (a weaver of fate). It's solid music, demanding in its way. But it's only one scene and then they're done for the night. If she stands out in that role, she may move up, you could say, to a Gutrune, and then later to *Brünnhilde*. The music is all of a type. It a question of stamina and the ability to maintain a beauty in the voice despite all of the attending punishment. Of these singers, Wendy Bryn Harmer strikes me as a future Brünnhilde. The part she is singing tonight does not command all that much attention. She is on stage a lot, but it's something of a thankless role. But at the end of the evening, Harmer unleashes a gorgeous sound, a gleaming, robust bloom of power as Gutrune. It's the kind of sound that makes a listener do a double take.

I don't know whether there is such a thing as muscle memory for the ear, but as Harmer sings that note, I remember quite distinctly hearing Deborah Voigt for the first time. The quality of the sound was identical, or at least, that's how I am remembering it. There's an astonishment to the realization that someone can have power like that in their voice without it turning hard. The only comparison I can think of is a man's hands. Someone who works with his hands and is very strong also has calluses to show for it. This kind of singing, as rare as it can be, is like unlimited power without calluses. Harmer is also singing in *Das Rheingold* and *Die Walküre* at the Met this season. What will Harmer be singing ten years from now? She acts well, looks beautiful on-stage, moves easily, and has a perfect sound. Since her debut as a peasant in Mozart's *Le nozze di Figaro*, she has sung more than 100 times at the Met, each role slightly larger than the last. I have heard her perform a half dozen times at the opera house, in *Die Zauberflöte, Jenůfa, War and Peace*, and now *Götterdämmerung*.

Everyone has an off night, and I heard her sing poorly only once. It was not at the Met, but at a Christmas concert at church, across the street. She sang from the Messiah, "I Know That My Redeemer Liveth." All of a sudden, there was an emotional catch in her voice, the hallmark of the onset of tears. She was in trouble. She was thinking of the text of the song, maybe too much. What a powerful moment it was, though. The audience also began to cry as they realized that this performance, for once, was not just about pretty singing. It was an avowal of belief. And as Harmer proceeded tentatively, her voice collapsed in a haunting, vulnerable way. Nobody would say it was the best performance of that music ever sung, but for me it is the most heartbreaking and touching.

Götterdämmerung

Let's talk immolation. In the score of *Götterdämmerung*, the final scene for Brünnhilde is 20 pages of brutally difficult music. She sings alone. Aside from the issues of stamina—the opera is now into its fifth hour, and when performed as a cycle, Brünnhilde has literally been singing for days—the scene is punishing any way you look at it. The orchestral accompaniment underneath this extended monologue is turbulent and thunderous, as befits the destruction of the gods. The musical themes of the opera crash together, and many of them are brass-heavy. As a result, Brünnhilde pours out her anger and anguish over the top of tumultuous music. And don't forget that she's not just standing still delivering a punch. With the backdrop of the destruction of the world, she's acting up a storm, on horseback, no less, in this production. It isn't impossible singing, but these huge phrases that culminate in high Gs, As and even a high B-flat have to have the strength of steel to cut through the orchestra. Not impossible, but the list of great Brünnhildes in history is rather short. Voigt sounds just like she did five hours ago. That's quite a feat. On the other hand, Stephen Gould, at the end, was sounding parched as Siegfried. He cranked out a few notes that were coarse and fraying. He was probably relieved to be murdered.

The opera is ending with the destruction of Valhalla. In the Gibichungs' hall, the funeral pyre is burning. Astride her horse, Brünnhilde finishes her marathon of singing and rides into the flames. For most of the night, the action has been very close to the front of the stage. The set, being so large, gives the impression that it is happening in deep recesses of the Met, but actually, it's quite forward—all the better for singers to carry over the orchestra. But the pyre is farther back, and the Immolation Scene is set back too. Brünnhilde takes the ring and calls to the Rhinemaidens. They are instructed to claim it from her ashes after the fire has purified it of its curse.

This production is quite realistic, but as far as the horse is concerned, it doesn't compare to the production in the 1940s when Brünnhilde, played by Marjorie Lawrence, a real-life equestrian, mounted her live horse Grane and took a running jump into the flames. Our Grane slides slowly—and I mean slowly—toward the pyre, and Brünnhilde raises her arms in joy and flings her head back. She is consumed by flames, well, by smoke and fire-colored lights.

In Wagner's libretto, he is quite precise about stage action. The directions are written into the musical score. Here is an English translation of the stage directions for Brünnhilde's suicide:

> She has jumped on to the horse and with one bound leaps into the burning pyre. The flames immediately crackle and flare up high, so that the fire fills the whole space in front of the hall and seems to seize on this too. Terrified, the men and women press to the extreme foreground. When the entire stage appears to be completely filled with fire, the glare suddenly dies down, leaving only a cloud of smoke that drifts towards the background and lies on the horizon like a dark pall of cloud. At the same time the

Rhine greatly overflows its banks, and its waters inun-
date the area of the fire. The three Rhinemaidens swim
past on the waves and appear above the pyre. Hagen, who
since the incident of the ring has been watching
Brünnhilde's behaviour with growing anxiety, is filled
with the utmost terror at the sight of the Rhinemaidens.
He hastily throws aside his spear, shield and helmet and
plunges, as if insane, into the flood.

I have a beef with the ending as staged by Lepage and the
Metropolitan. It simply isn't apocalyptic enough. Wagner intends
that the Gibichungs' hall catche fire and collapse. Then the Rhine
overflows its banks, extinguishing the fire, and the Rhinemaidens recapture the ring. As Hagan tries to stop them, he is dragged
to a watery grave. The people on the banks of the Rhine look to
the skies and see Valhalla afire. The gods are destroyed. And the
curtain falls. I suppose a director doesn't have to do everything
that's in the score. On the other hand, if it isn't cathartic, then
what's the point?

This production is hollow. It ends not with a bang but a yawn.
After Brünnhilde disappears, the rest is a muddle. The banks
don't overflow. If the Rhinemaidens and Hagen appeared, I
missed it, and as for the destruction of Valhalla, it's feeble. After
investing six hours at the opera (or 23 hours when the *Ring* cycle
is performed in repertory this spring), an audience can be forgiven feeling that this production's ending is a letdown. The fall
of Valhalla? Five statues of the gods tip over, heads explode,

swords fall. I don't understand how the director could spend this much money on a set and not have it do something more at the end. I don't think Wagner is very well served in the last thirty minutes of this *Götterdämmerung*.

Bleary-eyed the next morning, I'm still trying to arrange my thoughts about the opera. My initial impression is that it zipped by much faster than I thought it would. I guess I had allowed myself to be caught up in the stereotype of Wagnerian excesses, and in hindsight, it was a baseless fear. As to the story of the *Ring*, I am not as powerfully involved in the mythology as many people seem to be. It's not uncommon to hear the word "life-changing" when talking to Wagner fans about their introduction to the *Ring*.

Once, a few years ago, I worked with a young man who claimed to be royalty. He was from a Slavic family, if I'm remembering this correctly, which escaped Europe. If his country returned to a monarchy, he said, he would be in line to be king. At any rate, I was listening to Wagner one day at work, and I introduced him to the Ring cycle. He became consumed by its story. Having had access to private journals of his royal family, he was rather well acquainted with the Divine Right of Kings and other such thought systems. In our workplace, as he read the synopses of the Ring, he would mutter aloud, "Of course. Yes, that is right," and so forth. His belief of a system of Gods and their intervention with mortals (his family line) dovetailed with Wagner much more closely than my belief system does.

The *Ring* mesmerizes. Audiences are devoted to Wagner in ways that are hard to classify. It goes beyond fandom. Perhaps there are Rossini societies and Puccini clubs too (just as there are *Star Wars* and *Star Trek* conventions), but Wagner is almost a religion of its own. Listeners become devotees to Wagner, and to the *Ring* cycle in particular. Attendance at annual performances of his operas at Bayreuth is like a religious pilgrimage. The attitude of dedication, of giving oneself over to Wagner, is part of the festival's design. I don't know if I'd say that the music is greater than anyone else's music, but I am coming to think that the audience participates in Wagner's music differently. What I mean is that Wagner enjoys an unusual level of the audience "getting it" musically.

It has to do with the way an audience listens to Wagner. Upon first hearing, the audience hears that Siegfried is approaching, for example. The orchestra plays a tune that will be associated forever after in the *Ring* with Siegfried. Whenever other characters refer to him and when he is onstage, the Siegfried tune, or leitmotif, recurs. The audience associates the leitmotif with the character in a specific way. Later, when Siegfried uses a prop—a sword, say—it is given a leitmotif as well. And harmonically it relates to and comes from Siegfried's tune. Then, as other characters interact with Siegfried, as they fall in love with or give battle to him, their leitmotifs intertwine with Siegfried's. By intertwine, I mean it literally. The notes are extensions of each other. Leitmotifs are provided for animals too, settings, natural elements like water and fire, and for the emotions of characters. After all of these leitmotifs are in place, Wagner is able to use them to foreshadow things to come or to recall events that occurred earlier. A character will say he wants to kill Siegfried, and in the orchestra, his leitmotif will sound, even if only a few notes. Brünnhilde will recall meeting Siegfried, and his leitmotif will perfume the memory. It's not just in the text.

All of this adds up, in the ears of the audience, as a puzzle whose intricacies are complex and yet entirely knowable. More than that, as the component parts are assembled and loosed into the greater mythology, the character-specific sounds take on a bigger role. They come to feel like inevitabilities falling into place. Wagner once said that every musical measure of the *Ring* was connected to the measures before it. All the while, the audience has the feeling that they get it, regardless of the listener's previous acquaintance with music. They catch these leitmotifs, however fleeting, and they think that they understand Wagner's creative process. The audience even believes that they are participating in the music-making somehow, and relative to the passivity of other musical experiences—the going to a concert and letting the music wash over them without trying to figure it out—they are participating.

It's quite an achievement, if you think about it. However natural it feels to so closely identify a character with a given combination of notes, it's an ingenious and relatively recent invention musically. In Mozart, you hear a glorious tune, let's say the ending of *Marriage of Figaro* when the Count confesses to his wife and asks her forgiveness, and as a listener you think that the slow, cascading intervals are like the melting away of pride to reveal pure love. You give Mozart full credit as the genius that could pull beauty out of thin air. But what you don't say is that the notes combine into a symbol that is identifiable to the narrative. You don't recognize in that Mozartean moment that it has been coming and has finally arrived, a consequence of a build-up of notes and themes. You don't see the machinations of the composer. Those are tricks left to Wagner.

Wagner creates professional audiences. That is, he takes people who have studied music and those who haven't, and he gives them a language to talk about music. He says, This pattern of notes I'll assign to the Valkyies, and so when you hear them, think: Valkyrie. Another way of thinking about it is a maniacal sense of control, that Wagner gets into the head of his listeners and tells them what to think and when. He casts a bullying spell. Maybe that's unfair to say.

For composers today, coming after Wagner, the interplay of audience and music suddenly must have become more complicated. In 2012, does a composer embrace a leitmotif-leading system or go another way? And if they discard the close associations of tunes and subject, how do they get audiences to be as fully engaged in their music as they are with Wagner's? The dilemma is not unlike that of visual artists. A painter friend recently said to me, "When it comes right down to it, what I'm trying to do is to get somebody to stop and look for more than five seconds." How does a composer get you to listen? Most will have to concede, 136 years after the premiere of *Götterdämmerung*, that the majority of composers have no idea how to get an audience to negotiate the pathways of the music's creation like Wagner routinely accomplished. Mark Twain quipped that Wagner's music is better than it sounds. I'd argue that the opposite is true.

The review of *Götterdämmerung* in *The New York Times* is polite and laudatory without drumming up much heat. The production, according to Anthony Tommasini, is "the most theatrically effective staging of the four works". He likes most of the singing and referring to the orchestra, calls it "exciting." "Mr. Luisi's lucid, textured and urgent conducting was distinguished. He received a huge ovation." He agrees with me about the Mormon singers. Harmer "was a bright-voiced and affectingly volatile Gutrune", and the Rhinemaidens were "all excellent." Reading the review, it sounds like his biggest hesitation was with Brünnhilde,

Her singing in *Götterdämmerung* was sometimes patchy and tremulous. Her lower range continued to be a problem. And sometimes sustained midrange tones wavered. But through sheer force of will, she proved herself as Brünnhilde here, especially during the complex confrontation scene in Act II, when her character lashes out at Siegfried, who she thinks has betrayed her, with blazing phrases of accusation and bitterness. Ms. Voigt's sound was not pretty, but it sliced through the orchestra and throbbed with intensity.[10]

I am aware from talking to some of the cast members that Voigt had been ill during the rehearsal process. There was some doubt whether she'd make it. Two Brünnhildes were cast to alternate performances.

On February 7, Deborah Voigt pulls out of the performance. Her understudy is Nina Warren, another of the LDS singers at the Met this year and a friend of many years. Throughout most of the early rehearsal period around the holidays, Voigt had been absent and the cast practiced around her as best they could. It didn't surprise me that she sang the first performances of *Götterdämmerung* however. Too much was at stake for her. The role is being shared with Katarina Dalayman. But Nina is covering the role of Brünnhilde and, I assume, was pretty busy in rehearsals before Dalayman arrived and while Voigt was recovering.

The New York Times thought it was big enough news to report the withdrawal online on Tuesday, a few hours before the performance is to begin. It quotes a Twitter message that Voigt sent at midnight, "Hostess Twinkies. That is all." (Brünnhildes can be so cryptic when they tweet.) If Nina gets the call to step into the role, I'm determined to head back to the opera house to witness it. But ultimately, Dalayman goes on and the initial run of the opera ends. It comes back in the spring with the other three *Ring* operas.

CHAPTER 6

IT IS THE SEASON FOR GETTING SICK. Anecdotally, it seems like half of the city has one flu bug or another. In an opera house, a singer who is ill is replaced by someone farther down the food chain. But at other venues, there is less flexibility for vocalists. I purchase tickets to hear Erin Morley give a recital concert at Carnegie Hall. The performance is February 24. The initial run of *Götterdämmerung* is over, and Morley, liberated from her gymnastic Rhinemaiden performance, is to give a recital of art songs by Haydn, Schumann, Rossini, Poulenc, Barber and Rachmaninoff.

The concert is presented by Carnegie Hall, one of a series titled, Great Singers: Evenings of Song. It is sponsored by The Ruth Morse Fund for Vocal Excellence and is to take place at Weill Recital Hall, which is an intimate venue above the main hall. The promotional blurb for the concert is tantalizing,

> For Erin Morley, last season was what she called 'the year of the Queen': She wowed audiences in Santa Fe, Frankfurt, and Dresden as the Queen of the Night in Mozart's *Die Zauberflöte*. This season, the regal, young soprano appears in Robert Lepage's new production of Wagner's *Ring* cycle at the Metropolitan Opera—and gives a recital of songs by Haydn, Rossini, Schubert, and others at Carnegie Hall.

I love going to concerts at Weill. It's an intimate space, and everything seems to sound good there. It has 268 seats divided between an orchestra section (14 rows with 14 seats per row) and a small balcony (5 rows). There are no aisles in the orchestra to divide the seating. The stage looks like the main hall of Carnegie shrunk down to a more negotiable size, 33 feet by 15 feet. The room has a high ceiling that is decorated with arches and gold leaf ornamentation. It's an elegant space with columns and decorative panels, crystal chandeliers, and rich, blue velvet draperies with swags and pull-backs that give the illusion that the room has windows, which it doesn't.

By Friday the 24th, it has been raining heavily in the city for two days straight. The audience members at the concert are soggy but in high spirits. I see quite a few people whom I know. I suspect that many of those in attendance have personal relationships with Morley. So when Jeremy Geffen, the director of artistic programming of Carnegie Hall walks onstage, there is an added degree of disappointment. The first words out of his mouth are that Erin Morley is ill. I feel sorry for myself, having braved a stormy night for a concert that might be cancelled, but I especially feel badly for a friend. This recital was to be something of a coming out party for her as a concert artist in New York. Geffen calls Morley a trooper and says she is going to perform anyway. I don't know how to react. Is it wise for her to perform? There's always a possibility of hurting your voice under conditions like this. And then I wonder about the critics who are undoubtedly in the audience. Will they cut her any slack? Morley's a coloratura soprano. Head colds and high notes are like oil and water. For a bass, who cares if you have a cold? But for a high-flying soprano....

A few years ago, in 1991, I sat in Carnegie Hall to hear Luciano Pavarotti sing through Verdi's *Otello*. He had never sung it before in performance, and there had been a lot of hype leading up to it. Georg Solti led the Chicago Symphony in a concert performance of the opera. It was a farewell to the great Solti who was stepping down after 22 years leading the symphony. Decca Records was there to record the performance. It's too heavy and demanding of a role, really, for a tenor like Pavarotti was, but for one night, I expected that it would be very interesting. Unfortunately for him, he caught a cold before the performance. A chronic canceller of operas in Chicago, to the point that the Lyric Opera of Chicago banned him from the company permanently, I don't think even he dared cancel at that point, so Pavarotti sat in front of the orchestra on a chair, slumped over a humidifier with an enormous handkerchief covering his head. It was a bizarre night.

He had a table in front of him with snacks and drinks, and throughout the night, presumably to keep his throat open, the tenor munched on food like he was at a picnic, and then he covered himself with the handkerchief. Pavarotti would remain hidden until a few seconds before he was to sing. Then he'd emerge, somehow get through a scene, looking absolutely terrified, and then slink back to the humidifier and the comfort food. He sang from his chair part of the time while everyone else stood. Needless to say, it was odd. But surprisingly, it was also pretty good singing. I don't know how he ever got through it.

When Morley is announced ill, I have a flashback to Pavarotti. What am I in for? Right away, we find out what we're not in for: Haydn and Poulenc. Morley intends to sing but there are major cuts to the scheduled program. In addition to the above, she's omitting Rossini's "La danza", which was something of a calling card for Pavarotti back in the day when he would toss off the rollicking, tarantella showstopper with Neapolitan swagger. Probably a wise choice from an energy-conservation standpoint. As sad as I am to be hearing a truncated recital, by now I'm more nervous for the soprano than anything else. It's not an ideal emotion for the audience. The illusion of a recital—and a circus too, for that matter—is that however dangerous and precarious, the performer will ultimately be fine. Watching NASCAR is a crash-and-burn pursuit. Music is not.

Morley steps onto the stage, greeted by a rush of goodwill from the audience. She is wearing a lustrous purple gown with jeweled short sleeves and a voluminous train that allows for the kind of sweepingly grand entrance and exit that are the right of an opera singer. She doesn't look all that nervous to me. I would be terrified in her shoes. Her pianist is Vlad Iftinca. He is the staff music coach at the Metropolitan for the Lindemann Young Artist Development Program. Morley is a graduate of the Lindemann Program; that explains the connection.

What remains of the recital are groups of three or four songs in four languages: German, Italian, English and Russian. Had the Poulenc songs been included, it would have been five languages. That's not a coincidence. Recitals by young opera singers tend to have a component of auditioning to them. They are strategic. They are designed to show a variety of styles, in multiple languages, and the music tends toward the encyclopedic to traverse centuries and continents. These recitals fight off pigeonholing. They say, *I'm singing small parts now, but I've got the chops for more.* Being so cornucopia-like, a lot can go wrong.

The Schumann songs that open the recital are a gentle warm up. A sandman, a cow herder: these are sweet and simple songs about pastoral pleasures. Morley sings them with confidence and focus. They don't require anything too taxing for a high soprano. She sounds beautiful. During Schumann's "Leibeslied" (Love Song) I wonder whether Morley is sick at all. Maybe this is a tactic to lower expectations. Naw, that's a cynical New Yorker's thinking. But she is singing beautifully. It's not until Rossini's "La fioraja fiorentina" (The Florentine Flower Girl) that the concert really gets going for me. The song, about girl who cries out to sell flowers but in her head hears a poor, helpless mother crying for bread, is a stunner and shows off more of the dangerous side of her singing. Morley navigates the bel canto passagework with high notes that sound robust and almost easy. This ends the first half of the concert—it was only five songs long.

I consider getting up and stretching my legs during intermission, but compared to *Götterdämmerung*, this amount of sitting hardly justifies it. Instead, I watch the frantic retuning of the piano. This is something you don't see very often in the middle of a concert. Immediately after the house lights come up at intermission, a piano technician emerges with his instruments and begins tuning the piano. I can only imagine the conversation that must have taken place backstage. I hadn't noticed anything horrible pitch-wise, but what do I know?

Once I was talking to a concert pianist who was among the first to go to the Soviet Union sponsored by the U.S. State Department. He told me that the Russian audiences had an expectation that every recital should be a couple of hours long, but after that, encores should follow, and follow, and follow. It was not uncommon for him to play a dozen encores after a concert. Each was greeted with rhythmic clapping to encourage yet another piece. These were not little ditties either; he was expected to play a continuous string of major works. At the end of one performance, dripping with perspiration, he took leave of the stage and acknowledged that with all of the heavy playing, the piano was a full tone flat.

The pianist and soprano reemerge for the set of songs I'm most interested in hearing, Samuel Barber's *Four Songs*, Op. 13. Barber's aunt was the great American contralto Louise Homer. She sang 741 performances at the Met between 1900 and her retirement in 1935. Barber was an excellent baritone himself, and his love of poetry makes his large body of art songs especially rich. On his bedside table, Barber kept books of poems, and he read them every night of his life, before falling asleep, in search for texts that could become songs. He began writing art songs as a teenager and continued until the last decade of his life.

The *Four Songs* dates from 1937-1940, when he was nearing 30 years old. Morley sings them magnificently. They have real atmosphere to them. All are elegant, sustained, mini-rhapsodies of insight. She's a fine communicator, and the audience is into them in a way I haven't sensed so far. The best of the lot for me is "Sure on This Shining Night" with text by James Agee. She sings, "Sure on this shining night/I weep for wonder/Wandering far alone/Of shadows on the stars." It is melting pathos. It makes me think what Morley might do with the Barber/Agee master-piece for soprano and orchestra, *Knoxville: Summer of 1915*. With any luck, this work will be in her future.

The concert ends with Rachmaninoff's *Six Songs*, Op. 38. These are songs about nature and landscape. They have a wist-fulness to them. Some of the songs are stories of dreams and fairy tales. She returns for an encore, Schumann's "Der Himmel hat eine Träne geweint" (From Heaven Once Fell a Tear). The song tells the fable of a mollusk that finds a tear that has fallen from heaven. He finds and comforts it. The tear will be his pearl, he says. I assume that Morley isn't German, but she seems so at ease with these Schumann works tonight. Maybe the Russian and Italian are idiomatic too, they could be for all I know, but these songs pose no difficulties for her. Her bio doesn't mention it, but in graduate school, she was a dual voice and piano major. She is an excellent pianist—I know from experience in our church congregation—and I hope that she will become the kind of singer who revels in recitals of songs. Given her ability to search out music on her own and play through it, it would appear that the world of song literature is open to her.

With that said, I do have a reservation about the recital. Not of the singing—what a trooper, indeed—but of the material itself. I come away from the recital without knowing where her musical passions lie. I'm curious to know what will catch her eye as her career blooms. How will she put a stamp on music? With the luxury of learning whatever she wants, what will she sing in recital? Will she be a scholar of art songs, like a Cecilia Bartoli, Jan De-Gaetani, Dawn Upshaw, or Dietrich Fischer-Dieskau? Will she be the kind of singer who premieres a lot of new music? Is she curious about all kinds of music, like a Renée Fleming who jumps from opera to jazz to rock and back? Plenty of opera singers, when they give recitals at all, perform arias from their favorite opera roles. Will she be that kind of concert artist?

Part of the fun of watching a singer emerge is the slow unfurling of what makes them tick, personally. In the opera house they are offered this role or that role; they accept it or they don't. Recitals are different. If a singer could perform anything of their choosing, what would they sing? That's the fun of going to recitals.

I haven't heard Morley sing much contemporary music. I

don't know if it appeals to her, but she would be an ideal collaborator for a living composer because of her high degree of musicianship. I suspect she can sight read anything, for example. My guess is that challenging, modern music is not particularly difficult for her. She seems to find storytelling easy, too. I hope she tackles the big song cycles eventually because I suspect she'll be able to sustain a narrative tension in ways that will really captivate her audiences. Ultimately, she's an actress who sings. Time will tell.

On the 27th, *The New York Times* publishes a review of the concert. Predictably, it begins by citing Morley's decision to perform under unfortunate circumstances. "[She] still sounded remarkably good, though occasionally tentative in the first half of the program." The critic, Vivien Schweitzer, praises the Schumann songs "that showed her distinctive, silvery soprano to fine effect," and the Rossini extravaganza "complete with illness-defying radiant top notes." (There's a phrase I don't think I've ever seen before.) The critic praises her commitment to the texts and singles out the Barber as a highlight.[1]

Morley and Iftinka performed the same recital program in early November in Salt Lake City. (Morley is a Salt Lake City native.) I have friends who attended the concert given at the University of Utah's Libby Gardner Hall, and they were bowled over by it. I look up a review online and find one by Matt Dixon, writing for reichelrecommends.com (Ed Reichel is the former music critic for the *Deseret News*, which no longer has a music critic on staff, I believe). It begins, "Wow, what a musical partnership!" It's a glowing report. Here is Dixon's last paragraph,

> Concerts like this are difficult to summarize. Techni-
> cally, I couldn't hear a single note or inflection that
> seemed out of place, but my admiration extends far be-
> yond the performers' sizeable technical achievements.
> The intricate and inviting quality of the musical interpre-
> tations simply won over the audience who demanded, and
> received, an encore. These are two young performers to
> watch for in the future, and the concert became another
> feather in the cap of the University of Utah's excellent Vir-
> tuoso Series.[2]

The season at the Metropolitan rolls on. For a box office, the winter months are like sailing around the cape. There is momen-tum going into the December holidays, but the doldrums hit in January. November and December productions included rarities and risk-taking: Phillip Glass's *Satyagraha* (an opera about Gandhi performed in Sanskrit), *Nabucco* (Verdi), and *Rodelina* (Handel), sprinkled between favorites *Don Giovanni, La bohème, Madama Butterfly, La fille du régiment*, and *Hänsel und Gretel*. The tide of tourists shifts in January, however, and other than *The Enchanted Island*, which was a box office bonanza, it's time to play it safer. The Met goes with the tried and truly familiar: *Faust, Tosca, Barber of Seville, Aida, Ernani*, and a return of *Anna Bolena*, plus the new production of *Götterdämmerung*.

To some degree, the opera house is insulated from the fate that many Broadway shows face in January. Typically, the first Sunday after New Year's Day is Black Sunday on Broadway. Each year, several shows close on this day, unable to weather the box office drop-off of ticket buying that will abate with the spring arrival of a new wave of shows. The opera season is set to a different calendar. But looking ahead to the spring, excitement awaits: the complete *Ring* cycle, a new production of *Manon*, and two twentieth century operas: *The Makropulos Case* and Britten's *Billy Budd*.

For now, artistic risks bow to the realities of staying afloat. On February 25, the press announces the cancellation of Verdi's *Simon Boccanegra* starring Placido Domingo with The Opera Orchestra of New York. It was to have taken place at Avery Fisher Hall, home of the New York Philharmonic. The reason: "a loss of funding." Like many opera companies, The Opera Orchestra of New York is in transition. Its long-time music director, Eve Queler, stepped down last year at the age of 80. The organization, founded in 1972, serves a specific niche in opera. It performs the overlooked works in the repertoire, particularly rarely-heard works by major composers. Given in concert performances rather than fully-staged productions, The Opera Orchestra of New York frequently unearths forgotten treasures that later are given new productions at the Metropolitan. It also gives New York premieres of works by recognized composers that have been overlooked. Over the years, as far back as I can remember, the reviews for Queler as a conductor are never as impressive as the appreciation granted to her dedication to these rarities. The Orchestra—it doesn't use its logical acronym, TOONY, for some reason—also had a reputation for finding major singers and engaging them before they appeared at the Met. The Orchestra, when asked about the choice to cancel *Simon Boccanegra*, reveals that a donor withdrew a $250,000 pledge. Chairman of the board, Norman Raben notes, "we have a mandate to be fiscally responsible, and with the loss of funding for this production we were given no choice but to cancel."[3]

Finding the balance between risk and safety in operatic programming is a continuous struggle. For critics, the Metropolitan's risk aversion is a subject of party game speculation. Alex Ross in *The New Yorker* carps in the March 12 issue of the magazine that,

operatic news is being made elsewhere. Both London companies, Covent Garden and the E.N.O. (English National Opera), have offered contemporary pieces on contemporary themes. European houses from Bayreuth on down grapple with Wagner in serious terms. The San Francisco Opera, the Houston Grand Opera, and the Minnesota Opera pay more heed to American work. New York has yet to see Messiaen's "Saint Francis", Birtwistle's "Gawain", Saariaho's "L'Amour de loin", and a dozen other modern masterpieces. The city has, in truth, seldom been on the front lines of operatic art, but it now seems almost peripheral—even "out of town."[4]

But what about the consequences if these artistic risks don't pay off? Even one flop can cause an avalanche of trouble for an arts organization. It comes down to business management. Earlier in the season, the papers remarked upon the Met's balance sheet. The finances are not published in detail. It is noted that the annual budget is now $300 million. Joseph Volpe, the former Managing Director gives a slightly fuller picture in his memoir, *The Toughest Show on Earth*. These are statistics for the fiscal year 2005-2006. The budget then was $221 million. I am extrapolating that the numbers have risen, but the relative values have remained more or less constant. The largest item on the budget is the cost of producing the operas themselves during the thirty-three week-long season: $143 million. Other costs are touring, producing concerts of the Met Opera Orchestra at Carnegie Hall, summer park concerts throughout the city's boroughs, broadcasting, fundraising, keeping the opera house in working condition, and paying its share of Lincoln Center bills. Volpe notes that the sale of tickets accounts for 46% of the money to pay expenses—that's $101 million (again, for the 2005-2006 season). More money comes from the Met endowment, another $18 million. The Met's proceeds from the Lincoln Center garage and other shared revenue is $10 million more. The shortfall, then, is $92 million.

How is the hole filled? Not by government donations, to be sure. Federal, state and city support is less than one-quarter of one percent of the annual budget, or $375,000, according to Volpe. Five million people flock to Lincoln Center each year. The economic impact for the city is huge, estimated to be about $1.5 billion annually. 50% of the cash flow at Lincoln Center is through the Met. Therefore, $375,000 is not very much money. It's a miniscule investment in the city's profitability. In a nation of farm subsidies and corporate loopholes, I find the amount donated to the arts an embarrassment, particularly in relation to the revenues they generate for communities. The donation to the arts is a pittance, a rounding error on a gargantuan balance sheet that has become a political tug of war. For the Met, considerably more money arrives from foundations ($5 million) and corporate gifts ($7 million). The budget shortfall is still enormous.

Like any down-on-his-luck person who has exhausted other options, this is where the family comes in. According to Volpe, the Met has 125,000 private donors. It maintains a database of 1.5 million names. Approximately 300,000 to 400,000 of those names are considered active. $80 million comes from them in annual gifts that range from $60 to $500,000. That's a lot of rich New Yorkers, right? Actually, no. Two-thirds of these generous opera-lovers live outside of the metropolitan area. The Opera Guild has been incredibly successful reaching out to people through their publication, *Opera News*, through radio broadcasts, and now through HD broadcasts. Just like a grassroots political campaign, the Guild has 40,000 members, and small contributions add up quickly. The amount that the Met receives from the Guild is over $4 million annually. To be sure, there are also big players who live in the city. There is a group called the

Metropolitan Opera Club that donates $500,000 a year to the Met. It is comprised of 300 members who maintain reserved sections of the Dress Circle boxes. They even have their own dining room. This is a throwback to the days of the founding families of the old Met.

Every arts organization has a board, and the Metropolitan Opera has a fantastically active one. It isn't simply a question of donations, either. The Met board—which has no term limits—oversees all operations of the company. It rolls up its sleeves and gets involved in day-to-day operations. There are twelve working committees on the board, including an executive committee, as well as those for audits, artists, archives, investments, productions, upkeep, compensation, to work with the Guild, and to find new board members. The board raises funds, recruits new members, and it hires the general manager. Again, using the 2006 Volpe memoir for statistics, there are 105 board members, 37 of whom are managing directors. This title comes with an obligation to make an annual contribution of at least $125,000 to the Met. Board members also buy tickets, lots of tickets. 40% of board members annually purchase $25,000 or more worth of opera tickets each. The big payday comes from trustees who have long relationships with the company. It is they who write checks to produce new productions and give boosts to the endowment. An example is the $25 million Christmas present given to the Met by Texas billionaires Sid and Mercedes Bass in 2005, the largest unrestricted gift in the company's history.

People give money to the Met for many reasons, of course. Texaco began its historic sponsorship of the opera house in 1940 with Saturday afternoon radio broadcasts to repair its public image after it became known that it was selling oil to Hitler. Corporations and individuals burnish their reputations by joining with other society people. But it is not as calculated as all that. There are plenty of other social causes and organizations that these folks could become aligned with. The thing to remember is that opera means something to these people. They are passionate about it. This brings me back to a consideration of the balance of risk in programming. The board and other donors to the Met are ones to please, it seems to me, because without them, the entire endeavor collapses. Aside from their history as donors, they respond to the buzz about the Met. Critics must be pleased too. If it is viewed as a critically exciting place to be, then the contribution checks reflect that enthusiasm. If it goes to either extreme— too safe or too unfamiliar—there will be financial repercussions. A few years ago, audiences simply stopped going to see opera warhorses. Newer fare performed better at the box office. A few years later, things shifted, and old favorites trumped again. These preferences wax and wane. There's no single approach that will always work. For me, it boils down to leadership. As any organization that has been through reorganization knows, people will follow the passion of a visionary to change course. What they will not do long-term is stick with a sinking ship.

After 9/11, the Met fell on hard times. Ticket sales dropped from +90% sold out rate before the attacks to 82% the following year. Tourism in the city fell off sharply. Volpe notes that by 2004-2005, the box office was still depressed, at 79% of capacity. The average age of the Met ticket buyer is 66. That sounds like bad news too, but Volpe argues that the age has been stable over time (in contrast to the perception that the audience is "graying") and at the same time people are living longer. He also notes that 40,000 students tickets are sold annually (at least that was the number for the 2004-2005 season). As challenging as the demographics and tourism rates are, the fact is that the habits of buyers have shifted radically too.

A generation ago, 75% of the Met tickets sold were to subscribers. Financially, this is a great cushion to have. Subscribers prepay to lock in their seats, and the bundling of performances further spreads risk in that more challenging operas can be nestled in with familiar works to create a desirable series. But that approach of marketing is going away. Only 50% of tickets are through subscriptions now. And that number is on the decline. People still go to the opera, of course, but they are not planning in advance. Opera tickets are becoming an impulse buy.

The Metropolitan Opera announces its 2012-13 season on February 24. I am thinking about the balance of risk as I peruse a rather familiar list of operas. At least, that's my first impression. Here they are, in alphabetical order: *Aida* (Verdi), *Un ballo in maschera* (Verdi), *The Barber of Seville* (Rossini), *Carmen*

(Bizet), *La clemenza di Tito* (Mozart), *Le Comte Ory* (Rossini), *Dialogues des carmélites* (Poulenc), *Don Carlo* (Verdi), *Don Giovanni* (Mozart), *L'elisir d'amore* (Donizetti), *Faust* (Gounod), *Francesca da Rimini* (Zandonai), *Giulio Cesare* (Handel), The *Ring* cycle—*Das Rheingold, Die Walküre, Siegfried, Götterdämmerung* (Wagner), *Maria Stuarda* (Donizetti), *Le nozze di Figaro* (Mozart), *Otello* (Verdi), *Parsifal* (Wagner), *Rigoletto* (Verdi), *La Rondine* (Puccini), *The Tempest* (Thomas Adès), *La traviata* (Verdi), *Les Troyens* (Berlioz), and *Turandot* (Puccini). Next year is the 200th birthday of both Verdi and Wagner, and the Met's six Verdi and five Wagner productions are proof that the Italian and German masters still hold a central place in opera programming.

As a whole, the list is a little disappointing at first glance. Only *The Tempest* is a premiere. This opera by Thomas Adès was commissioned and performed by the Royal Opera House Covent Garden in 2004. After the London premiere, it had multiple productions in Europe and in 2006, in Santa Fe. The Met will create a new production it will share with La Scala in Milan, which will present it the following year. Adès is a forty-one year old British composer, pianist and conductor. His first opera was *Powder Her Face* (1995), a chamber opera about the scandalous Margaret Campbell, whose 1960s divorce trial became a lurid window into sexual inhibition. *The Tempest* was an acclaimed follow-up. In the Met's production, the action of Prospero and his band of castaways will be transported to the 18th century and the Milan opera house. I haven't heard the opera yet, but I'm intrigued. The libretto follows Shakespeare closely, but I've read that the authors trimmed the language in interesting ways while maintaining its Elizabethanisms. For example: "Full fathom five thy father lies/Of his bones are coral made;/Those are pearls that were his eyes" is altered to "Five fathoms deep/Your father lies/Those are pearls/That were his eyes."

The New York Times' announcement of the 2012-13 Met lineup bears the heading, "What Happens in Vegas Will Also Happen at the Met Next Season." The lead story of the article is the decision by director Michael Mayer (whose Broadway musicals *Spring Awakening* and *American Idiot* sought to make musicals edgier entertainments) to set *Rigoletto* in the milieu of the 1960s Las Vegas Rat Pack.[5] I'm not afraid of gimmicks in the opera house. Maybe this will work. I suspect that more rewarding evenings will be spent with a whole host of operas that are performed less frequently, and although they are somewhat standard fare, the Met is lavishing them with luxury casting. New productions will probably garner the attention initially, but in keeping with the Vegas metaphor, I'd rather put my money on a few underdogs.

CHAPTER 7

THE METROPOLITAN OPERA National Council Auditions Finals Concert (a mouthful) is coming up. This year, it will take place on Sunday, March 18 at 3:00pm. I think I'll go. To the best of my knowledge, there aren't any LDS singers in the group of finalists, but several excellent Mormon singers have broken into the Met through the annual competition in recent years, both as winners and as finalists. How do you get to Carnegie Hall? The old joke's punch line: "Practice, practice, practice." How do you get to the Met? You audition.

The company holds auditions for dancers, chorus members, orchestra players, and singers at various times throughout the year. The Met's website gives details and procedures. For orchestral musicians, for example, there are no regular auditions. For an instrumentalist, playing in the Metropolitan Opera Orchestra is one of the plum music jobs in America. Its pay is at the very highest echelon of symphony orchestras, its reputation is stellar, and it provides opportunities for teaching at Juilliard across the street and other free-lance gigs without the pressures of much touring. One of my son's friends in elementary school is the son of a member of the Met's horn section. I became friends with the father. He would occasionally invite me to performances at the opera as his guest, and we frequently talked about the lifestyle of a member of the orchestra.

I assume that musicians at the Met are well paid. I don't know exactly how to quantify that impression. Opera is a business, and to the extent that Mormon musicians are players in the organization, it seems to me that I should delve into the issue of wages in order to understand how the puzzle pieces fit together. Opera singers are not salaried. They negotiate payment for each performance, based on the subjective nature of their artistic stature. I've never had the nerve to ask a singer about the size of their paycheck, but I come across the union agreements for the orchestra, which I imagine to be somewhat comparable to the singers' pay.

According to the International Conference of Symphony and Opera Musicians Settlement Bulletin of September 30, 2011, the current agreement for the Met's orchestra is the following: $138,562.32 annual salary (52 weeks) for performances only. Orchestra musicians rehearse approximately 300 hours annually, which is additional income. The 2011 bulletin doesn't specify the wage amount for rehearsals, but the previous year, it was $80.11 per hour of rehearsal with an average of 10 hours each week. Pensions are paid at 2% per year of service to a maximum of 30 years of base year salary. (The pension is approximately $75,000.) There are 10 weeks of vacation. The orchestra has 90 musicians.

As nice as that package sounds, the big deal in the bulletin is the amount that the orchestra players receive for all of the Met-HD and other media initiatives. This is the underappreciated union concession that has allowed the Met to considerably expand its performances into new media possibilities. Orchestra members receive $13,000 guaranteed revenue sharing listed as "yearly media salary." One assumes that for participants in profit sharing, the extra revenue could be substantial as that portion of the Met's programming continues to grow.

To put the Met Orchestra salary in context, the Utah Symphony annual salary (52 weeks) is approximately $65,000, the Chicago Lyric Opera (24 weeks) is $59,160, New York City Opera (29 weeks) is approximately $38,000, Dallas Symphony (52 weeks) is $90,034.36, San Francisco Opera (23 weeks) is approximately $79,000. Only a handful of symphony orchestras are on par with the Met Orchestra: L.A. Philharmonic (52 weeks) is $143,260, and the New York Philharmonic (52 weeks) is approximately $135,000.[1] That means that the Met's a pretty great gig to land, nice work if you can get it. I can see why auditions are rare. Who would want to leave?

Auditions are held for the Met chorus each year. Singers send resumes and have the option of sending an MP3 audio file of an opera aria to the Met in advance of the auditions. Based on the resumes, those selected are invited to audition for open positions. The singers do not have to be union members (American Guild of Musical Artists) in order to tryout, but they have to be legally eligible to work in the U.S., and if they are offered a job, they must join AGMA. There are five sessions of auditions, all told, about 19 hours of auditions. That indicates to me that there are quite a few people invited each year. At the auditions, each singer performs two arias in different languages, from memory. I have friends who have auditioned unsuccessfully for soloist roles and also for the chorus. Getting into the Met chorus is another in-demand job for a musician.

I want to grasp how the performers function at the opera house, but it's a little tricky to figure out. The Met has a company of dancers, but in addition, others dancers at the Met are hired for each opera individually, I think. I can't quite understand it. The Met posts auditions for the operas that require dancers nearly a year in advance. Essentially, it is the same as any short-term job. Auditions, callbacks, rehearsals, and performances are specified, and any additional requirements are noted then, for example, whether it requires ballet, modern dance, and/or acrobatic training. It seems like dance hiring at the Met is a la carte. That probably makes sense. I'm not sure how the house ballet company fits into that model. The majority of the operas I've seen recently have not had dance in them. Or if they do, it's a couple of dancers rather than a company.

The Metropolitan runs a children's chorus program as well. Boys and girls participate in the Operatic Music Appreciation Program. Children ages 7 through 10 can audition for singing roles at the Met through the Children's Chorus Program. There is no fee to participate in these programs, but the children are held to professional standards of attendance, punctuality, and behavior. The classes meet twice a week from September to mid-May. They are divided into beginners and intermediate (with approximately 20 children each) and advanced (with up to 50 children). The advanced class feeds its participants into auditions for opera roles at the Metropolitan.

All of the above auditions are conducted behind closed doors, of course. But the Metropolitan Opera National Council Auditions, on the other hand, are like American Idol meets Miss America. It is the most visible classical voice competition in the U.S. To my mind, this is an extraordinary system that shows American artists at their most democratic. The National Council Auditions begin each year on a district level. Winners move up to a regional competition and then those winners come to the Metropolitan for two final rounds. The first is a semi-final concert given in front of an audience of officials at the Met. The semi-finalists are whittled down to about a dozen who are given an intensive week of coaching at the opera house before a final concert. A panel of judges selects the winners who receive a nice paycheck and a whole lot of recognition. Winning the competition isn't a prerequisite to landing a spot on the Met roster; that's not the case by a long stretch. On the other hand, the National Council Auditions have an excellent track record of discovering vocal talent.

It's a pretty great system, really, if you think about it. The idea that somebody can come along who's essentially a nobody and through sheer talent become "discovered" in these annual contests—I find that wonderful. The process is not unlike sports, with their system of scouting, recruitment, tryouts, minor league franchises, and so forth. But there is one crucial difference. Unlike a young professional baseball player who has been at the game since he was four or five, it's not at all uncommon to hear a National Council Audition winner say that they had never seen a live performance of an opera until they were cast in one. That is, people without exposure to opera can take voice classes as adults and find themselves onstage in an art form they've never witnessed first hand. It would be unfathomable to hear a professional athlete state that he had only been playing a year or two, let alone that they had never seen the game before; it happens in opera all the time.

In 2007, a documentary called *The Audition* was filmed by Susan Froemke that told the story of the National Council Auditions. It was produced by the Metropolitan Opera and shown on PBS nationwide. I have a copy of the DVD, and I pop it in to watch it before heading off to the finalists' concert on Sunday. I'm looking for two things in the documentary: how are singers discovered, and to what extent are Mormon musicians involved in this entry-level stage of performing opera?

The documentary opens with one of the aspiring singers, a tenor from New Jersey, in a coaching session with Bill Schuman. I haven't seen Schuman in person before, but we have many mutual friends. He is a graduate of BYU and comes from an LDS background. For those in the opera business, he is one of the most important people on earth. He is an internationally famous voice teacher, a legendary figure, really. He's worked with everybody in opera and on Broadway and many in Hollywood. His reputation is that he's extremely knowledgeable, has a laser-sharp ability to fix minute problems, and that he's unusually kind. He set up his voice studio in New York years ago and has been on faculty of prestigious music schools as well. Schuman is one of those people that many singers credit as life changers and voice savers. I have close friends who, when they hear his name, start to well up with emotion. He enjoys that kind of status in the opera world.

The documentary trails the semi-finalists and finalists of the National Council Auditions. Of 1,800 contestants across the country (and some international singers, too), 22 singers have made it to the semi-final round, having already competed at the district and regional levels. From the semi-finals, a dozen will be selected for the final round. Then, a few—some years it has been only three and other years up to six—will win a cash prize of $15,000 each. Of course, getting the attention of the opera world is more important than the prize money. They will be labeled "the stars of tomorrow" by agents, producers, and opera management teams. Peter Gelb says to the camera, "It is the way that these young talents, the five or six who win, get recognized. It is the first step in building a major career." The judges of the semi-final round sit in the orchestra section of the opera house. One of them, Jonathan Friend, who is Artistic Administrator of the Metropolitan Opera notes, "What we're looking for mostly is somebody who has something to say. It's about communication not just about singing." Before the judging, the singers walk onto the stage for the first time. Several of them are emotionally overwhelmed from the experience. They test out the acoustics of the empty house by singing a minute or so from their competition arias. Each singer has selected four arias to bring to the competition and will perform two of them for the semi-final round with piano accompaniment.

One of the 22 contestants is Nicholas Pallesen. I'm not thinking that he is representing the Church as he sings, not exactly, but I am aware that he's LDS, and I think it would be great if he were to be a finalist. I've heard him sing numerous times and have a high regard for him. He's studying at Juilliard and has been cast in big roles in their productions, most notably as Falstaff in Verdi's *Falstaff* and as Klinghoffer in John Adams' *The Death of Klinghoffer*. I'm a fan of both operas, and I'm a fan of Nicholas too. For the semi-finals, he sings Rossini, "Largo al factotum" (Make way for the man of all trades), the bravura aria for baritones that I find unsingably hard—how does a mouth get that many words out so fast? Pallesen is tossing it off like it's nothing. He's animated, effervescent. He has short black hair, a goatee, and wire-rimmed glasses. He's wearing a dark suit, a blue dress shirt with an open collar, and I notice that his belt strap has come loose and is bouncing all around while he sings the tongue-twisting patter at break-neck speed, "Ah, bravo Figaro! Bravo, bravissimo;/Ah, bravo Figaro! Bravo, bravissimo;/a te fortuna (a te fortuna, a te fortuna) non mancherà...." Even though it is a short snippet on film, I can tell there's great joy in the performance.

It is a documentary, and the camera lingers over singers who have a dramatic personal story to tell, who have erratic personalities like a reality show contestant, or who are going to be the eventual winners—since by nature, these stories are told with the advantage of hindsight. The shots are full of tensions. One soprano sums it up, "Four years of work for, like, ten minutes."

At the end of the semi-finals, all the singers are gathered together under the Chagall murals near the balcony. Eleven finalists are called. Nicholas is the second to last one named. There is a big smile on his face as he accepts a certificate and the congratulations of others. The singers who don't advance in the competition are encouraged to "come back next year." I wonder how many of the eventual singers will be first-time competitors. The nature of professional musicians is changing. A couple of generations ago, a classical musician—a pianist, for example—used to rent a small theater and give a recital. It was a way to garner press attention. They emerged having studied with famous artists who lent credibility. After the recital, they sank or rose quickly. That system has mostly disappeared, replaced by competitions.

I know of older professional musicians who bemoan the current system. They think that students who should be expanding their repertoire in schools are, instead, concentrating on a single, flashy concerto to wow a competition judge. There are stories of pianists who have won major competitions who literally can only play a handful of pieces. The fear is that if their careers take off, they will have even less time to grow and mature as artists.

The expectations are different for vocal competitions. These are clearly gateway events, designed to identify young artists to join apprentice programs at major opera houses. As the judges discuss contestants during *The Audition,* a recurring theme is the contestant's likelihood of growing into an artist of distinction rather than an attempt to identify ready-made stars. Still, as one of the competition organizers says, it's not all about potential, "What have you got to put on the table and how good is it today?"

The finalists of the National Council Auditions are given a week to prepare for the Grand Finals. It will be a performance with the Met Opera Orchestra on the main stage, with the house full of paying attendees. During the week, the singers work individually with the conductor Marco Armiliato and are coached by him. They are given a dramatic coach as well, and they attend a breathing technique class. If it weren't for the fact that there is so much pressure on them, the finalists are at the classical music equivalent of Disneyland: access to the wonders of the Metropolitan Opera and all its resources. They are costumed for the concert. The men are wearing tuxedos—hopefully with collars that aren't so tight as to restrict their throats—and the women are in evening gowns. Generally speaking, the women with large voices have large body shapes. There is some discomfort in the way they negotiate looking their best. Those, like Angela Meade, age 29, who are on the larger side, also voice a concern that however populist opera becomes, and however much producers want their opera singers to be camera-friendly, you still have to have voices big enough to sing these roles. This is an on-going debate, and it's not new. But the prevalence of HD broadcasts and other visual technologies have stirred the pot. What should an opera singer look like?

There's a scene in the documentary that shows the men sitting down together. It's a great moment because even though they are competitors, they simply want to enjoy each other's company. They have such respect for each other, particularly among the lower voices, the baritones. There appears to be a rivalry between the tenors. One of them, Alek Shrader, decides at the last minute to replace his competition aria with the untoppable, "Ah! mes amis", (Ah, my friends) from Donizetti's *La fille du régiment*, although he's never sung it in public before. It has nine high Cs in it, for one thing. It's a crazy choice, and the professionals look at him like, *Hey, if you can do it, knock yourself out.* The other tenors are more competitive, like, *Are you kidding me?* But back to the baritones, they are all sportsmanlike, affable, colleagues. Nicholas is funny, humble, and self-effacing. He says that he could never sing the difficult songs his competitors are singing. And they answer that they couldn't sing his aria either.

One of the tenors has an especially touching story. He's Ryan Smith, an African-American tenor who's had a tough life. More than any of the other singers, this is a redemptive moment for him. At the end of a coaching session he says that this experience, "validated my confidence. Made me feel like I belong." I get the impression that for this vocalist and the others, too, that the experience of singing at the Met has changed them all. It's made them feel like maybe they do belong on this stage. However confident a singer is, such a statement can't be made until they walk into the wings hearing applause at their backs.

Three days before the concert, the singers run through their arias with orchestra for the first time. On the day of the concert, they sing with orchestra again, although some of them choose not to sing full out, to save their voices. The concert begins at 3:00pm. The judges are given an admonition to look for budding artists. They use the word "investment". One says, "Age doesn't make a difference," but the statement is qualified by someone, "forgiving a younger singer who hasn't got it together yet," meaning that an older singer might not get quite the benefit of the doubt. The judges are Craig Rutenberg, Director of Music Administration at the Met; Sarah Billinghurst, Assistant Manager, Artistic at the Met; Jonathan Friend, Artistic Administrator at the Met; Brian Dickie, General Director, Chicago Opera Theater; Sheri Greenawald, Director, San Francisco Opera Center; and Diane Zola, Artistic Administrator, Houston Grand Opera. The judges are told they can choose five winners from the finalists, and "Six, if we want."

The documentary shows brief moments from the concert. Nicholas appears again singing "Largo al factotum". It makes me want to hear him perform the entire role. I'm reminded, watching him, of the stereotype of early American hucksters selling snake oil on the frontier. He oozes bravado, charm, wiliness and agility. Angela Meade sings "Casta Diva" (Pure Goddess) from Bellini's *Norma*. It's beautiful, and she holds out the last note forever. If this woman doesn't have a huge career, I'll be surprised. The boyish Alek Shrader bounces around stage and lets his showstopper fly. The nine high Cs are crystal clear, and he wins a huge ovation. It's almost like he's too young to realize what's at stake. It's angst-free singing. After the performances, I try to imagine myself in the judges' chambers. Whom would I select? And how would I speak about the contestants? To use the *American Idol* model from a couple of years ago, would I be a nice guy like Paula Abdul or a cut-to-the-bone critic like Simon Cowell?

They're frank, all right. One judge says of the tenor Michael Fabiano, a full-throated, emotive singer, "He's either going to be fantastic, or dead." For some of the singers, it's not only a question of their training but also the realities of their prospects in the current marketplace that are in doubt. One soprano's voice, according to a judge, has "a beautiful top, but with the size of houses in this country, can this voice project?" The judges want to be encouraging, but this is not pampering: "There's a fine voice...in there somewhere." And they don't shy away from talking about body size after a Meade sings Mozart and Bellini, "A girl of that size in that repertory isn't going to cut it anymore. You know? I mean, that's not going to happen." I'm a little stunned to hear that. Behind the statement is the assumption that it's an indisputable fact. Mozart gets the skinny singers;

Wagner gets the heavy ones, period. I don't know what that says about audiences and producers. How much do I care what a singer looks like? This is opening such a can of worms. Aren't the Arts supposed to be a place where prejudice takes a back seat to talent? It's a naive notion. On the other hand, haven't I enjoyed looking at sexy singers singing sexily? These issues are certainly not new, but they are compounded by the emergence of HD video-taping. The product that the Met (and many other opera companies) wants to put out is being packaged in the same way that Hollywood frames its starlets.

It is time for the winners to be announced. There are six. Unsurprisingly, they are the singers that the documentary has focused upon most: Jamie Barton, Amber Wagner, Alek Shrader, Angela Meade, Ryan Smith, and Michael Fabiano. The documentary ends with updates of all the finalists, not just the winners. Sadly, it notes that Ryan Smith passed away from cancer after the competition. Some of the finalists and winners went back to training for careers in opera. Others began singing in regional opera companies in the U.S. Of Nicholas Pallesen, the documentary says, "...at the time was training at Juilliard Opera Center." This is a good warm-up for the National Council Finals that I'll be seeing on Sunday. But before that, I have *Khovanshchina* on Tuesday, March 13.

Man does not live by bread and butter operas alone. To the predictable diet of *Carmens, Toscas, Bohemes, Butterflies,* a few more exotic dishes have to be added to maintain the interest of the die-hard fan. *Khovanshchina*, an opera by Modest Mussorgsky (who wrote the libretto and composed the score) was first produced at the Met in 1950. Lawrence Tibbett led the cast of American singers. After four performances, it disappeared until the current production premiered in 1985. Mussorgsky is known for a small numbers of works: "Night on Bald Mountain," "Pictures at an Exhibition," art songs, the operas *Boris Godunov* and to a lesser degree, *Khovanshchina*. *Boris* has been a repertory staple in the U.S. since 1913 when the opera commissioned by Serge Diaghilev made its American debut at the Met, but *Khovanshchina*, Mussorgsky's last opera, was only known for its "Dance of the Persian Maidens" until the 1950 premiere. The composer died in 1881, at the age of 42. He left a pile of music unfinished. Much of the music we know by Mussorgsky has been delivered to us through the efforts of other composers who arranged his music for orchestra. Most famously is the orchestration of "Pictures at an Exhibition" by Ravel but also by over two dozen other composers for orchestra and an even greater number of other versions for jazz band, guitar, organ, wind ensemble, brass ensemble, jazz orchestra, and even voice.

Khovanshchina has its own complex origins. At the time of his death, Mussorgsky had finished the libretto and had composed all of the opera in piano score except for two numbers. He had orchestrated only two excerpts from Act III. The story is drawn from Russian history, from a moment of rebellion: the

Moscow Uprising of 1682, in the time of Peter the Great. Rimsky-Korsakov, who had once been Mussorgsky's roommate, completed the score for *Khovanshchina* and orchestrated it. The Rimsky-Korsakov version was published two years after Mussorgsky's death. It was his view that Mussorgsky's talent was only matched by his dilettantism, and therefore, the deceased composer's work required sprucing up.

The premiere took place in 1886 in St. Petersburg. For decades, this was the version that was performed, including the Met's production of 1950. Mussorgsky's music was essentially Romantic, but modern composers in Russia held him in high esteem and were greatly influenced by him. Those younger composers, Prokofiev and Shostakovich, in particular, reacted to his strong Russian point of view and his embrace of Russian history as source for his music. Shostakovich took *Khovanshchina* and reorchestrated it to excise the floweriness of Rimsky-Korsakov and to return the work to Mussorgsky's purer musical voice. Mussorgsky composed the opera in five acts, with Act IV divided into two scenes. In the Met's current production, the opera is presented in six scenes using the orchestration by Shostakovich (for the first five scenes) and Stravinsky (for scene six).

I obtain my ticket in my new, favorite way. Two hours before the performance is to begin, I walk over to the Met box office, stand in line for five minutes, plunk down my $20, and walk away with a seat toward the back quarter of the orchestra. I've seen the opera before, but it's been a long time. I remember liking it a lot and being moved by the final, mass suicide scene in which the believers set themselves on fire in the woods. I am in my seat a few minutes before the lights dim and the Swarovski crystal chandeliers fly up to the ceiling.

The house looks like it is mostly full. On one side of me is a librarian from one of the city's elite private schools. On the other side sit three Russians. Two, a man and his wife, I suppose, look to be in their mid-fifties. They are accompanied by a large, elderly woman dressed in an enormous coat, which she does not remove, and an elaborate babushka wrapped around her head and tied under her chin. She doesn't remove that either. As the rest of our row is turning on the subtitle system, they sit and speak in Russian to each other.

Unlike the 1950 production of the opera in New York, this *Khovanshchina* is packed with Russian singers. A few of them are familiar to me, including Ildar Abdrazakov, whom I liked so much as Henry VIII at the beginning of the season, and Olga Borodina, who has been singing leading mezzo-soprano roles like Carmen and Delilah for fifteen years. One of the few American singers in the cast of principles is Wendy Bryn Harmer, who finished the run of *Götterdämmerung* about two weeks before *Khovanshchina* began performances, and she will jump back into Wagner (*Das Rheingold* and also more *Götterdämmerung*) two weeks after *Khovanshchina* is done.

Tonight's performance will be in Russian. I click on the button to activate the English subtitles on the back of the seat in front of me. I haven't noticed a message like this before, but for this opera, the Met acknowledges, "A generous grant of Lila Acheson and DeWitt Wallace" on the subtitles screen. I wonder if advertisements will make their way to these displays someday. Anyway, back to the opera. First, I smell smoked salmon. Either the Met is also experimenting with smell-o-vision, or.... I turn to my left and watch my neighbor unwrap her sandwich of smoked salmon on pumpernickel bread. *What, no borscht?* That's a first for me. I chalk it up to authenticity.

The opera begins with a prelude that sometimes finds its way into symphony orchestra programs. This is marvelous Russian music. I don't know what that term means, when it comes right down to it. I would be hard-pressed to get technical about how this sounds Russian and not, say, Polish or Slavic, but there's a brooding quality to the music, a stately darkness. I love Russian choral music and as I remember, *Khovanshchina* will offer plenty of exercise for the Met chorus.

The story begins bleakly. In late 17th century Moscow, Russian ex-police, called streltsy, bully the public under the command of Prince Ivan Khovansky (Khovanshchina means the Khovansky Affair). The people sing—and how they sing!—a lament for Mother Russia. She is under attack, not from outside forces but from internal strife. It is, essentially, a three-way civil war: the young tsar against the police and religious conservatives—these groups are resisting the modernizing reforms of Tsar Peter—and members of high society who support the tsar. The streltsy are decommissioned elite forces, loyal to Prince Ivan Khovansky. The Old Believers are Russian Orthodox Christians who have quit the church, which followed Tsar Peter, to form their own sect. Dosifei, a prince who renounced his title, leads the Old Believers. Shaklovity, a socially prominent aristocrat, champions the tsar. In the opera, all three forces are led by basses. Only in Russia.

In scene one, Ivan's father, Andrei Khovansky, chases a Lutheran girl named Emma. This is Wendy Bryn Harmer's role. She is only saved from being ravaged by Andrei when Marfa, a member of a sect of Old Believers, appears. Father and son demand that Emma be taken to the palace, but they are interrupted by Dosifei, who saves her. He then sings to God a prayer of protection and help. The end of the scene means the end of the night for Harmer. Her character doesn't appear again. Now's a good time to praise her singing. Emma's an intense part. The music is big, dramatic, and difficult. Harmer lets fly some amazing sounds. It is glorious singing. Once again, impressive.

The opera continues in scene two in the home of Vasily Golitsyn, a nervous nobleman. He is the intersection of the battling forces because he has sympathies in each of the camps. Golitsyn hires Marfa to tell his fortune. She prophesizes betrayal, dishonor, poverty, and exile. He is joined by Dosifei and Khovansky. Each of these men urges a united front against the tsar. Shaklovity enters and announces that Tsar Peter has begun a crackdown of his enemies. This spells the end for Khovansky and Dosifei. The rest of the opera is the bloom of their demise.

In scene three, the Old Believers and the streltsy realize that their way of life is ending. In frustration, each group turns inward and attacks itself with denunciations and petty squabbles. News arrives that the tsar's guards have attacked the nearby streltsy. Terrified, they plead for help from Khovansky. When he urges them to align themselves with the tsar, they pray to be delivered. It is another extraordinary choral moment, sung a cappella; it is a heartbreaking anthem of despair. The harmonies come in waves. A single, plaintive tune grows deeper and darker and richer. This is extraordinary music.

I love the simplicity of this score. When the orchestra plays, it is something like a droning foundation of sound. The orchestra has a continuous wash of color, but all of the movement comes from the voices on top of it. The contrast between this and Wagner's *Ring*—the two composers died within two years of each other—could hardly be more pronounced. In Wagner, the orchestra is itself a vital character; in the Mussorgsky, the orchestra is rich, velvet wallpaper in front of which the action happens. I suspect that the Rimsky-Korsakov orchestration wasn't like this. If I had to characterize the difference between this Russian point of view and other opera, it's that in the Mussorgsky, the voices are exalted. The singers are not trying to sound like musical instruments; rather, the orchestra, when it plays at all, is trying to sound like a voice. I understand that the orchestration is by Shostakovich, and I am trying to hear his distinct sound in *Khovanshchina*. But it's hard to find him in this, which is a compliment. For him to be this deferential to Mussorgsky must have been a mark of true admiration.

In the "Dance of the Persian Maidens", I hear more of the sardonic bite of Shostakovich. In scene four, Khovansky knows that his position is unsustainable. To distract him from worry, he calls for his slaves to dance for him. The dance is sort of silly, but opera and ballet have a long, tangled history. At the very least, it's a break from singing. The question is whether I want a break from the singing.

The choreography is by Benjamin Millepied. I've watched him over the years dancing at the New York City Ballet across the plaza from the Met. He was a virtuosic dancer, and when he started making dances of his own, they were often complex and athletic. As far as the public is concerned, he's best known as the choreographer of the Natalie Portman horror flick, *The Black Swan*. These Persian maidens are not at that level of intensity. The eight of them prance around, kick their legs into the air, make nice patterns of lines, and look appropriately aerobic in compacted stage space. The music is not jarringly different from the rest of the opera, but it is set apart, sonically. For me, the only interesting thing onstage during the dance is Khovansky who drinks and dances with the maidens. Shaklovity interrupts the revels and brings a message from the royal palace. Khovansky is dressed in royal robes. As he is about to leave, a rifleman assassinates him.

The fifth scene portrays the downfall of Golitsyn. He is taken through the streets into forced exile abroad. A word about the set. This production looks pretty old and creaky. I don't remember much of it from the first time I caught a performance, but components of the set look incomplete and haphazardly designed. In opera terms, this is an elderly, rickety production, past its prime. I can't imagine, however, that the Met would spring the money for a new production. If it's a question of keeping the opera in the repertoire or getting rid of it because the set looks bad, I'll vote for keeping it, rusty set and all. At any rate, Golitsyn is taken away, and word comes from Marfa that the Old Believers are to be killed. They learn of Ivan Khovansky's death. Dosifei urges Marfa to talk to Ivan's son Andrei to convert him before it's too late. Marfa makes an appeal to Andrei who refuses at first. Then, when he sees the streltsy marching to their execution, Andrei escapes with her.

Scene six is the outlier of the opera. It is the only scene that takes place away from the city, for one thing. The Old Believers are gathering at their hermitage in the woods. It is the first time in the production that nature is depicted. More importantly, the sound of the opera is different in scene six. There's some musical history here. In 1913, Diaghilev mounted a production of *Khovanshchina* in Paris. An orchestration was prepared by collaborators Igor Stravinsky and Maurice Ravel. At the time, Stravinsky was finishing "The Rite of Spring", and he called upon Ravel to help him. For the ending, Stravinsky replaced the brass-laden finale of Rimsky-Korsakov with choral chants that Mus-

Khovanshchina

sorgsky left in his manuscript. As he composed, Stravinsky took themes that occurred throughout the opera and developed them into new material. But the famous bass Feodor Chaliapin apparently refused to sing his role (Dosifei) with the new orchestration. For him, it was Rimsky-Korsakov or nothing. Still, the producers wanted to use the new Stravinsky/Ravel music. The result was a hybrid of an opera that is already a hybrid. After the production ended—it was considered a failure—the new orchestration was forgotten and lost except for the Stravinsky finale, which survived and was published in 1914. The Shostakovich orchestration was written in 1959 and first presented at the Kirov in 1960. The Met used the Shostakovich orchestration for their revived production in 1989, but they cut nearly an hour of music. By now, it's a confused muddle. It's hard to know who wrote what and furthermore, which Met performances used which version. The program notes explain that this 2012 revival is the first to use the Stravinsky *Khovanshchina* ending.

The orchestra is considerably different in scene six. It's easy to hear the distinction. For one thing, it puts away the deferential attitude and becomes an active commentator on the characters' stories. The instruments in the orchestra double the singing voices more, and there is a large shift in the way that it presents counterpoint and harmony. I have a Stravinsky "Firebird" flashback as I listen to it. As the plot of the opera is winding down, the orchestra is waking up. It doesn't get to a modernist "Rite of Spring" vitality, but I hear Stravinsky in every measure. Despite all of the historical territory that the opera covers, the first five scenes unfold slowly. But this is different. These characters are rushing toward their own destruction.

The Met production of *Khovanshchina* always had a limited budget. It would be hard to justify it otherwise. But the producers sprang for some showiness in this final scene. The two-story hermitage is on a rotating platform. As the Old Believers walk up a spiral ramp into the building, it rotates to show the enormous Met chorus crammed into the two levels. The sect follows Dosifei who pronounces that they will enter the hermitage and sit it aflame. They will be martyrs. Marfa coaxes Andrei to join with them. He is unaware that at the last minute, the tsar has pardoned the streltsy. Inside the building, they light a fire and, as the flames and smoke overcome them, they sing a magnificent chorale. It is a bloodcurdling image, truly unforgettable. The opera begins with dawn and ends with a tragedy at twilight. Musically, it ends with a slow fade.

I can't help but compare it to the bloated production of the *Ring* cycle and Brünnhilde's immolation in *Götterdämmerung*. I found the staging of Wagner's apocalypse almost boring in contrast to *Khovanshchina*'s final moments. The Russian opera and the experience of seeing it run counter to business as usual at the opera house. This is an uncompleted opera burdened with complex, historical plot, a mishmash of an orchestration, a cast full of powerful basses, much static choral stand-and-deliver singing, and a narrative that sometimes doesn't make a lot of sense. And yet, and yet. At the curtain calls, the principal singers receive extended ovations. Olga Borodina (Marfa) and Ildar Abdrazakov (Dosifei) are especially warmly greeted. But the biggest cheer of all goes to the chorus and the Met Opera Chorus director, Donald Palumbo, as it should be in this extravaganza of choral singing.

I have a few days before I return to the Met for the National Council Auditions concert. It's March Madness, and I catch a couple of basketball games. I watch BYU lose by a wide margin, and I catch the ending of a great game with Kentucky coming from behind to win in the final minutes. Although I'm completely unqualified to predict a NCAA winner, I'm going with Kentucky. On Sunday afternoon, it's time to return to the Met for the opera equivalent of March Madness, the Metropolitan Opera National Council Auditions Grand Finals concert. I decide to make a game of it. I'm my own pool. I'll rate the singers as they perform on a scale of 1 to 10. Each of them will sing. Then, there will be an intermission. And the singers will return and perform again, in the same order, in the second half of the concert. The judges will deliberate, and the winners will be announced, hopefully before very much time passes.

I climb up to the balcony to my seat. Many of the people around me are friends and relatives of the contestants. It is something of a reunion for them. People are grouping in the aisles and chatting. It's a leisurely Sunday afternoon atmosphere. I open my program to discover that this year, there are only nine finalists. I assume that means only four or five winners. In the program, there are short biographies and photos of the singers. Their ages and hometowns are listed. I feel like a handicapper at a horse race. It looks like six of the singers are still in school and the other three have landed residencies at regional opera houses. It makes me laugh to read bios of young musicians. They don't really have outstanding credits yet, so they pad their resumes with things that they think will sound important. It's not dishonest, but they tend to make a lot of a little.

I'm intrigued by a few singers who sound good on paper at least. Margaret Mezzacappa, a 24 year-old from Euclid, Ohio, has won a few important singing competitions. In 2012 she was the winner of the George London Award. The year before that, she won the Licia Albanese-Puccini Foundation International Vocal Competition. Will Liverman, who is 23 and comes from Virginia Beach, Virginia, is a baritone who has sung more contemporary music that the others. One of his selections today will be "Batter My Heart" from John Adams' opera, *Doctor Atomic.* That should be good. There is a countertenor on the program named Andrey Nemzer who hails from Moscow, Russia. He is one of the oldest singers we'll hear today, 29, and he's also won a few competitions before this one. The nine National Finalists have already won in their district and region. Cash prizes vary at the district level, but the first place winner of the regional audition receives $800. Semi-finalists who don't make it to the final round get $1,500.

Finalists who don't win received awards of $5,000. The Grand Winners announced at the end of the competition today will get $15,000. The Met notes on its website that there is a mandatory 30% federal withholding tax from winners outside the U.S.

The Met also gives additional financial support to these singers. Those who make it to the National Semi-Finals and beyond can apply to audition for Educational Fund assistance. First time National Semi-Finalists, Finalists and Winners are eligible for further financial assistance of up to $5,000 from the National Council Education Fund over a period of three years after the competition.

The Met spells out the requirements for competitors on its website. Singers are to be between 20 and 30 years old. The goal of the National Council Auditions is threefold:

1. To discover exceptional young talent; 2. To provide a venue for young opera singers from all over the country and at all different levels of experience to be heard by a representative of the Metropolitan Opera and to assist those with the greatest potential in their development; and 3. To search for new talent for the Metropolitan Opera and the Met's Lindemann Young Artist Development Program.[2]

There is no limit on the number of times one may enter the National Council Auditions, as long as the singer is under 30 years old. Auditions are open to U.S. and Canadian citizens. But how is the Russian allowed in? The website explains, "Foreign applicants must show proof of one-year residency or proof of full-time enrollment in a college or university in the U.S. or Canada."

This isn't the only way that young singers can audition for the Met. Auditions for soloists are held periodically during the opera season. These are for small and mid-sized roles. It's not an open call. Singers send a photo and resume to the Met. A panel reviews the materials. The Met screens applicants and declines to hear any that it deems insufficiently qualified.

The Grand Finals concert is ready to begin. The house lights dim, although not completely. I appreciate that gesture because I intend to make notes in my program, and I imagined I'd have to do it in the dark. The conductor of the orchestra today is Andrew Davis. The host is Eric Owens. He's having a breakout year in the *Ring* cycle, and as a previous Finals winner, he is a dangling carrot for the contestants. He welcomes the audience to the Grand Finals and notes that this is the 59th annual competition. At the Met this year, 120 of the singers on the roster have come through the National Council audition process.

The stage is mostly bare. There are seven wooden panels arranged in a semi-circle, like a room dividing screen. When the orchestra beings to play for the first contestant, he doesn't appear onstage. What gives? He's Anthony Clark Evans, and the aria is "Si può? Si può?" (A word, a word). I get it. It's the aria sung in front of the curtain of *Pagliacci*. Soon enough, Evans bounds onto the stage. It's a clever bit of programming. The audience cheers loudly after his virile, "Incominciate!" (Let's begin). I find his lyric voice underpowered. The orchestra drowns him out. From an acting standpoint, it's a little boring. To me, his final high note was uncomfortable. I give him a 7.

Lauren Snouffer, a 23-year old Texan, is next. She is tall and thin, and she wears an obligatory bright red dress. Snouffer sings an obscure aria from *Idomeneo.* Her vibrato is fast and bird-like. It's an odd choice of music. There's no phrasing. Many of the short bursts of phrases end with pitch problems. The fancier passagework is sloppy. The audience doesn't respond to her much. I mark down a 6, and I feel generous about that.

Matthew Grills, from Connecticut, is 25 years old and seems to have lots of friends in my vicinity. Whoops and hollers. His aria from Mozart's *Così fan tutte* is pleasant enough. He's young and sounds like it. Not a pro, at least, that's my first impression. His voice has a tightness to it, like he is extremely nervous, and there is no shading. The entire aria is delivered at the same volume. Not as impressed as the audience seems to be: 6.

Margaret Mezzacappa—there's a name made for opera—displays a ton of breath control in her aria, again unknown to me, from Gounod's *Sappho.* Her singing creates a fine atmosphere despite a wobble in her vibrato that I find troubling for a singer who is only 24. She goes for a high note and cuts in short. Maybe it's an unfair stereotype, but her mezzo-soprano voice is smaller than I expected it to be given that she is a large woman. I'll give her a 7.

Michael Samuel is unlike the other singers in that he stands still and delivers his aria, from *Don Giovanni* (more Mozart). He is from Texas and is 26 years old. I don't mind his performance approach. All of the acting is happening in his voice. Unfortunately, it's a nothing-special voice. It's odd for a baritone to have the low notes disappear like his. And as they like to say on TV singing competition shows, he's "pitchy." There's a lot of Mozart on the program this afternoon. Of the 18 selections, six are Mozart arias. The good news is that the Met orchestra loves playing Mozart. Conversely, they sounded like they were sight-reading *Sappho*.

Kevin Ray is taking some risks. No Mozart for him. The 26-year old New Yorker is singing an aria from *Die Walküre*. The orchestra is gearing up for a *Ring* cycle, so they're more than ready to accompany this singer with a lengthy introduction. When he does start singing, I like his voice. It's good. The dramatic moments, in particular, carry over the orchestra. I've had the feeling with some of the singers that the orchestra is playing with a lid on it. Happily, they can wail here. Good enough for an 8, my favorite so far.

Stop the presses! The real news of the concert to this point is Janai Brugger, an Illinois soprano, age 29. Within a couple of seconds into her aria from *Louise* (Charpentier), the audience loves her. This opera was a favorite of turn-of-the-century sopranos. The composer has fallen out of favor these days, but the aria, "Despuis le jour" (Since the day I gave myself) is built to impress. Brugger has a Renée Fleming-like sound—floating high notes, lushness. The voice is big in its way. This is hard to explain because it doesn't try to bowl you over. The voice simply carries easily because it is focused so perfectly. She's got a great stage presence too. She's regal. The orchestra isn't holding back. She's developing low notes in an interesting way, but this aria is all about the jumps to high notes, and she's a pro. The audience unleashes a roar of admiration. She rates a 9.

Of the arias to be sung today, I'm most eager for the next one, "Batter My Heart" by John Adams. It's sung by Will Liverman, who is 23 years old. The Virginia baritone has a big sound. The orchestra seems to be really into this music, and it begins with that turbulent Adams sound that I really like, a sort of jacked-up, propulsive minimalism. Liverman is comfortable singing high and low. He sounds like an adult in a group of students. He is easily heard over the orchestra. For whatever reason—maybe it's the contemporary music aria choice—the audience doesn't like him as much as I do, an 8.

The final singer is the Russian countertenor Andrey Nemzer. According to his bio, he was a tenor who only began singing as a countertenor four years ago. He is 29 and looks like a lumberjack. For that reason alone, it's disconcerting to hear his aria from *Giulio Cesare* (Handel). Everybody does a double take when he opens his mouth. Does he have a soprano hidden under his tuxedo? At any rate, he is a big, bold, loud singer. Completely castable. Many of the countertenor roles are kings and monarchs, and he would be a strong presence on stage. There is power throughout his range, from the lowest chesty notes up into the stratosphere. The trill's a bit shaky. Most of the technique seems to be in place. The audience loves it—a big ovation. An 8.

After intermission, the singers come back in the same order and perform their second selection. Evans, the baritone, sings Mozart (*Figaro*), and it's fine, in a boring and predictable sort of way. There's nothing distinctive. It's perfectly acceptable and proper, although he can't navigate through complex passages with much ease. I keep thinking about the documentary, *The Audition*, and the counsel given to the judges to find singers with something to say. There have to be hundreds of baritones that could sing this as well as this 27-year old from Kentucky. It's a 7.

The red-dressed Snouffer returns with Ravel (*L'enfant et les sortilèges*). I like it. She's got some great agility. Her notes ring out high and clear. I respond to the brightness of her sound. I'll give her an 8.

Next up is Grills, the tenor. Yikes! He's singing "Ah! mes amis." Oh dear, this could end badly for him. There was nothing about his first aria that suggested he'd be able to get through this throat-buster. His bio is the only one of the finalists that includes a lot of musical theater. I wasn't even sure he was committed to opera. Still, he begins well. He's relaxed. How is that possible? Maybe he doesn't know what's coming? He's worked on characterization too, and he's adopted a sweetness that fits the role. The quality of the voice is unusual. It sounds like he's singing in a canyon. It's an Italianate sound, an emotional catch in the voice.

That's his approach to this French song. I find it a little distasteful. Maybe that's too harsh a word. The nine high Cs are packed into the last portion of the aria. He lets the first two fly, and they sound solid. As he ticks them off, 4, 5, 6, each gets scoopier than the last. This is an Italianism too. And I don't love it. His high notes are all accompanied by little grace note swoops. Still, when he arrives at the C, it's good. I can feel the audience getting wrapped up in it. By the time he gets to the final high C, which is held out for a while, the crowd is completely with him. There is an explosion of applause. I don't love it as much as everyone else does: 8.

Miss mezzo Mezzacappa arrives next. She's singing a Handel aria from *Semele*. It's an opera I really like, packed with beautiful songs. But this one, "Hence, Iris, hence away!" sounds off. Essentially, her voice has a similar quality to Marilyn Horne, the American mezzo-soprano who reclaimed a big chunk of this repertory from oblivion a few decades ago. Specifically, Mezzacappa sounds like Horne when she was getting older and ready for retirement. It's a threadbare kind of voice, almost. No agility in the runs and scales. And if you can't do that, why sing this repertoire? I almost feel angry listening to her. How is it possible that she's won all of those competitions? I just don't hear it. She can't manage the Baroque-ness of the music. To my mind, it's an embarrassing performance. I rate it a 6.

The bass-baritone Samuel, another Texan, sings an aria from Rachmaninoff's opera *Aleko*. Talk about obscure. Rachmaninoff completed three short operas in his lifetime, but the Met's never performed any of them. I don't know why he would choose this. Russian baritones have a relatively distinctive quality in the sound. It's a burnished beauty with a lot of power behind it. I suppose that it's completely possible that an African American Texan can possess that sound too, but Samuel, unfortunately, doesn't have it. It's shaky from the start. As a performer, he lacks authority. I see it in the way he carries himself. He doesn't appear to know what to do physically as he sings. It's a 6.

Ray, who sang the Wagner in the first round, returns with Wagner-lite, that is, an aria from *Der Freischütz* (Weber). This isn't a competition that favors big, German tenor sounds. The heldentenor voice type tends not to appear with 20-year olds. Ray is still a student. Nevertheless, he has a heft in his voice. To my taste, it's also blustery, especially for someone his age. I can't imagine that the judges are going to overlook that weakness because it hints of problems to come. But he makes a really nice impression on the high notes. They are bright and clean. Elsewhere, he tends to bark a bit. 7.

The expectations are high when Brugger, the soprano, returns to the stage. She is greeted by warm applause. She's singing one of the high-flying Queen of the Night arias from *The Magic Flute*. I'm surprised that if she wanted to sing Mozart, she didn't choose a more lyrical aria, but she is definitely impressive here. She's got phrasing to burn. In complete control. I can't get over the ease of its projection. Why can I hear her so readily? It's not loud per se, but it just cuts through the air. Mozart leaves nowhere to hide, and although it's not perfect, Brugger is easily one of the winners today. I write down: 8.

Liverman, who sang the *Doctor Atomic* aria earlier, is back with *The Magic Flute* too. He's doing the aria with the pan-flute sung by Papageno in the opera. It's really fun to watch. There are a few flute glitches, but he has this character firmly in place. His bio doesn't mention that he's performed this role before in a production, but it wouldn't surprise me to learn that he has done it. He gets some good laughs from the audience with his antics. It's a consolation prize, I suspect. He's not going to win. By the way, this orchestra sounds terrific today. Their Mozart is so light and fresh. I'm not rating them, but I give Liverman a 7.

Last up is the countertenor from Russia. He's performing "Ratmir's Aria" from *Ruslan and Lyudmila* (Glinka). I'm not sure why he's performing it. It's written for a contralto, the lowest of the female voice ranges. In the opera, it's a pants role, and I suppose Nemzer decided to make an honest man out of it. There's a problem. The voice sounds fine, but I question the integrity of the choice. What does he mean by singing it? I don't understand what he adds to the music, as a countertenor. At the very least, it doesn't tell a prospective director much about the repertoire for which he is likely to be considered. Is he saying that he'd like to move away from the countertenor repertoire and start singing women's roles altogether? It's gutsy, if that's the plan. How to put this in a nice way? It's a fine drag performance. I say, a 7. The audience disagrees and would give him an 11 if they could.

While the judges deliberate, the master of ceremonies, Eric Owens sings. Throughout the afternoon, he's been a light-hearted host. It's been a relaxed, Sunday afternoon, kind of a concert. No suit and tie required. Owens lets fly a beautiful, extended aria from *Don Carlo* (Verdi). To the best of my knowledge, he hasn't ventured into the Verdi villain territory onstage before, and this makes me anxious to hear him in those roles, and I predict it won't be a long wait. This is how a voice is supposed to sound. For some reason, his body is turned slightly away from me for the entire aria. Maybe he's singing directly to someone on the other side of the house. But I can hear him easily, way up in the rafters where I'm sitting. This is exactly how all of the big voices didn't sound today, although they pushed hard to make it seem so. As he finishes, the audience pours out the love.

The Metropolitan Opera General Manager Peter Gelb comes on stage to announce the winners. The singers are waiting in the wings, and as their names are called, they come to the stage, one by one. There is not a set number of finalists nor is there a set number of winners. I have tallied my scores. My picks are Janai Brugger (17 points), then Will Liverman, Andrey Nemzer, and Kevin Ray (each with 15 points). Gelb announces five names, "in no particular order": Janai Brugger, Anthony Clark Evans, Matthew Grills, Margaret Mezzacappa, and Andrey Nemzer. I'm no expert, it appears. I only had two of the five. I will enjoy watching these careers blossom, or wither, for that matter. The next morning, there is nothing in the newspaper about the winners. It is not news, I guess.

For Mormon singers, however, these audition concerts have been the open gate to singing at the Met. There were no LDS singers in this year's audition concert, but in recent years, nearly all of the LDS artists at the Met have been emerged from these auditions. The public is generally unaware of the young singers, at first. It is not like a professional football player who goes in the first round of the draft and is immediately a star. A winning singer from the auditions still has a long, long way to go.

CHAPTER 8

TODAY, I ANSWER THE AGE-OLD QUESTION, can you go to the Met in your pajamas? The answer, I am happy to report, is a solid "yes." But you must take your iPad with you. This month, the Met announced its new iPad app, Met Opera on Demand. I'm going to give it a whirl. First, I download the app, which is free. It takes about 30 seconds to have it ready and functioning. The app doesn't do anything, however, without subscribing to the Met's streaming services. The Met already had a free app called The Metropolitan Opera for iPad. I download it this morning too—yes, in pajamas—and discover that it's nothing more than a brochure of the season's operas. But what a beautiful little brochure it is.

I'm fascinated about the possibilities of watching opera anytime, anywhere. Throughout this season of discovery, I've become increasingly aware that the Met is doing everything it can to dismantle the barriers people might have to experience opera. They're trying their best to maintain quality and integrity while expanding audience. It seems to me that technology is the keystone here. That solution might sound obvious, but for decades, fine arts organizations have tried to reach more and more people by diluting their product. They reach for blockbusters in a pandering way. To me, at least, this online initiative doesn't condescend. At the same time, the Met isn't falling into the internet trap of giving content away for free and undermining their financial business model.

The app, Met Opera on Demand, is cool. I hestitate to give a play-by-play of how it works and drown in the minutiae of tabs and clicks. But at the same time, I know that I can't understand the current Mormon opera singing phenomenon without delving into history. And Mormon singing's past has landed, literally, in my lap, on my iPad.

Here's how it works: the app is downloaded free, but to activate it, one needs an On Demand subscription account. This isn't free, and at first glance it's pricey. A full year subscription is $149.99. Monthly subscription is $14.99. If someone is a member of the Met—I presume this comes from joining the Met at the Member or Patron levels—a six-month subscription is $49.99.

All of these services come with web and iPad access. The Met also has opera rental. Once you rent an opera, you have 30 days to start watching or listening to it. Operas are $3.99 or $4.99 for the HD productions. For now, these rentals are only available on the web. I don't know if you have to watch them on a computer or on any smart phone or tablet accessed through the Met's website. There's another level of subscription, a 7-day free trial. In fact, the Met encourages people to try the 7-day version of the subscription prior to committing to anything long-term. I take that to mean the Met's confident about its service. So I sign up as a 7-day trial member. If I don't cancel it in a week, it will automatically roll over to the monthly $14.99 rate. I'm good with that.

Having established an account, I open the app, Met Opera on Demand. I type in my username and password, and up pops a page of 105 videos organized, depending on my preference, by performance date or title. I can browse all videos or only high definition videos. The top row of thumbnail images is under the banner, "Featured Video Performances." I am looking at the other videos listed alphabetically.

Under A, for example, there are nine videos available: *Aida* (10/24/2009 with Violetta Urmana) *Aida* (10/07/1989 with Aprile Millo), *Aida* (1/03/1985 with Leontyne Price), *Andrea Chenier* 10/15/1996 with Luciano Pavarotti), *Anna Bolena* (the 2011-2012 season opener), *Armida* (5/01/2010 with Renée Fleming), and the documentary about the National Council Auditions, *The Audition.*

I continue flipping down the alphabet of operas, and I'm impressed. There are excellent selections. It's a fine balance of fan favorites, more exotic offerings, brand new productions, and some Met classics. A few operas have multiple videos available. This will make some comparisons fun. The videos go back to about 1978, it looks like at first glance. The operas that are available in high definition have a little green logo superimposed on the thumbnail photograph, "HD."

Let's take one for a test drive. I tap on *The Ghosts of Versailles.* It was an opera I saw at its premiere. The video is listed January 10, 1992. It was commissioned by the Met to celebrate its 100th anniversary. I always thought it was a grand act of contrition after ignoring, for the most part, contemporary composers for decades at a time. At any rate, the opera by John Corigliano to a libretto by William M. Hoffman got a first-rate treatment at its premiere. Levine conducted. It starred Teresa Stratas, Håkan Hagegård, Marilyn Horne, and featured a young Renée Fleming who had only sung one performance at the Met before this.

It's the kind of production that's terrific to put online because it's unlikely to be seen very often. After an initial run of seven performances in 1991-92, the opera was revived only once, in 1995, for six more performances. It wouldn't surprise me if this opera is never seen again (although Corigliano authorized a cut-down version that regional companies can more easily manage). So as I tap on the title, a nostalgic happiness washes over me.

On screen is a small window with a playback bar. There are options for subtitles (English only for *Ghosts* but English, French, Italian, German, Spanish and Portuguese for most of the operas on the app), a pull-down menu to "Share" the fact that I'm watching with Facebook, Twitter, or Email friends. I tap on the email icon and a template appears with my return address. Its subject heading reads, "Met Opera on Demand iPad App". The message says, "I'm enjoying 'The Ghosts of Versailles' on the Met Opera on Demand iPad App." It continues with some additional marketing texts and information about how to subscribe. That's ok, I guess. I can't imagine that I'll use it very often. My friends wouldn't care whether I'm "enjoying" an opera or not. Perhaps I need new friends. There is also a little, white star next to "Share".

When I click on it, I discover that it toggles on or off. It is a button to take any of the operas I'm watching and place them in a "Favorites" page. I can return to them without having to browse through the entire list of operas on demand. That's a good idea. These Met programmers are pretty smart. The last button is to enlarge the viewing box to full screen size.

This can all be viewed in portrait or landscape orientations by turning the iPad on its side. I slightly prefer portrait for this previewing mode. The image takes up the top of the screen. Below it are an overview of the opera, a listing of its cast, and some fun facts about it.

On the right side of the screen is a column of gray rectangles. In each box is listed the scene and its duration. For example, after the Opening Credits, the next box is: 2. Act 1: Mon coursier hors d'haleine, 8:30." That's the aria that starts the scene and its running time. I glance down the list of scenes by flicking my finger. Every so often there is a box of a different shade. Number 6 is highlighted as "Featured". It is Act 1: "There's Figaro! Oh no! Here we go again!," This opera is divided into 45 of these boxes. Four of them are designated as featured highlights.

I know the opera well enough to know that the featured scenes are the high points of the production. That's a good attribute of the app. If I want to watch the entire opera, I tap on the arrow in the center of the preview box, and it begins without any buffering, immediately. It's very smooth. Elegant. If I want to jump at a specific scene, I tap on its box, and it likewise begins immediately. To enlarge the video to full screen, I tap on the button (and tap it again if I want to return to preview mode). Although the scenes are divided this way, when I start actually watching, the movement is seamless between the sections.

I remember that *The Ghosts of Versailles* was recorded and broadcast for PBS. The problem with PBS broadcasts is that they only show them once and then they disappear. Sometimes these Met/PBS videos are released on VHS and later DVD formats, but not always. *The Ghosts of Versailles*, for example, was released with a list price of $40.00. To be able to pull it up in about ten seconds and watch it for free is pretty swell. Once I begin watching it, the navigation bar disappears after a few seconds or so. To bring it back, I tap anywhere on the screen. I can jump back or jump ahead from scene to scene, and there is the information about the act, scene, duration, and all the sharing icons. If I want to, I can drag my finger across the bar to move to any place in the scene that I want. Standard stuff for iPad playback, but as a user, this functionality adds a sense of interaction that opera doesn't usually provide. I'm really liking this experience.

It's not perfect. If you try to send an email about how much you're liking it, the video doesn't remember where you were. You have to retrace your steps to begin again. A couple of times, when I move around the apartment—why watch an opera without snacks?—I lose the playback, presumably because my Wi-Fi has a hiccup. I relaunch, and it only takes a couple of seconds to be back in business. Maybe it's just good luck, but I don't experience any computer crashes while viewing.

I jump to three scenes of the opera that I remember best. The first is a show-stopping, zany aria sung by Marilyn Horne. She plays a, well, it would take too long to describe it. It's a silly thing really, "Limatha hajartani" (My love, my life, why did you leave me?). It's a riff on Mozart's *The Abduction from the Seraglio*, I think. She sings some Turkish stuff, dressed like a bejeweled Pasha in a turban, and she goes all wacky. It's very funny, but vocally, it's a fireworks display. She's obviously having a terrific time sending up the bel canto and baroque music that made her one of the most famous singers ever to come from America. The audience goes crazy for it.

The other two selections are ensembles that begin with Renée Fleming singing a wistful tune that grows into duets and quartets in the way that Mozart developed tunes. They are simple and beautiful moments, "Look at the green here in the glade" and "Give me back the stolen years." I'm not saying these performances made her a star, but they showcased the floating ease of her virtuosic soprano singing. For years afterwards, the Met could hardly sneeze without casting Renée Fleming in a lead role. I love being able to relive the moment that I discovered her singing.

What else have we got here? There's a "back" arrow tab on the top left that returns me to the full list of videos. I tap on *Aida*, January 3, 1985. If I'm not mistaken, it's...yep. The description reads, "This was one of the most emotional evenings in Met history—the night Leontyne Price bid farewell to opera...captured here forever." Cool. I was a college student, I remember, when this was broadcast on tv. At the end of her big aria, "O patria mia".... Let's see if I can find it. Ah! I flick to it. It's "Featured." They got that right.

I tap and there is Simon Estes, Aida's father. He was great singer back then. He was the first Porgy I ever saw live. He's African American, had a huge baritone voice, and was tall and regal. A perfect guy for this production. Well, almost. He's probably younger than Leontyne Price, who was in her late fifties. Here she comes. She wears a beautiful blue gown. The opera is almost over and she will soon be trapped with her lover Radamès in a pyramid and die.

She sings of the green hills and fragrant streams that she will never see again. "O patria mia" (My homeland). It's gorgeous singing. There's something in the air that's different about it. The audience knows that this is her farewell performance, and being one of the great singers of her day, and a true trailblazer for singers of color and American singers, for that matter, there's an enormous weightiness in her message. She is saying goodbye, but this is on her terms.

She is standing stock-still. Then she takes a seat on a step in front of the pyramids. "But now love's dream has vanished," she sings in Italian. "I shall never see my homeland again." Here come the soaring high notes. Wow! A high C as clear as a bell, and she holds it and without cutting off slides into the next phrase. *Take that young whippersnapper sopranos,* she's probably thinking. *Try that when you're my age.*

The aria is winding down. The final note she holds for what seems like forever. It's an astounding moment. At the cutoff, her jaw closes, pointing upwards in defiance, and those dark eyes gleam out inpenetrably. The audience goes absolutely crazy. I've never experienced anything like it. The camera doesn't move, and she doesn't move. She starts swallowing hard but refuses to budge. The camera zooms in tight, and we see her eyes tear up and her lips tremble; otherwise, she is a statue. Almost nothing is happening visually, which only makes the viewer strain to see every tiny tremble. The ovation goes on and on. She looks down to the conductor in the pit and starts to cry. The movement is almost inperceptible. Her head is bouncing a little. It is all sinking in, what this moment means for her. The brows furrow as she tries to control her emotions. She slowly looks back up and out, all at a glacial pace. The ovation goes on still. It sounds like a riot is breaking loose. The cheers are like yells of a mob that feed upon each other to grow more ferocious. She looks down and then up to the ceiling. As she does so, as if in prayer, she falls to her knees and places her hands over her chest. It is accompanied by a tidal wave of cheers. She is breathing hard. She is not breaking character and refuses to make eye contact with the audience.

It is a sensational moment. In all, three and a half minutes have elapsed, which in real time onstage feels like forever. Finally, she turns and moves into position for the opera to continue.

The orchestra begins to play, and the scene moves on. Somehow she manages to sing through it. Incredible.

I grew up with a funny notion in my head about history and video. It had to do with eternal video playback. Maybe some Sunday School teacher implanted the notion. I don't recall exactly where it came from. But anyway, I imagined that I would someday face a video transcript of all the things I've said, done, and thought. What this movie would be rated would be up to me, I guess. This childhood fantasy comes back to me as I watch opera on the iPad. I feel like I am reexperiencing pivotal moments from my life. That's silly, because I don't appear in any of these videos, obviously, but they generate vivid memories, nonetheless. For a fan looking to discover Mormon opera singers, on the other hand, the app is like the entrance into a wide landscape of musical history.

Throughout the weekend, I open up the app when I have a few minutes free. I explore performances I saw at the opera house and want to relive, as well as performances I regret having missed. I am surprised how many of these operas featured Mormon singers. A few of the warhorses have multiple performances available for viewing. And because the operas queue up so quickly, I play a game of comparisons. Which is better: the Jean-Pierre Ponnelle production of *Figaro* with Levine; Carol Vaness, Kathleen Battle, Frederica von Stade, Thomas Allen and Ruggero Raimondi of December 14, 1985 or Jonathan Miller's production with James Levine; Renée Fleming, Cecilia Bartoli, Suzanne Mentzer, Dwayne Croft and Bryn Terfel of November 11, 1998?

What an embarrassment of riches this is. I switch back and forth. I listen to Mentzer sing "Voi che sapete" (You who know what love is) which is perfectly fine and then von Stade's rendition, which is flat out perfection. How about Fleming vs. Vaness, and so on? I have fun watching Kathleen Battle in 1985, almost a decade before the Met will fire her for excessive diva-ness. She does sound incredible. But then again, Bartoli is so much fun to watch in the same role in 1998. She sings a rarely-performed alternate aria at the end of the opera, and her musicianship makes my head spin.

In the same production, I watch Jennifer Welch-Babidge, just getting started in her career at the Met, singing a small role. In Act III, she is one of two peasants who sing to the Count and Countess, "Amanti constanti" (Lovers true). She was in our ward at the time, and I have fond memories of her bright personality and warmth. All of it comes across in this little scene. She is a go-for-it actress, fearless, really. It's hard to watch anything else on the screen. What a vibrant singer!

I'm not perceptive enough to notice the differences in Levine's conducting of the two works more than a dozen years apart, but I love the idea that scholars can so easily study them back to back. If I had to name my favorite moment from all of the operas that I've ever heard in my life, I'd probably say it's the ending of

Figaro when the philandering count asks his wife's pardon. I don't know exactly why, but it always gets to me. For me, it is a miraculous moment—music so simple that a rising and descending pattern of intervals in the strings feels like those eight notes can wash away all the bitterness in the world. I view both endings and decide that however much I like the singers of the 1998 production, Thomas Allen breaks my heart and Carol Vaness heals it, in the 1985 version.

The Met Opera on Demand app provides plenty of opportunities for comparison games. There are three versions of *Aida, La bohème, Don Giovanni, Lucia di Lammermoor, Otello, Simon Boccanegra*, and *Tosca*, for example. If I wanted to, I could view the entire *Ring* cycle in the 1989-1990 Otto Schenk productions, or watch concerts honoring Luciano Pavarotti's 30th anniversary at the Met, various opening night galas and other concerts. And this is only the beginning, according to the Met. The opera house plans to add to the video catalog continuously. The app isn't merely a shelf of favorites. I'm pleased to see that Met Opera on Demand also has more unusual offerings, too.

Anybody with a VCR, I suppose, could also have all of these things recorded already. They were broadcasts from Lincoln Center that appeared on Public Television across the country. But realistically, I don't know anybody who has a collection of these things at home.

One of the little surprises of the Met is that, as a media content producer, it has more power than people realize. It puts on shows. That's the main thing, and it's capitalized to continue with live performances. These are expensive endeavors, budgeted to break even (fingers crossed). And yet.... There's this catalog of recordings in the vault, over a hundred years' worth of them. Many of the works are long out of copyright. The Met owns them outright, or nearly so, and however great it is to see live performances, there is a constant interest in singers and performances of the past. If they play their cards right, this could be a gold mine.

I am interested in the iPad app for another reason apart from nostalgia: it allows me to see performances by LDS singers I completely missed. There are six Mormons singing at the Met this year, but that's less than half of the members of the Church who have performed at the Met. How can I discover the others now, years after their performances? The app is one answer. I saw some of them live, but I've also missed some. Here's a chance to catch up.

I pull up *Doctor Atomic*. It's the John Adams opera about the building of the first atomic bomb. Because of my family's tragic history with atomic testing, I skipped the opera when it premiered in San Francisco and later when the production came to the Met and was broadcast in 2008. That meant that I missed the Met debut of the LDS tenor Thomas Glenn in the role of Robert Wilson, the questioning scientist at Los Alamos. I'm a fan of the composer. I've seen productions of *Nixon in China, The*

Death of Klinghoffer, I Was Looking at the Ceiling..., as well as plenty of orchestral and vocal music. My iPod is relatively well stocked with Adams recordings. I don't love everything of his, to be honest, but I can look back at my adult life and punctuate moments with memories closely associated with Adams, I guess— the same way that people consider songs by Bob Dylan, Frank Sinatra, Bruce Springsteen, Willie Nelson, Madonna, or Justin Bieber, for that matter, to be the soundtrack of their own history.

The Met ignored Adams for a long time. The same could be said for other excellent, contemporary composers, both American and international. For a long time, it dodged the issue by blaming audiences. Ticket buyers, they'd say, won't come to works by John Adams, Philip Glass, Steve Reich, William Bolcom, John Harbison, and so forth. But other opera companies outside of New York staged their works again and again, and sought out a new generation of opera composers while the Met sat on its check-signing hands. In New York, the City Opera was historically the place to see new American opera, but their decline has slowed that river. In the last ten years or so, however, the Met's been trying to catch up.

Doctor Atomic tells the story leading up to the first atomic tests in Los Alamos, New Mexico in 1945. After Germany's defeat in the war, American scientists grouped to form the Manhattan Project, which developed the bomb that would be dropped on Japanese cities. The libretto of the opera comes from the scientists' diaries, testimonies, transcripts, and a broad collection of world poetry. Wilson, Thomas Glenn's role, is something of an ethical agitator. He organizes a group of the scientists to discuss the political, social and moral ramifications of the project, and he circulates a petition to the President of the United States that a controlled test of the bomb should be observed by all to deter the enemy. The military, instead, plans to target populous cities in Japan to create maximum panic.

Thomas Glenn sounds great as the young, earnest scientist. Like many contemporary tenor roles, it forces the voice up high and keeps it there. As one of the leads of the opera, Wilson is its moral center in many ways, and Glenn portrays it brilliantly. He's particularly strong is his final sequence, "I dreamed the same dream several nights running." In it, Wilson recounts his foreshadowing vision of falling from a bomb tower.

The idea of an opera about a bomb might sound like an odd choice to some people, but it means a lot to me. My awareness of the consequences of atomic bomb testing began only with the diagnosis of my father's cancer. As I landed in Las Vegas to see him one last time, I was reading the morning newspaper at a friend's house and I discovered a small advertisement for the Smithsonian's National Museum of Atomic Testing. Yes, there is such a thing.

It probably wasn't the smartest thing I ever did, on the verge of losing my father, to go to a museum that chronicled the testing era and congratulated itself for its accomplishments, but I went anyway. My friend accompanied me to the museum. I sat in a recreation of a testing bunker and watched a video made of a test. By the time the tape was filmed, the tests were conducted underground. Upon detonation, the ground and everything upon it—trees, pick-up trucks, houses, telephone poles—convulsed. The surface of the ground became as malleable as the waves of an ocean. I was sitting on a concrete bench that was wired to tremble. Afterwards, a former employee of the Nevada Testing Site approached me, seeing that I was upset. I held my tongue while he extolled the program and its effectiveness as a military deterrent. More propaganda followed. "The testing was one of the shining moments in American history," he crowed. To which I replied, "My dying father might disagree."

My response to an opera about atomic testing is that I have deep feelings about it and equally high expectations, unfairly so, probably. I want to put a human face on this moment of our history. Ultimately, *Doctor Atomic* is about waiting. There is tension in that, and Adams' music makes the most of the nervous suspense. From a plot standpoint, the opera is almost completely static. Characters stand there, not even singing, just thinking and waiting while the orchestra pulses beneath. There is a large chorus that more or less dwarfs the principal characters visually. They stand in cubicles arranged vertically, like an expanded, sinister version of the old game show, *The Hollywood Squares*.

The video recording of the opera is likely much more effective than a live performance would be if only because the camera is constantly in motion—panning, zooming, cutting from one face to another. The camera compensates for what otherwise is dramatic flatness and emptiness.

I like the music. I really do. But Adams has an almost resolute aversion to character development. People appear onstage. They are not introduced. They just exist. They speak language that has little to do with what is going on around them. In this case, spouting lines from poetry as diverse as John Donne and the Upanishads as if they were their own thoughts. These have innate power—and "Batter My Heart" is a complete knockout to end Act I—but they are wholly removed from linear storytelling. They come off as non sequiturs, like the absurd, random lines of Gertrude Stein that happen to have been dropped like bombs.

I lay the blame with Adams because he chooses librettists who refuse to be narrative. In this case, Peter Sellars, his longtime collaborator as a director, cobbled together the texts. For me, they don't add up to anything nearly as powerful as what might have been. It's lazy writing, to my mind. I contrast the experience of seeing *Doctor Atomic* with the play by Aaron Sorkin, *The Farnsworth Invention*. Both dramas are about scientists and emerging, world-altering technologies. The Sorkin play, which came to Broadway in 2007, is about Philo T. Farnsworth, the inventor of television. *Doctor Atomic* premiered in San Francisco one year later. I wish Adams could take a cue from Sorkin and embrace stories rather than merely putting contrasting things side by side in his operas—Nixon and Mao, Palestinians and Israelis, and Manhattan Project scientists and the military—and hoping that their inherent tensions will supplant the need for dramatic construction.

I'm in Adams mode, and my next app stop is *Nixon in China*. It's an opera I already know well. I've sung it—okay, I've sung along with the recording of it—since it was released in 1988. Last year, my wife bought Met tickets to *Nixon* for our anniversary. President Nixon stepped into China on my tenth birthday, and that gives the opera a little extra meaning for me. And here are two more LDS singers in the cast. In the opera, three secretaries of Mao are like a mini, Greek chorus. Ginger Costa-Jackson and Tamara Mumford are two of the secretaries. They are dressed in drab—what else?—Mao jackets and pants. Their hair is pulled tightly to the back of their heads. They stand side by side and comment on the action. It sounds like a small part, but the roles are substantial. They are onstage for much of the opera. Their music is challenging. I find it difficult to distinguish which woman is singing what, but that's the point. It's an excellent mix of tightly harmonized sound.

In the opera house, the entire production of *Nixon* is miked. It's weird, and I confess that I don't love how microphones change the experience. At intermission, I remember, I went down to the orchestra pit. There was a microphone alongside every instru-ment. The singers had microphones too. This is a choice of John Adams, clearly, the composer who was also making a debut as the conductor of the Met orchestra. To be fair, the opera is really too small for the Met. It's essentially a chamber piece. The orchestration is small and thin, by design, and I could argue that the voice writing doesn't aspire to fill a hall as large as the Met's. I could quibble, too, with casting. James Maddalena, who created the role fourteen years ago, played Nixon. He sounded tired to me. And he had problems vocally on the night I saw it. He was altering the vocal part just to get through it.

The HD broadcast was made during the six-performance run of *Nixon* in 2011. On the iPad app, it looks better than it did in person. The camerawork makes it feel more alive, and although I lost some of the bigger moments when the stage fills with chorus and dancers, the zoom into the faces of the principals allows me to feel like it is a more intimate production than it really is. The sound, however diminished from the three tiny iPad speakers that my thumb occasionally muffles by accident, is at least less patchy than it was in the opera house.

A final word about Costa-Jackson and Mumford. The production was choreographed by Mark Morris, one of the great modern dance choreographers to emerge in recent memory. There are moments in the production when professional dancers shine, but there is a lot of designed movement throughout the performance for the singers. The three secretaries, for example, are asked to be synchronized physically for much of the opera, and that includes holding unusual poses for extended periods and making quick, ritualized shifts of movement. It's a lot to ask an opera singer to do, and they perform splendidly.

Singers at the Met become well known by audiences who attend regularly. Particularly in the supporting roles, it's not un-common for a singer to be heard multiple times each season, year after year. A happy consequence of the HD initiatives at the Met is the frequency with which these singers are seen by audiences outside of New York. Ginger Costa-Jackson is an excellent exam-ple of this phenomenon. To date, she has sung in six operas at the Met since her debut in 2008: *Thaïs* (Myrtale), *Cavalleria Rusti-cana* (Lola), *Lulu* (multiple roles), *La fanciulla del West* (Wowkle), *Nixon in China* (Nancy T'ang), and *Manon* (Rosette). Of those, two are available on the Met app (*Thaïs* and *Nixon in China*). For the 2008 season, the Met Opening Night Gala featured an act from three separate operas. The third act of *Manon* was the occa-sion of Costa-Jackson's debut, and it is also on the On-demand app. Furthermore, *La fanciulla del West* was broadcast on PBS but not yet available on the app. I suspect it will be added before long. For many of these emerging singers, the Met is essentially video-documenting their entire careers, step by step.

I wonder if these vocalists realize how lucky they are to have these beautifully-made recordings of their work. Some years ago, as my mother was getting older and could no longer sing, as she would say, "predictably," I asked if she had any recording of her younger days. By that time, I was getting into classical music, and I was eager to hear her singing in her prime, even if it was just a short excerpt of a performance. I thought there must be something—maybe an old cassette tape, or a reel-to-reel, since my parents had dozens of those lying around. The answer was that there was not a single audiotape of her singing until the technology of handheld video became commonplace. But by then, she was in her seventies.

For someone desiring to get an introduction to Mormon singers at the Met on the fly, the app's the most convenient route to exposure. Here is Jennifer Welch-Babidge singing in *Fidelio*. Beethoven's only opera is a stunner. It's about a woman who disguises herself in men's clothes to search for her abducted husband in prison. It's a political work filled with beautiful music. In this performance from October 28, 2000 led by James Levine, the stage is packed with one terrific singer after another—luxury casting. Welch-Babidge sings the role of Marzelline who is the jailer's daughter. Particularly in the first act, she is prominent. Every moment of her singing in arias, duets, and ensembles, is full of excellent acting and singing. I remember seeing her in this production at the Met. My eyes were glued on her whenever she was onstage. There's such life to her singing. She is coquettish one second, bashful the next. Her voice is girlish in one phrase and then becomes a powerful force of nature immediately thereafter.

One of the drawbacks of operas on stage is the distraction of having performers break eye contact and look down at the conductor. For me, it's a necessary evil. Obviously, it's better than getting ahead or behind the orchestra. With Welch-Babidge—and I don't know exactly how to articulate it—it's different; she doesn't appear to be acting or performing at all. She exudes these tremendous sounds and emotions, seemingly without any artifice. To accomplish it, there must be an incredible security of her ability.

For example, the beautiful, "Mir ist so wunderbar" (It seems like a miracle) begins with Marzelline pining for Fidelio, who is actually Leonore, sung by Karita Mattila, dressed as a man. Welch-Babidge sings sweetly, tinged passionately. She colors each phrase masterfully by adjusting dynamic levels constantly, by pushing and then pulling back. Leonore joins in a plaintive canon. Marzelline's father enters, sung by bass René Pape, noting his daughter's love for Fidelio. It becomes a trio. Then Marzelline's suitor, sung by Matthew Polenzani, rounds out the quartet. (Those are, by the way, some of the best singers in the world.) The vocal lines arch and billow. One singer's part takes the lead and then another, and another. What terrific music this is! Too soon, it is over, but the quality of moments like this one continue throughout the opera. Wunderbar.

I can't watch this performance of Welch-Babidge without thinking of her portrayal of Lucia at the City Opera in September, 2003. Six months pregnant at the time with her first child, the performance became front-page news in New York. Anthony Tommasini wrote, "Yet she acted with a physical involvement and intensity that belied her condition, and sang with authority, agility and bright-toned beauty, winning an enormous ovation from the audience."[1]

In performance, it was crazy subtext: pregnant Lucia goes mad after hurriedly marrying the wrong man. Instead of trying to hide her pregnancy, the director chose to embrace it. The effect was pretty shocking, and Welch-Babidge, true to form, tore up the stage with a ferocious abandon that verged on creepiness. I wasn't entirely convinced that the concept worked—pregnant Lucia going mad—but I was quite sure, watching this excellent LDS singer who was living in my ward at the time, that she was Wonder Woman.

On the iPad app, I move next to watch excerpts from *Peter Grimes* by Benjamin Britten. When this production was new in 2008, Erin Morley generously gave me a couple of tickets to see it. Even though they were excellent seats in the parterre boxes (and as I remember, we had the place all to ourselves), I am able to see more of Morley's performance in the video than I could live. The staging is another example of a grid-designed verticality, and Morley's character of a gossipy young girl appears frequently above the stage in a cubicle. The camera zooms in, and I see what a sparkling presence Morley is onstage. She moves great, but her face is especially evocative. Whatever her bratty character in *Grimes* is thinking, you see it before you hear it. She's another excellent actress.

Yesterday in church, Erin gave a talk to the congregation. She mentioned that she is an opera singer, and she said that recently her mentor at the Met approached her and said he wanted to study Mormonism. She asked him why, and he replied that he was now aware, with all of these Mormon singers at the Metropolitan, that there is something different about them. He noted the happiness that they seem to have, and he wanted to learn about it. I was struck by that story for several reasons. In writing about these singers, I have wondered whether it really matters. So what? There are six LDS singers at the Met this year. What about it?

To some degree, Erin's story is the answer: a critical mass appears and allows a community to form. When others look at it, they start to make generalizations that would not be possible in isolation. One nice person is just an anomaly; a group of nice people, or happy people, or angry people, for that matter, speaks to their sameness and invites inquiry. It makes a difference.

The other resonance for me in Erin's story takes me back to an opera I heard in New Haven about twenty years ago. I had always wanted to see a production of Aaron Copland's *The Tender Land*. With my wife, I traveled north and caught a Saturday matinee. It was a beautiful production. I loved the performance of the leading soprano whose name was Jamie Baer. One day, a couple of years later, into church one Sunday walks Jamie. We become friends, and I hear the story of her conversion to the gospel.

It was the spring of 1987, and Jamie was cast as Laurie in a new chamber music version of *The Tender Land* at the Long Wharf Theatre in New Haven. She had just finished a year as an apprentice with the Lyric Opera of Chicago, and this was her first Equity show. At the first rehearsal in late March, the entire cast was together for a read-through. The woman who was playing

Laurie's mother, Kristen Hurst Hyde, was only 8 years older than Jamie. She made an impression because she not only had a fabulous voice and was a wonderful actress, but she was really together as a person, and as Jamie put it, "was way too happy to be an opera singer!" She was a stark contrast to the egos and angst Jamie had encountered at the Lyric Opera.

Kristen and Jamie were the only two in the cast not from Connecticut or New York, and they became roommates. They stayed at the Hotel Duncan, a rather run-down hotel that had assorted crazy characters both working and living there. The two women did their best to spend as little time as possible in the hotel when they were not rehearsing. They went on long walks together, shared meals and explored the area. During these months together, they became good friends, and Jamie began asking many questions about why Kristen seemed so happy. Jamie relates that Kristen had everything that Jamie wanted—respect as an artist, a husband and a child, plus, she had joy.

Jamie tells the story this way, "Through our conversations I learned what was the source of her joy: the gospel of Jesus Christ. I had been raised Roman Catholic, but since I was 15, I had been searching for the truth in other faiths. I always came back to the Catholic Church because it felt familiar. Often during our conversations, a light would go off in my head—I recognized truth and realized I had always known it, but was just now, through Kristen being taught it."

The two women parted ways in early June as the show ended, and Kristen went home to Los Angeles, and Jamie went on to her next singing engagement with the Santa Fe Opera. Kristen gave Jamie The Book of Mormon, The Doctrine and Covenants, *A Marvelous Work and a Wonder*, and her phone number. During her first couple weeks in Santa Fe, Jamie read all the materials and called her new friend often, but then she got caught up in all the drama of a summer in Santa Fe. Near the end of the engagement in New Mexico, Kristen called again to check in, and she could hear the edginess and fatigue in Jamie's voice. "I want you to know joy," Kristen said. And she invited her to visit in Salt Lake City while she was visiting family and then spend a week with her at her home in L.A.

Jamie met Kristen's family, her extended family, and to her surprise saw that they were all happy people. There was no pressure about joining the Church. The last Sunday that Jamie was with them, she asked to accompany them to church. She recounted to me that when she walked into the chapel, she felt like she had come home. "It was an overwhelming feeling and that moment I decided I would one day join the Church. I knew it would be hard on my very Catholic family, so I would have to do this slowly and carefully," Jamie said. From that Sunday on, she stopped drinking alcohol and coffee and started cleaning up her "potty mouth", as she called it. She went off to another singing engagement, this time with Virginia Opera for two months. She and Kristen spoke nearly every day, and Jamie faithfully read the scriptures and prayed.

About a month after arriving in Virginia, Jamie received a phone call early one morning from Kristen telling her that she had been unable to sleep all night because she felt that the Spirit was telling her that she needed to tell Jamie to meet with LDS missionaries. Jamie balked at first, but she trusted her and said "Ok, I will call them and meet with them just once." Jamie met with the elders at a member's home in Portsmouth, Virginia and immediately was impressed with the strength of the Spirit. They began with the first discussions, but Jamie, having already finished reading the books that Kristen supplied, wanted to cut to the chase. Jamie turned the tables and gave the missionaries a list of questions to answer. Ten days later she was baptized at the Newport News Ward, with no friends or family present.

She had not even mentioned the fact that she was investigating the Church to her family. "But it felt like the right thing to do," she said. "I felt like I was making a clean start with my life. When I told my parents and siblings at Christmas over a month later, they were saddened and shocked. It was a hard time. But each time they saw me as I was growing in the Gospel, they recognized that it was the right choice for me. By the time I met my husband, four years later, they embraced him and the concept of Temple Marriage. Friends and fellow singers were also curious and concerned about this change, but again as time passed they realized it was a good thing."[2] This was 25 years ago. The mezzo-soprano who changed Jamie's life started it all by simply being a happy person and being willing to explain why she felt that way. And it shifted the path of Jamie's life.

Earlier this year, as I began writing about Mormon singers at the Met, I sat in a chair in church for a stake choir rehearsal. A man I didn't know sat down next to me. As soon as he opened his mouth, it was evident that he was an opera singer. He introduced himself. He had been singing in the chorus of the L.A. Opera and then decided to try to make a career for himself as a soloist. He had sung larger roles in regional opera houses, and he was in New York to audition. As we talked, he said that he had joined the Church only a few weeks before. As it turns out, he took a singing job in Logan, Utah last summer with the Utah Festival Opera. And while he was there, he fell into the warm camaraderie of the company, led by Michael Ballam and quite a few performers who are also LDS. Over the course of the summer, while performing, he listened to the missionaries, and before the season of *Boris Godunov, Don Giovanni, Oliver!,* and *South Pacific* ended, he was baptized.

I have wondered whether it matters that a singer is LDS or not. In the case of the Mormon singers at the Met, they are taking roles that don't exactly smack of virtue all the time. (Playing prostitutes is something of a rite of passage for many of these female vocalists, in fact.) And yet, as professionals, they are interacting with hosts of other performers, technicians, designers, management, and so on. It is on that stage, as a professional, that they seem to be having the most influence. Maybe the same thing is happening in other industries. Perhaps stories will emerge about politicians who come to join the Church after brushing shoulders with LDS politicians, business people, and athletes. The Mormon operatic moment is not about public relations, but the relationships they are building within the global artistic community.

I finish up my video-on-demand exploration with the opera that started the Met's Live in HD metamorphosis. It was *The Magic Flute*, an abridged, English-language production from December 2006. The fanciful production by director Julie Taymor was filled with her bag of theatrical tricks: masks, puppets, animals. It was unusually popular. The Met produced two versions of the opera simultaneously. The full-length version, *Die Zauberflöte*, in German, and a more family-friendly, holiday-branded, reduced-length version in English. We took our kids to the *Flute*. They were seven and twelve years old then. Kate had already seen it as part a school trip, but she went again with us.

On December 30, 2006, the Met broadcast the production, not on PBS, but in movie theaters around the country as a live performance. At the time, it was seen as a risk, the kind of permissive venture that Arts institutions permit new general managers when they begin their tenure but later curtail if they prove unprofitable. Peter Gelb took over as General Manager of the Met in August 2006. Aside from his first production, a critically lauded production of *Madama Butterfly*, the Live in HD theater broadcast would be a defining event in his tenure as the 16th General Manager. He predicted that HD would transform the Met, and he has been correct. Some critics say it is a negative thing. My point of view is that as a democratizing tool, this iPad app is proof that the reaches of HD performances continue to spread to anyone with a computer. I suspect it will be transformational for opera itself.

I watch *The Magic Flute* again on my couch, with the iPad in one hand and a bag of peanuts in the other. I smile at the two performances of LDS singers, Tamara Mumford and Wendy Bryn Harmer, as Ladies of the Queen. The costumes are pretty great. These women carry masks that they detach and move about with the effect of disembodied heads floating above the action. Mumford and Harmer are two of a trio of women who propel the action in the Mozart opera forward. The HD technology and how it will change the way the opera house functions is an historical moment for the Met.

However cool the videos in the app are, the deeper trove is found by tapping on the "audio" button at the bottom of the iPad banner. Here are audio-only performances of operas captured live at the Met. If the Live in HD operas represent the best moments in recent memory, the audio performances take a broader historical approach. This is enough to get any opera fan salivating. It is the equivalent of finding bootleg videos of full baseball games played by Babe Ruth, Lou Gehrig, Ty Cobb, and Shoeless Joe Jackson.

Currently, there are 256 opera performances available on the app, searchable by title or performance date. The oldest here are four operas performed in 1936 and 1937: *Samson et Dalila* (Wettergren, Pinza, and with Maurice Abravanel conducting), *Götterdämmerung* (Lawrence, Melchior), *Siegfried* (Flagstad, Melchior), and *Carmen* (Ponselle).

Navigation of the performances is identical to the video offerings. That's good news. I had worried that there would be a three-hour recording that I'd have to wade through. Instead, each scene is broken down, highlighted, and described separately. To jump to a favorite moment, I tap, and I'm there. I choose the "Truaermarsch" (Funeral march) from *Götterdämmerung* conducted by Artur Bodanzky. There's a little bit a surface noise, but not much. Definitely not scratchy like the old LPs I grew up listening to. The big moments of the orchestra sound full and lush. It's a compressed sound, but much more dynamic than I expected. I get chills.

The Metropolitan was founded only a few years before Edison invented the phonograph in 1878. It should come as no surprise that opera singers jumped on the technology early. Why sing for an opera house full of people when you can sing for a nation full of living rooms of people? Caruso made dozens of short recordings from the turn of the century until 1920. And he wasn't the only one to tiptoe into the recording studio, of course. The Metropolitan made a famous batch of recordings on wax cylinders between 1901 and 1903 eventually named after the company librarian,

Lionel Mapleson. The more than 100 Mapleson cylinders form an early cache of documents by singers who left no other records. Caruso's recordings, by the way, were the first recordings of any kind to be digitally remastered by computer, in 1976. So far, the Met Opera app doesn't go back beyond 1936, but they've got the goods in the vaults somewhere; it's a question of when rather than if.

I find myself wanting to listen to more things than I have time for. The offerings are live broadcasts, and they sound terrific: Lily Pons 1940 *La fille du régiment*, Jussi Björling 1949 in *Manon Lescaut*, Eleanor Steber 1949 *La traviata*...it's a long list. Most of these recordings have been available over the years in one form or another, but the searchability and, frankly, the economic value of having them right before me, is pretty attractive. The trickle of offerings from the 1930s and 1940s turns into a deluge from the 1950s forward. Nearly ever year is represented by four or five performances. I wonder if these are the Texaco Radio broadcasts. Probably. At any rate, with 265 available and more on their way—eight operas from 1947 to 2007 are featured in a menu bar marked "new"—this is an almost-unending feast.

Just for fun, I click on the "Search" function button. Up pops a message, "Search the Met Opera on Demand catalog by opera title, composer, conductor, or performer." I type "Ariel Bybee". The response is, "Sorry, there are no results for 'Ariel Bybee.'" That's odd. I try again: "Bybee". Nothing. Upper case, lower case gets the same result. Maybe, I think, the search function isn't up and running yet. I type "Pavarotti". A listing appears with 33 audio or video performances from 1976 to 2001. Hmmm? I know that Bybee made her debut with the Met in a production of *Rigoletto* October 31, 1977.

I type "Rigoletto". And one of the many results is a video dated November 7, 1977. Could she be in it? I tap and within thirty seconds I am listening to Bybee sing what was her third performance at the Met. I see and hear the hallmarks of her talent: a focused, full richness, a visual intensity and sensitivity to the characters around her, and an understanding of how she fits in sonically to the fabric of the music. She is beautiful looking in the role, and she sounds just as beautiful.

The search function of the app must be shallow. That is, not all of the performers in each opera trigger a searchable response. To get a fuller list of what might be possible to hear, I go to the Met opera archives online (archives.metoperafamily.org/archives/frame.htm). Under "Key Word Search", I type "Ariel Bybee". The result is an interactive listing of the 466 performances Bybee gave between *Rigoletto* of 1977 and *La traviata* in 1995. All of the opera titles are links that connect to complete cast lists of each performance and an added index of subjects and names. As I scroll down Bybee's list (each performance has its own horizontal column of information), I see other icons. There is a "Met Player" logo next to 11/7/1977 to indicate the performance is available on video. When I click on the logo, I'm directed to the

Opera on Demand page of the Met's webpage. A little clunky. It would be cooler if it took me directly to the video.

I notice other icons. Here is one for "Opera News" for *Die Frau ohne Schatten*, 4/1/1978. I click on the link and I'm taken to a two-page spread of the magazine. There is the cast including Bybee, a servant, and photographs of the production. The Met archive list informs me when the performance took place on tour, and where. Wait, there's another Bybee *Opera News* link. She is a servant again in *Elektra*, 12/30/1978. Young singers must pay their dues by servitude, I guess. And then another video available: *Luisa Miller*, 1/20/1979. And one week later, another video link as well as "Rhapsody" "Opera News 1", and "Opera News 2". The "Rhapsody" link takes me to information on the Met's site that describes radio subscription options.

I tap on the video link to *Luisa Miller* and within ten seconds, I am watching Bybee, in peasant costume complete with white apron and bonnet. Her featured moment is short but powerful. It's a big sound, surprisingly large, to my ears. And look at that smile! I skip to the Act I finale. Bybee's holding her own against Sherrill Milnes, Placido Domingo and Renata Scotto with a young, afro-coiffed James Levine conducting. By tapping on the scene selection, I find all of Bybee's moments immediately. I watch each one. She's terrific in the beginning of Act III in an extended, featured scene. It's so cool to me to be reliving what must have been an exciting moment for this pioneering Mormon artist.

I look for more operas with Bybee in them. There are more

photographs from *Madama Butterfly* and *Rigoletto* in 1979, and then a full audio recording of *Parsifal*, 4/14/1979. She is playing the Second Esquire. It's only an audio file, and I worry that I won't be able to recognize her voice when I hear it. No need to worry. There it is in Act I, a burly, dark sound, with Wagner's German text muscling its way through the orchestra. Bybee had an ability to shake your seat underneath you as you listened. I wondered, before I opened these historic recordings, whether that ability grew as her voice matured. I wondered what she sounded like before I moved to the city, and before I started attending the same church congregation that she and her family did. To my ears, her mezzo-soprano voice didn't change that much over time. It always had that distinctive gutsiness to it. There was an emotionality to the singing too, as if she were ripping her heart out and presenting it to you. There is danger in her voice, and that's what makes it so thrilling. Her role in *Parsifal* is large. I make a mental note to come back and listen to the entire performance, headed by Jon Vickers, Christa Ludwig and Martti Talvela—all singers that were heroes when I was growing up.

And so it goes, perusing Bybee's performances in the Met archives and listening to each that is available on the Opera on Demand app. There's a broad list of operas here including many favorites of mine, *Dialogues des Carmélites* and *Eugene Onegin*. I didn't know that she sang Hänsel in *Hänsel und Gretel*. But she played that role often. And then there's the big break, the March 30, 1981 performance of Jenny, the starring role in Kurt

Weill's *Rise and Fall of the City of Mahagonny*. She stepped into the role replacing Teresa Stratas on short notice. The archive notes that a second performance by Bybee on April 4 was broadcast as a Saturday matinee, but so far, it's not available on the Met app.

I do tap on the *Lucia di Lammermoor* starring Joan Sutherland and Alfredo Kraus. Neither of these lead singers was in their prime by 1982, but it's a treat to hear them. Granted, they are not the greatest actors who ever strode the stage, but it is a class of singing that stands apart. Bybee plays another handmaid role, which becomes her bread and butter type. In a way, the roles are not killers. It doesn't take me more than a few minutes to play the scenes in which she sings. The trick is balance and stamina, and in this regard, Bybee towers above many of her peers.

Although there are not pages and pages of her singing, when she does have something, it is often intense and part of a larger scene with the (usually) heroine launching into a climactic moment. If the supporting singer isn't of sufficient caliber, the entire thing feels off, like a tawdry showstopper in a regional production. In Act I of *Lucia*, for example, Bybee's character, Alisa, begs Lucia to renounce her love. It's big music sung by Bybee that gets even bigger when Lucia jumps into the main aria that ends with a high D natural that is practically atomic-powered. Without a big dose of vocal support from the mezzo, the aria is just as great, but it isn't as dramatic.

One of Bybee's strengths, and I witnessed this over a period of years in the audience, was a marathon-like ability to remain intent upon the star in the limelight. She is onstage a long time. She doesn't draw focus, but it's a statuesque earnestness that she provides as a foundation for the higher flights of bravura singing of her colleagues. Any mezzo-soprano will tell you that it's not easy going toe to toe with great sopranos like Sutherland, and Bybee succeeds memorably again and again. In the famous sextet that ends Act II, however, all the singers are equally matched in a game of melodic tag.

By this time, Bybee had already sung 220 performances at the Met. There were more of the lady-in-waiting roles to come, certainly, but in the mid-1980s, she also had larger parts in *Les contes d'Hoffmann*, (which has been broadcast on Sirius radio but is not yet on the iPad app) and revivals of *Mahagonny*. She sang in other houses besides the Met, of course, and in these places she sang more leading roles, including Melisande, Carmen, Poppea, among others. I don't have any of those recordings, but I click on the Met's *Carmen* from March 21, 1987, and I listen to an amazing performance with Agnes Baltsa, José Carreras, Samuel Ramey, Dawn Upshaw and Bybee, led by Levine. It makes me wish I had heard Bybee's Carmen in San Francisco, early in her career. I went to a party once, and everyone was supposed to bring a song to sing. Ariel was there, and she sang a sexy aria from *Carmen*. On stage, I bet she was a knockout.

I arrived in New York in 1985, and I saw many of Bybee's Met performances. I was a fan before I discovered that she was LDS.

I saw her in the roles that are now on the Opera on Demand app. Moving through her career chronologically, at this point the recordings are less historic and more nostalgic for me. I listen to the opening scene of *Eugene Onegin* and Bybee's rich voice is unmistakable. Unlike the urgency that is a part of her Italian characterizations, there is a sadness in this Russian characterization. It's an exquisite effect. For some reason, although she continued to sing in multiple operas each season until her last, in 1995, there are no audio or video recordings of her operas available yet on the app from her last six years. That's unfortunate, and I hope that in time the gaps will be filled in. Fans talk about Bybee as a dramatic singer, and of course that's true, but she could also be very funny. One of her roles that I loved was a covetous neighbor in Puccini's *Gianni Schicchi*. I remember vividly how she chewed the scenery in that delightful one-acter.

Using the app, I compare the same opera filmed in different decades. Acting styles, camera work, and technology have changed. In the *Luisa Miller* of 1979, for example, the close-up shots reveal the stars with sweat dripping down their faces. The singers don't know exactly where to look. They haven't recalibrated their acting styles for the camera, and it is all big and melodramatic to the point of clownishness. Occasionally, the camera cuts off parts of the singers' bodies and leaves out singers who are singing solo lines.

If anything, the Live in HD recordings are staged to the camera, almost to a fault. The productions are aimed with the camera rather than the live audience in mind. As I watch the more recent Met productions on the app, I repeatedly think that I'm enjoying them as movies more than I enjoyed them as operas in the opera house. What I mean is that although I miss the sound and atmosphere, being able to zoom in makes the experience as rich as theater. I think it's something like the breakthrough of having the librettos projected as subtitles on the backs of seats at the Met. There were naysayers at the time, but the operagoing experience was enhanced so radically that there is no going back. I suspect that the same is true for the video revolution.

The last stop on my app journey is a search for recordings by LDS tenor Stanford Olsen. Of the Mormon singers, it was he who sang the biggest roles regularly at the Met. His career was not unusually long. He sang 165 performances from 1987 to 1997, but many of them were leading man roles. Olsen and Bybee had careers that overlapped, and they performed together twenty-five times in three operas: *La traviata, Lucia di Lammermoor,* and Puccini's *Il Trittico,* although in the latter, they were in separate one-acts. Olsen's voice is the high, flexible tenor. For some reason, I missed most of his career at the Met. I saw him a few times in opera and also in concert performances elsewhere. At the Met, his principal roles were in *L'elisir d'amore, Lucia di Lammermoor, Il barbiere di Siviglia, Così fan tutte, Die Entführung aus dem Serail, Don Giovanni, Semiramide, I Puritani, Falstaff,* and *Die Fledermaus.* This is an unmatched accomplishment among Mormon singers at the Met. So I am excited to see that two of Olsen's performances are available on the Opera on Demand app: *Il barbiere di Siviglia* and *Die Entführung aus dem Serail*.

First, I listen to his aria from the first act of *Barbiere*, "Ecco ridente in cielo" (There, smiling in the sky). It has such a transparency of sound. So refined. It sounds so easy for him. But I know Rossini music enough to know that the complex passage work of trills, roulades, and runs strike terror into most singers. As the aria progresses, I am enveloped in this wonderful cushion of articulated air. It swirls in my ears. When he gets to the faster, devilishly-complex sections, his voice never strains to negotiate the bramble of notes. He reaches the finish line of the aria with an intricate scale leading up to a gleaming, crystalline high C, which he holds out for what feels like a very long time. He is a powerful singer. Many light, Rossini and Mozart tenors have beautiful voices, but they sometimes have difficulty projecting in a big opera house. That's no fault of theirs, but the realities of large architecture make it a problem. Olsen's voice, though, is bright and bold. In the performance of *Barbiere*, he is joined by American opera titans, Frederica von Stade, Samuel Ramey, and Thomas Hampson. Olsen is their vocal equal in every way.

Using the Metropolitan Opera Archives' searchable database, I make a listing of all of the Mormon singers that I know about, and I look up their performance histories. During the course of the year, I've asked experts about this group of singers. "Who do you know who is LDS and has sung at the Met?" It's a straightforward question, but it's not as simple as that. I don't know, for example, if there have ever been LDS singers in the Met Opera Chorus. The archive doesn't list chorus members' names, and so even if I did hear of their names, it would be difficult to verify.

Over time, the archive has shifted the way it lists performances. Sometimes it includes concerts with the Met orchestra performed elsewhere. I've decided not to include those in my tallies of performances; I view them as just another concert gig. And recently, the archive began to include the National Council Grand Finals concerts too. For my purposes, I decide not to include those competitions as part of my statistics because it gives short shrift to those who may have competed on the stage of the Met years ago and are unreported in the archive. But I have included the Met performances on tour and also stagings of special events at the opera house such as gala commemorations. Essentially, I have limited my accounting to actual opera performances.

At any rate, I become aware that there have been 15 Mormon singers who have performed roles at the Met. It is a rarified group any way I look at it. To have a season with six on the Met roster, therefore, is staggering. Here is a listing of all the Mormon singers, the span of time they performed at the Metropolitan Opera, and the total number of performances. Several, obviously, are in the process of racking up numbers.

Fittingly, the first (alphabetically and statistically) is Ariel Bybee. Ariel Bybee 1977-1995, 466 performances; Carla Rae Cook 1984, 13 performances; Ginger Costa-Jackson 2008-present, 45 performances; Kent Cottam 1978-1983, 25 performances); Thomas Glenn 2008, 9 performances; Wendy Bryn Harmer 2005-present, 130 performances; Brian Montgomery 1992, 2 performances; Erin Morley 2008-present, 52 performances; Tamara Mumford 2006-present, 132 performances; Stanford Olsen 1986-1997, 163 performances; Sue Patchell 1999-2004, 8 performances; Glade Peterson 1975, 2 performances; Nina Warren 1992-1994, 25 performances; Jennifer Welch-Babidge 1998-2006, 101 performances; Carla Wood 2003, 1 performance.

The story of Carla Wood shows just how bizarre Met performances can be. On February 13, 2003, Wood was covering the small role of a Maid in *Jenůfa* sung by Diane Elias. In the third and final act of the opera, Elias became unable to continue after beginning the act. Carla Wood stepped in and replaced her for the last section of the act. That was Wood's Met debut. And to date, it's her only performance at the Met.

Brian Montgomery's story is like Wood's but with a different outcome. In 1992, he was covering roles at the Met, Verdi's *Don Carlo* and Philip Glass' *The Voyage*. The archive notes that he has performed two times at the Met, but both of those performances were leading roles, Rodrigo in *Don Carlo* and Columbus in *The Voyage*. He's just a lucky guy. The majority of people who cover roles never get to perform them. Nicholas Pallesen is one of these, so far. Other LDS Met covers who haven't gone on include Marie Te Hapuku, who was a Met cover during the 2010 season, but was not fortunate enough to go on.

I note that there have been 15 singers from the Church at the Met, but that's not a definitive number. I speak with a friend over the weekend, and as I tell her about my year of opera going, she asks me whether I've come across her brother-in-law, Kent Cottam in my research. We look through the archives together, and sure enough, there is Cottam with 25 performances in 1978 and 1983. He sang in *Thaïs* for his debut at the Metropolitan and then continued in the role as it went on tour. In 1983, he sang the Lawyer in *Peter Grimes*. An online search notes that after his LDS mission to Brazil, Cottam came to New York. He sang in the choruses of the City Opera and the Metropolitan Opera. It appears that at some point, he took on roles at the Met as well. Come to find out, Kent Cottam and I went to the same high school. Small world. All of this sleuthing makes me more nervous than ever about putting a fixed number of LDS singers on the Met scoreboard, so to speak.

I think it's worth mentioning that other LDS opera singers have been associated with the Metropolitan without performing roles with the company. These include Lindsay Killian and Rachel Willis-Sørensen, both of whom were National Council Grand Finals Concert winners in 2000 and 2010, respectively. Diana Walker sang a lot with the New York City Opera and performed in the Metropolitan Opera House with the National Ballet of Canada. Jamie Baer Peterson sang with the Metropolitan Opera Guild for a few years in their educational outreach program.

I begin to wonder just how many opera singers there have

been in the history of the Church. It's an unknowable figure. I imagine walking into a rehearsal at the Mormon Tabernacle Choir and asking, by a raise of hands, how many of them have sung an opera onstage and got paid for it. And I imagine traveling back in time and asking the same question to the Choir in 2000, 1990, 1980, 1970.... Think how many opera singers there must have been!

I go to mormon.org and type the word "opera" in the search window. Dozens of members of the Church worldwide, who have posted their own stories and beliefs on the website, note that they have been professional opera singers. The posts include only their first names, but I'm able to track down a few and discover that, sure enough, they have sung with opera companies here and abroad. A few have been fixtures in opera company choruses, and others are performers of roles in companies in their communities. Many of the women who post on the site note that they were professional singers but they stopped performing when they began to raise a family. I'm pleasantly surprised to see that dozens of young Mormons on the site are studying vocal performance at college and plan to be opera singers. All of this makes me wonder about the future. Is this new critical mass of professional singers—at the Met and elsewhere—going to impact a younger generation to aspire to duplicate their successes?

I am focusing on Mormons at the Met because, being somewhat lazy, I am Mormon and live a few blocks from the Met; it makes sense to me to attempt to tackle the topic. At the same time, I know personally many brilliant opera singers who are Mormon who have not performed at the Met. It is not only a question of quality, either. Some musicians began a career and then decided they preferred the lifestyle of academia, for example, or they made any number of choices that took them in directions away from the Metropolitan.

I ask friends who are singers to help me compile a list of Mormon opera singers who have performed professionally at some point in their lives. I reach out to accompanists, voice teachers, and regional opera singers with LDS connections. Together we come up with a list of current and historical opera singers from the Church: Carol Ann Allred, Christi Amonson, Marcus Arbizu, Ray Arbizu, Darrell Babidge, Jamie Baird, Michael Ballam, Michael Belnap, StacyLyn Bennett, Joy Berta, Olivia Biddle, Justus Bonn, Susan Alexander Boren, Barry Bounous, Elaine Brewster, Doris Brunati, Ariel Bybee, Megan Cash, Betty Jeanne Chipman, Michael Chipman, Hyun Soo Choi, Christopher Clayton, Connie Cloward, Carla Rae Cook, Debra Lynn Cook, Ginger Costa-Jackson, Kent Cottam, Bryan Davis, Brandt Curtis, Alexis Defranchi, Liriel Domiciano, George Dyer, Karen Early Evans, Cecily Ellis, Ruth Ellis, Gary Fisher, Aaron Foster, Thomas Glenn, Shawna Gottfredson, Marie Te Hapuku, Wendy Bryn Harmer, Christopher Holmes, J. Arden Hopkin, Isaac Hurtado, Kristen Hurst Hyde, Camella Northrup Iund, Denise Jensen, J. Delos Jewkes, Angela Johnson, Jubal Joslyn, Tony Kibbie, Lindsay Killian, Clara Hurtado Lee, Carolyn Tueller Lewis, Laura

Garff Lewis, Jon Linford, Jennie Litster, Felicia Marie Lundie, Gabriel Manro, Nancy Peery Marriott, Maughan McMurdie, Chad Millar, Dan Montez, Brian Montgomery, Anna Mooy, Erin Morley, Tamara Mumford, Ryan Olsen, Stanford Olsen, Melissa Otani-Jensen, JoAnn Ottley, Amy Owens, Shea Owens, Stephen Pace, Nicholas Pallesen, Cynthia Pannell, Sue Patchell, Curt Peterson, Glade Peterson, Jamie Baer Peterson, Robert Peterson, Stina Peterson, David Power, Gabriel Preisser, Alta Rae, Diane Thueson Reich, Clayne Robison, Adam Russell, Roy Samuelsen, Lisa Hopkins Seegmiller, Bonnie Seeholzer, Bruce Seely, Celena Shafer, Gwendolyn Soper, Brian Stucki, Patricia Swasey, M. Ryan Taylor, Sam Thompson, Andrea Thornock, Eugene Tueller, Noel Twitchell, Kathleen Van de Graaff, Peter Van de Graaff, Lisa van der Ploeg, Lawrence Vincent, Nina Warren, Jennifer Welch-Babidge, Kay Welch, Rachel Willis-Sørensen, Gretchen Windt, Carla Wood, Amanda Woodbury, and Margaret Woodward.

This is a cursory, skim-the-surface list. And it's possible that a name or two is added to the above in error. That said, as I research these names, I find that all of them have significant performing credits and some of them have performed in the best opera houses in the world. Quite a few of the above are currently pursuing careers, and it's exciting for me to note how many of them are involved in the premiere of new works. It would not surprise me to discover, a decade or two from now, that these singers were considered pioneers in their way.

CHAPTER 9

THERE WERE OTHER MORMON VOCAL PIONEERS. Emma Lucy Gates Bowen is the earliest that I've learned about. She was born in Utah in 1882 and enjoyed an opera career in Europe until World War I brought her back to the U.S. She received offers from the Metropolitan Opera, but she chose Chicago instead because they promised her leading roles in her coloratura repertoire. She made recordings, too, with Columbia Records, and I listen to one posted on YouTube. It's called "The Nightingale's Song."

It was recorded in December, 1916. The sound takes me back. It's that great old, scratchy, antique sound. The song itself is silly. And the producers have layered goofy, bird twittering over the music that sounds to me like a Disney *Sleeping Beauty* castoff sound effect. At any rate, her voice doesn't bowl me over. It's not a question of technology either, although the aged sonics do get in the way. I have plenty of recordings from this period, and I don't think her voice is particularly great in comparison. Her sound is kind of mealy and thin. When she swoops up to high notes, there is almost no vibrato, and her departures of pitch are a little glaring.

I look up a review of Gates (she married Albert E. Bowen in 1916). On February 4, 1902, Emma Lucy Gates made her debut at Carnegie Hall. Her first public concert had been only one year earlier, with the Mormon Tabernacle Choir in Salt Lake City. The Carnegie Hall concert was with orchestra, conducted by Emile Paur. Gates shared the program with "boy violinist" Florizel Reuter. Gates sang three selections: "Caro Nome" from *Rigoletto*, "Pastorale" by Bizet, and "Sing Sweet Bird" by Ganz. The review, reprinted in the *Deseret Evening News* the next morning describes her contributions to the concert this way:

> Miss Gates followed, rendering the aria from "Rigoletto" which was counted one of her strongest productions in her home concerts. She was given a full orchestral accompaniment. That the audience was delighted was shown by the fact that she had four recalls, and that three handsome bouquets were handed her over the footlights. For an encore she gave the German "Nachtigal Lied." During the evening Florizel was recalled nine times. Miss Gates was recalled six times, and after the concert people crowded upon the stage to congratulate both artists.[1]

Emma Lucy was the sister of B. Cecil Gates, a prominent composer in the Church. They were grandchildren of Brigham Young. After her return to the States, she and her brother formed the Lucy Gates Grand Opera Company. It toured the country for several years, and at the same time, she began recording with Columbia Graphophone Company. According to articles written about her, she was a very popular recording artist in her day. She continued her career through the 1920s and 1930s. When her husband was called to be an apostle in 1937, she began to curtail performing and shifted to teaching (she would have been about 55 years old at the time). Her last public performance was in 1948, a concert given to celebrate her career. She died in 1951.

I read an excerpt from a letter that Emma Lucy Gates wrote to her parents from Europe. It is deposited in a sizable archive of her materials in the Utah State Historical Society. At the time of the letter, Gates's parents were trying to convince her to come home. She had gone to Germany to study piano but was convinced to switch to voice: "Where would I have been studying at home—J. Reuben Clark, Reed Smoot, and everyone else. No one ever amounts to anything in the eyes of the 'Brethern' until someone else away from home has seen and acknowledged their worth."[2]

A valid question to ask is whether the careers of singers like Gates, Bybee, and Olsen have made a difference to LDS singers today. What is their legacy inside the Mormon community? To begin with, there was status. In the case of Bybee and Olsen, the Met stars sang with the Tabernacle Choir, performed (and still perform) concerts on Temple Square, and they gave any number of interviews with Church publications about their abilities to meld religious belief and professional success. Those are the kinds of questions that, early in the development of any culture, serve as a launching pad. As Mormon fine art culture moved from a cloistered provincialism to an embrace of international possibility, it was assuring to aspiring performers that someone had led the way. It could be done. It sounds silly to think in those terms. This idea of trailblazers and pioneers bumps against a contemporary feeling that anybody can do anything if they really want it. But in my lifetime, I've seen plenty of barriers fall, and in each case, there was an individual, not even a political figure, who set it all in motion.

My mother told me about Marian Anderson, the African American contralto who sang her way into history, taking the steps of the Lincoln Memorial in 1939 after the Daughters of the American Revolution refused her admittance to sing in Constitution Hall. Anderson sang for a gathered crowd of 75,000 people and broadcast the concert to millions worldwide. Without saying anything about race, she called attention to the unfairness of her situation. As cracks in the wall of tyranny go, she offered a tremendous, early blow. Although she was one of the most celebrated singers of the 20th century—I have some of her recordings that are simply rafter-rattling—she was not allowed to sing a role in an opera onstage. The one exception was at the Met in 1955.

Anderson became the first African American to sing at the Met. The Opera on Demand app has the performance. I tap on her aria, "Re dell' abisso, affrettati" (King of the Shades, hurriedly). There is applause when she enters. Her voice is strong. She is almost 60 years old by then, and the vibrato is a bit wide, but at the climatic note of the aria, I am blown back in my chair. This performance meant something. And it means something to me now. It signaled a shift in the public's intolerance for racism. Anderson's sermonizing was to open her mouth and let the music speak. At the end of the aria, there is an eruption of applause. This is the musical equivalent of the Berlin Wall falling down, of Rosa Parks taking a seat on the bus.

I have heard it said for years that classical music is irrelevant to the broader American culture. Anderson and the people she affected would argue against that point of view. Since then, many classical artists have emerged who have pushed the boundaries of what a star should be like. It now includes people with severe physical disabilities, artists from remote areas of the world, and people of all races. That is progress, and however non-progressive classical music appears to be on the outside, it has sometimes been a catalyst for change in the larger landscape.

I hesitate to mention Anderson and the Mormon singers back to back. Their social accomplishments are unequal. And the challenges they face, particularly the prejudice that aimed to snuff out singers of color in the U.S., have no parallel in the LDS community. That said, there is an insidiousness in the ways that members of a community hold themselves back until someone shows them a way to break through. In Anderson's day, the barriers were placed by others; for Mormon singers, the barriers were mostly self-imposed. The idea was to circle the wagons, think small, stay safe. The attitude prevailed in Emma Lucy Gates's day and it persisted in Ariel Bybee's. I draw connections between pioneering artists like Anderson and Bybee because I have witnessed that repressive attitude disappear in their wake.

In the Harris Fine Arts building at Brigham Young University, students go to classes, attend concerts and seminars, and meet with their professors. Prominently displayed in a foyer of a recital hall in the building is a larger-than-life portrait of Ariel Bybee. To say that young LDS singers are unaware of her pioneering foundation would be foolish. If they think that a Mormon artist can't have it all, the portrait robs them of the delusion. Unless they view Bybee as a complete fluke, they are stripped of the excuse that a career in opera (or whatever world stage) is incompatible with a Mormon lifestyle. The painting is a symbol of it.

As time passes, the breakthroughs become increasingly less significant. A Mormon singer at the Met (or a Mormon ballplayer in the World Series, or a Mormon on the moon, for that matter) is no longer unthinkable because all of those breakthroughs have happened already. This transformation of expectation is happening quickly. It was only ten years ago that a friend who is an opera singer won the Met National Council Auditions after graduating from BYU as a vocal major. Her family encouraged her not to pursue a career in New York, even though her father was a singer with international credits. Her parents were frightened for her spiritual well being.

For the group of young LDS singers emerging today—those at the Met and also at other opera houses around the world—I don't think that the question of "should I or shouldn't I" has anything to do with moral issues any more. And if the cultural shift is the case, the young artists have a few people to thank for that. Conversely, the life of an opera singer might indeed be a bad choice for some people. But that's not a judgment for me to make. I do care, however, about the possibility of venturing out into the world, far and wide.

To the minds of many in LDS circles, the leading man of Mormon opera is Michael Ballam. He had a big opera career and sang all over the country—at the Chicago Lyric, San Francisco, Santa Fe, Dallas, Washington, Philadelphia, St. Louis, and San Diego opera companies. He did not sing at the Met, but his robust website lists a string of impressive accomplishments that stretch over four decades.[3]

Ballam, perhaps more than anybody else, has most successfully integrated his beliefs and his music-making into a public persona. He returned to Utah and founded the Utah Festival Opera in 1992. Ballam has been a tremendous force inside the LDS community as a popularizer of opera. He now hires opera singers and travels constantly to audition musicians for his opera company. I suspect that Ballam, better than anybody else, knows what Mormon singers can do.

It is unsurprising that within a church that so values music—what other organization would make a 200-voice choir its primary media ambassador?—that a number of fine classical singers would emerge from its rank and file. There have been many fine singers throughout its history, both classical and popular musicians. It's beyond the parameters of my Mormon/Met exploration to do them justice, but I'm aware that they form an important foundation for what is happening now.

Speaking of the choir, the Mormon Tabernacle Choir sang with the Met once, too. On April 4, 1905, the Met stopped in Salt Lake City. At the tabernacle, Arturo Vigna conducted the Met orchestra in a program of opera arias and incidental music. They performed Rossini's *Stabat Mater*. The Met archives are a bit unclear about it, but it looks like the Met Opera chorus was joined by the Mormon Tabernacle Choir and its conductor, Evan Stephens. In those days, the Met performed the *Stabat Mater* frequently on its Sunday Night Concert series. It calls for a large chorus and soloists. Traditionally, opera singers who rarely ventured into the oratorio repertoire would nonetheless perform the Rossini work.

Utah has established itself as a regional player in opera. The state's opera companies have Mormon members of the board, management personnel, and performers. Glade Peterson, whose career was mostly in Europe, which was the case for many American singers fifty years ago, founded the Utah Opera. Peterson sang at the Met for only two performances, in 1975. He performed in the Ring cycle's *Das Rheingold*. He took the part of Loge.

The New York Times review accompanying the performance had this to say,

> Of three artists making their Met debuts, Glade Peterson as Loge made the strongest impression. Mr. Peterson's voice is ample, and his nefarious skulking about as Wotan's Secretary of State for Intrigue marked him as a

real find for the company. Loge is the perfect corporation lawyer, with a loophole ready for any occasion, and Mr. Peterson had him down to perfection.[4]

However auspicious that Met debut was, he did not return. He spent almost all of his career abroad. Aside from roles at the San Francisco and Houston Grand Operas, Peterson stayed in Europe. He was the principal tenor of the Zurich Opera for a dozen years and sang in companies in Paris, Milan, Hamburg and Vienna. Peterson's Met performances actually came toward the end of his career. He left Europe after 15 years to return to his native Utah. He founded the Utah Opera in 1978. Peterson died at the age of 61, in April 21, 1990. There had been opera in Utah before, but Peterson's Utah Opera was the first professional company of scale. It continues to this day, having merged with the Utah Symphony in 2002.

I met Peterson once. He was an excellent promoter of opera, and one of his duties in fund raising was to travel around the state with members of the Utah Opera company to perform in public schools. I met Maurice Abravanel of the Utah Symphony in the same way. Peterson visited 70,000 students each year with these trips. Because of his reputation as a European star, he was an excellent fundraiser. The opera company started off quickly and stabilized into a leading regional presenter of five or so productions each year. That was an ambitious undertaking, and it would not have been possible without Peterson's performance history cachet. Emma Lucy Gates was his voice teacher, and in

1948, she took him to Abravanel. That led to his debut performances after his return from military service in Korea. I look up and read his obituary in the *Deseret News.* I'm struck by the praise he receives from the governor and other state dignitaries, and also the way they comment on his visits to their church congregations to sing. Interesting.

Enough about history, I have work to do. The Met season is winding down. There are only four weeks remaining. The final performance of the season is May 12. I make a list of operas that I still need to see. LDS singers are in five operas going on right now. I've already seen *Götterdämmerung*, so that leaves four. But I want to see two other operas too. That's a whole lot of operas, and a lot of hours of opera. *Manon* is four hours long, and then the Wagner..., well, you know. I draw up a tentative schedule: *Manon*, April 17; *Das Rheingold*, April 26; *Die Walküre*, April 28; *Siegfried*, April 30. Those are the works with Mormon singers. If worse comes to worst, I could sit at home and listen to a couple of them as radio broadcasts.

I walk over to the Met to get a $20 seat for tonight's *Manon* by Massenet. I don't know the opera. I'm better acquainted with the Italian version of the same story, *Manon Lescaut,* by Puccini. I arrive an hour before the tickets are to be sold. That's more or less the timing I've used before. When I get to the Met, I realize that I've miscalculated. Maybe it's the fact that the season is coming to a close, maybe the tourists are running out of non-Wagner options; whatever, the line is much longer than I've seen before. I have doubts that I'll get a seat. Someone does a head count, and they say that I'm number 110. There are less than 200 tickets available. If everyone in line buys the allowable two tickets, I'll be left out in the cold. And if 50 of those tickets are already sold to the 65-and-older patrons, it's even more unlikely. But I have a magazine to read, so I plop myself down amid the chattering hordes.

It is not my lucky day. Earlier, I walked into a glass door at the gym while holding a Russian kettlebell, and I have a headache even before I line up behind a man who hasn't taken a bath recently, and who will sing incomprehensibly under his breath for the next 90 minutes. Shoot me with a crossbow, somebody. When we finally get toward the front of the line, a Met security guard announces that all of the tickets are gone. It wasn't meant to be, I guess. I imagine that I might have been stuck sitting next to this guy tonight, and I somehow feel relieved to be ticketless.

After I walk home, I go to the Met's website, look at the next performance of *Manon,* which is Friday night, and I prowl for tickets. It's a pretty sweet ordering system. The tiers of the house are represented graphically. By scrolling over them, a pop-up box notes the price range of tickets, and if there are none remaining, it gives a "sold out" posting. When I select a section of the opera house, a full seating chart appears. Each seat is represented by a dot. A gray dot means "sold", a white dot circled in blue means "available". When I select a seat, the dot turns orange and all the other seats that are still available at the same price turn white with an orange circle around them. Additional information is available, and this is shown by white dots with a little black dot in the center of them. This information includes wheelchair accessibility, partial views of the stage, etc. I start at the top, the Family Circle, which has the lowest-priced seats. Of the entire section, there is exactly one seat left. It is $25, with a $5 handling fee and a $2.50 "facility fee".

Some of the other tiers are completely sold out. I look at every tier above the orchestra level and find there are only 16 seats left in all, with prices ranging from $25 to $475. The orchestra has quite a few more remaining seats. They are between $141 and $375. Thinking of my budget and the many operas still to come, I click on the Family Circle graphic. I select the only seat left, the farthest section and the last row in that section, Row K, seat 219. I pay my $27.50 with a debit card, and print out a record that will serve as my ticket at the door. I'm done.

The Met has not been in the news much lately. That's a bad thing. At the end of March, the Met sent out a press release that it would be broadcasting the complete *Ring* cycle into theaters around the world from May 9th to 19th. On May 7th, the Met will also present *Wagner's Dream*, a documentary by Susan Froemke, who also helmed *The Audition*. International screenings will continue into the late summer.

The *Times* notes, "This is said by the Met to be the first time a 'Ring' cycle has been presented on a big screen, though the production will be not be entirely unified, since the first two operas were recorded with James Levine conducting, the last two with Fabio Luisi."[5]

Two days earlier, the *Times* had published its review of *Manon*, starring Anna Netrebko. It was not a glowing notice. About her, Anthony Tommasini wrote, "The problem area of her singing these days is pitch. Her plush, throbbing sound has a focused vibrato, making even slight pitch deviations noticeable. Still, it is a small trade-off for such sumptuous singing." He ends the review by noting that the production comes from Covent Garden where it premiered in 2010, also with Netrebko. At the Met on opening night, "When the production team took bows in New York, the reaction was a mix of tepid applause, some isolated bravos and scattered boos. That seemed about right."[6]

On March 31, the Met sent out another press release hours after Juan Diego Flórez sang an encore during the Saturday matinee performance (and radio broadcast) of *L'elisir d'amore*. After the big tenor aria, "Una furtiva lagrima" (A stray tear), Flórez sang it again. The press release noted that the unusual occurrence took place most recently in 2008 (by Flórez, again) and before that, in 1994 by Luciano Pavarotti. To my eye, that's hardly big news.

An opera house mounting a complete *Ring* cycle is supposed to be an international event. I can imagine the Met's frustration that as it geared up for it, the local press is giving it a shrug. On

April 4, Tommasini wrote an extended article about Peter Gelb titled, "The Met, the 'Ring' and the Rage Against the Machine." He noted that Gelb invited him to the Met for an interview. In hindsight, that might not have been the best public relations strategy.

The critic launched into a replay of all the criticism the four productions received separately. He noted Gelb's acknowledgment about the set's "persistent clankiness." Tommasini took it further. He called it a "glitch-prone machine that probably needs this warm-up 'Rheingold' more than the cast and the orchestra." It's an awkward back and forth interview of criticisms followed by meek defenses. Still, it provides Gelb the opportunity to rebut Alex Ross's stinging evaluation of the *Ring*, in *The New Yorker*, from which the *Times* article reprints: "Pound for pound, ton for ton, it is the most witless and wasteful production in modern operatic history."[7] The Met attempts to use the interview to deflect the barbs by looking to a brighter future. Gelb spends the last portion of the interview dangling productions as far as four years away. Some of them will be directed by the Met's Ring-man, Robert Lepage.

On April 6, the Met launches a multimedia feature on its website around the *Ring* cycle. It enlists its critics and other staff writers to post essays and musings on the site. It includes video highlights, photographs (which look gorgeous to me), and links to additional information about Wagner doings. I was curious to see the reactions of readers because it could indicate a groundswell of excitement. It is a bomb. After two weeks, there have only been 42 comments by readers, and many of them have absolutely nothing to do with the Met's new *Ring*. In contrast, any given article about politics gets hundreds of reader postings within hours. The readers that do comment about the *Ring* talk about how much they like Wagner, how much they don't like Wagner, their nostalgia for great performances of the past, and more than anything mindless rants on strange tangents. A few are interesting to me. Barbara Mauer from Seattle writes that she's seen the *Ring* 21 times.

Many of the writers jump onto the anti-machine bandwagon. I have the impression that most of them have not seen the production live. Others talk about the experience of seeing the Met productions in movie theaters. By no means is this a booming message board. Each day there are two or three new posts from the public. That's about it. A few bloggers report things that the Met surely prefers they hadn't. Jimmy from Queens writes about the performance he saw on April 13 of *Die Walküre* and the computer software glitch that projected the Microsoft symbol across the set in Act III while Wotan and Brünnhilde stormed in front of it.

When the *Times* interview with Gelb appears, few of the bloggers come to his defense. As a resource, however, the multimedia feature is excellent. There are articles about history, other productions, and links to resources that could enhance the audience's understanding of the music. One helpful citation is a link to a catalog of leitmotifs that can be read in a score or listened to as audio samples. There is a *Ring* primer that uses sound recordings to preview the cycle of operas. There's no way for me to know if other readers are finding it worthwhile other than by posting their own comments.

The *Times* publishes a critic's thought piece on April 17 in the paper. The *Times* calls these "Critic's Notebook". This one is by freelance music critic, Zachary Woolfe. He writes about the Cirque du Soleil circus spectacle *Ka*, and he draws similarities between it and the Met's *Ring*. Both were directed by Lepage. He writes, "It is no surprise that Mr. Lepage's dazzling ultimately dull 'Ring' looks and feels so similar to the dazzling, ultimately dull production it followed and consciously echoed. But it remains a grave disappointment—even, given the official $16 million price tag of the Met's 'Ring,' a disgrace—that with Wagner's incalculably greater dramatic and musical material, Mr. Lepage just provided more of the same."[8]

I wish that people could get past the machine of this *Ring*. I've seen this kind of momentum play out before in productions in opera houses and on Broadway. When the press reports on stage problems—accidents, delays, turntables that get stuck, lighting cues that fail, performers who have troubles learning lines or just getting along—the story grows until it overwhelms and swamps everything else.

There's no turning back from the downward PR spiral. *Spider-Man,* the musical will always be about actors rushed to the hospital, and I suppose this *Ring* will always be about the temperamental machine that is its set. I'm sure the Met was very excited about the contraption in the beginning. And they hyped it in the press as the biggest, heaviest, most complex, etc. Now, they have to live with it. I wonder if it is possible for critics and audiences to react to the music of this *Ring*. I hope they can. I hope that I can.

I was quoted in the *Salt Lake Tribune* yesterday.[9] An article written by Sean Means discusses Mormon artists. I wasn't aware that the article came out. It's not a paper I subscribe to. But a friend on Facebook said to me that he liked my "thoughtful comments"; otherwise, I would have missed it altogether. Means approached me for an interview last week. In his email to me, Means cited Neil LaBute, Richard Dutcher and Elna Baker as examples of formerly-Mormon artists. He asked if I would make myself available for a telephone interview to discuss, as he phrased it, "The trend is that artists who are Mormon and explore Mormon themes in their art have a tendency to leave the church."

I receive queries like this from time to time. As the director of Mormon Artists Group, I guess some people see me as an expert of sorts. I wasn't exactly offended by the generalization Means was making, but it didn't ring true to me and my experience working with Mormon artists, either. I haven't met the three examples that Means wanted to use as source material, but I have mutual friends of each of them. I didn't want to be in a position to judge them or to rationalize their choices either, for that matter. I declined the interview, but I did write a paragraph for him to use or not, as he wished. Ultimately, the article turned out to be an interview with the filmmaker Dutcher on the occasion of a rerelease of his 1999 film, Falling. The article does quote a couple of my thoughts.

Here's what I wrote in an email to Means (italicized is the material printed in the article),

I have a database of more than a thousand fine artists who are LDS. They live all over the world. They're serious, well-trained, and to varying degrees, ambitious. The perception that LDS fine artists who explore their beliefs abandon them is no more true than a similar statement might be about LDS historians, carpenters, or salesmen.

It's been my experience that the danger in this clichéd generalization is the unnerving message it sends to young Mormons who are considering careers in the arts, and for that matter, their anxious parents. You can be righteous anywhere and you can be unrighteous anywhere. I wouldn't dream of judging people who distance themselves from participation in the Church. Nor should you, frankly.

In a post-Prop 8 world, there are realities for an LDS artist who needs to sell art to the public in order to pay the rent, so I won't take it upon myself to give a list of terrifically gifted LDS composers, painters, poets, filmmakers, authors, sculptors, etc. But they are out there in the most influential galleries, museums, concert halls, and libraries in the world. My point is that advocacy of LDS artists is more important than undermining them with tired provincialisms or limiting them with ideas of what they should or should not be creating.[10]

Tonight I'm off to see *Manon*. It strikes me that I don't know all that much about French opera. *Manon* is by Jules Massenet (1842-1912). Of his 25 operas—he wrote 34, but some have been lost or were left incomplete—I've seen just one, Werther. I am such a neophyte. It makes me feel slightly better about myself to say I've heard bits of *Hérodiade, Le Cid, Thaïs, Cendrillon,* and *Don Quichotte*, but don't ask me to hum anything from them. Massenet comes in and out of favor. I could say the same thing for all of French opera besides *Carmen* and *Faust.* There are fads in opera, just like anything else in popular culture, and periods go by when the Met has produced a lot of Massenet and then a decade can pass with nothing. In the last eight years, the Met has produced his three most popular works, *Werther, Manon,* and *Thaïs.* Relatively speaking, that's a lot for the Frenchman who was encouraged by Liszt, Tchaikovsky, Gounod and his mentor, Ambroise Thomas. Generally speaking, these operas get staged when a star is behind their production. They are sometimes seen as star vehicles. Without such wattage, the productions seem to go into cold storage.

I wouldn't say that French opera has ever been at the center of the Met's repertory, and it certainly isn't now. Although the Met has embraced other Baroque works recently, it has never staged early French operas by Lully; only two by Charpentier, but nothing since 1948; nothing by Rameau until a couple of arias were grafted into this season's *The Enchanted Island*; only three French operas by the Gluck; nothing by Adolphe Adam; nothing by Daniel Auber, since 1902.

For a while at the turn of the 20th century, the French-language works by the German Giacomo Meyerbeer enjoyed wide popularity—*Robert le diable, Le Prophète, Les Huguenots, L'Africaine,* as well as a few curiosities that played once or twice and then disappeared. Since 1933, the Met's offered only one Meyerbeer opera, *Le Prophète*, and nothing since 1979. Hector Berlioz has fared slightly better with *Les Troyens* and *La Damnation de Faust*, as well as a one-off for Berlioz's bicentennial celebration in 2003, *Benvenuto Cellini*.

The average opera fan, when asked to name a French opera, will first say *Carmen*, by Georges Bizet. (They might also say *La bohème*, but Puccini would probably turn over in his grave at the thought.) The Met has performed *Carmen* a few times. Well, 198 times, but it has never staged Bizet's other operas, including the exquisite *Les pêcheurs de perles*. The Met used to perform a sampling of Charles Gounod, but in the last few decades, it has restricted itself to productions of *Faust* and *Roméo et Juliette*. That sounds pretty good, but Gounod wrote thirteen operas.

Likewise, Offenbach's only modern production at the Met is *Les contes d'Hoffmann*. It's a long list of neglected French composers. Ambroise Thomas? Nothing since 1949; Camille Saint-Saëns' only Met opera is *Samson et Dalila* although he wrote a dozen other operas. Léo Delibes (who wrote 26 operas) hasn't had an opera at the Met since *Lakmé* in 1946. Édouard Lalo? Nothing since Le Roi d'Ys in 1922. Chabrier? Zéro. Chausson? None. Claude Debussy? *Pelléas et Mélisande*, thank goodness, but there are other Debussy works that could be produced too. Gabriel Fauré? Nope. Paul Dukas? Not since 1912.

The Met staged Ravel's one-act *L'heure Espagnole* once, in 1925, and it performed *L'enfant et les sortilèges* in 1981, 1982, 1985, and 2002. Darius Milhaud wrote 17 operas, some of them said to be overlooked masterpieces, none of them performed at the Met. Francis Poulenc has been better represented. Of his three operas, two of them have been seen at the Met: a one-act, *Les mamelles de Tirésias*, and the wondrous *Dialogues des Carmélites*, which has had 54 performances since its premiere in 1977.

That the Met still hasn't produced Oliver Messiaen's *Saint-François d'Assise* can only be described as a black eye to the Met's ambition as the world's leading opera house, since many people consider the opera one of the great works of the 20th century. Erik Satie? Only one opera, *Parade*. And there have been no contemporary French composers at the Met.

Just for the fun of it, I look up the schedule at the Opera

Bastille, the largest of the French opera companies, in Paris. During the 2011-12 season of 19 operas, they performed these French works: *Faust* (Gounod), *Hippolyte et Aricie* (Rameau), *Manon* (Massenet), *La Cerisaie* (Philippe Fénelon, based on Chekhov's *The Cherry Orchard*), and *Pelléas et Mélisande* (Debussy). It's logical to think, well of course they're doing French works at Opera Bastille, they're French. But I take another look at the Met's current season. How many American works are there? One. It was Philip Glass' *Satyagraha*, sung in Sanskrit. The only works in English are British: *Billy Budd* (Britten) and *The Enchanted Island*.

I get to my seat for *Manon* with my heart pumping a little extra—more from the exertion of climbing so many stairs than for excitement about the evening to come. I'm right up to the ceiling, and when I stand up in front of my seat, I can touch the gold leaf of the ceiling with my elbow. Looking straight ahead, I am above the proscenium arch. The ceiling, by the way, is in moderately bad shape. It looks like water damage from the way it's peeling and flaking in large swaths. It has been patched in places repeatedly, sometimes with gold colored paint instead of the gold leaf that adorns the rest of the Met's ceiling. The colors don't match. The eleven rows of the Family Circle are so steeply raked that the subtitles are not inset into the backs of the seats in front of me. The top of the seat hits me about shin height. Instead, there are railings that go across with each row of seats, roughly at knee height of the person who will use it. The subtitle screens, identical to those elsewhere in the house, are mounted on the velvet-covered railings.

When I open my program, out falls a slip of paper. It's a substitution notice. This is a bit unusual in the opera house. Generally, decisions about cancellations are more last minute. It says, "In this evening's performance of *Manon*, the role of Lescaut will be sung by Michael Todd Simpson, replacing Paolo Szot, who is ill." That's too bad. I like Szot. He became famous in New York when he played the role of Emile de Becque in the first Broadway revival of *South Pacific*, at the Lincoln Center Theater in 2008. He won a Tony award for best actor in the musical. It was a great performance, and I looked forward to seeing him again.

My section of the house, the Family Circle, is full of a curious cross-section of people. There are tourists—one tries to take a photograph, and an usher rushes up the aisle and sternly says, "No photos!"—and there are others who are clearly opera fans who attend the performances often, even though by their dress, they don't appear to be wealthy. I am seated by a group of young people who look like they are in college. Before the lights dim, they are chatting and texting simultaneously. Even though the Met's seating chart reported the section was sold out, I have empty seats on my immediate left and right.

Met opera playbills always contain excellent information. Whether they are trying to save on electricity, I can't say, but tonight the lighting level is so dim that I can't easily read the articles in the program about the opera's history, its composer, an analysis of the music, and the Met's history of its performance. I can almost read the synopsis of the opera, but not quite. *Manon* is five acts long. It is to begin at 7:30 and end at 11:25, with two intermissions. The production is new this year, and the premiere was given on March 26, 2012. The production is being shared with Covent Garden, La Scala, and Toulouse. They spread the costs between them. The title role will be sung tonight by Anna Netrebko, who also performed in the Covent Garden run in London last year.

Aside from plugging a hole in my opera-going ignorance, I'm here to see Ginger Costa-Jackson, the only one of the LDS singers that I've not seen yet this season. I have seen her in the past, and just last week, I watched her scenes in the iPad app's excerpt from *Manon* that was part of the 2008 season opening night. The earlier production has been retired and replaced by this one, by Laurent Pelly. Fabio Luisi will be the conductor. I know in advance, that Costa-Jackson's role, while important, isn't too large. I wonder what it is like for her to sing the same role in two different productions at the Met so close to together. If a singer's career lasts long enough, he or she will run into this situation inevitably. I wonder what it's like to have one set of costuming, blocking, choreography, and other directorial ideas in mind and then have to switch and adopt a new set of ideas. I think I'd find it confusing.

The curtain rises to reveal the set of *Manon,* featuring a large, barren courtyard at ground level and a large, stone stairway leading to a street and buildings above it. On stage left sits a large tavern. This is French opera: food matters. And sure enough, in the first scene the characters talk about pastries and other edible goodies with the same passion that a politician talks about his country's flag. Now that I think about it, if I were to make a checklist of French stereotypes—food, fashion, flirting, etc.—they're all on display here.

Ginger Costa-Jackson isn't French; she's Italian. To me she looks like a young Leslie Caron, but feistier. I missed the performance that put her on the map in New York, last summer's Glimmerglass Opera production of *Carmen*. Tommasini of the *Times* wrote, "The Carmen was Ginger Costa-Jackson, a ravishing mezzo-soprano from Italy, just 24, who easily conveyed the allure and willful recklessness of Bizet's Gypsy temptress. Her voice has dark, rich colorings and considerable body."[11] In *Manon*, Costa-Jackson is a coquette supreme. She giggles and teases, unleashes beautiful music and then dashes away from suitors and their extended arms.

The opera is the tale of Manon, a teenager on her way to the convent who impulsively falls in love with the Chevalier des Grieux. (So much for life as a nun.) The trick of performing this role is the scope of its character. She begins as a know-nothing child and ends up a life-battered adult. In the evening, we witness a lot of transformation, mostly a sad devolution. In the beginning, Anna Netrebko plays Manon as an energetic teenager. Netrebko skips, spins, and dances her way through Act I. She stops whirling just long enough to sing a spectacularly marvelous aria. And by that, I mean she sings the aria marvelously. She is a wonder. That's no surprise, but who is the tenor? Piotr Beczala. I'm unfamiliar with him, but I'm loving his voice. It reminds me of the young José Carreras so much that it almost feels like a reincarnation—a youthful, ardent tone but with a tinge of heartbreak in it. Never straining, his top notes spill out like passionate bloodletting. This could be a good night.

In Act II, des Grieux writes a letter to his father and asks to marry Manon. His aria is thrilling. His father arrives with a nobleman, de Brétigny. The latter tells Manon that des Grieux's father plans to kidnap his own son. He offers her wealth and a life of luxury if she will leave her lover for him. Manon, who has always wanted to live such a life, can't resist the temptation. She sings, "Adieu, notre petite table" ("Farewell to our little table"). As Netrebko performs it, I can't help but think it is one of the most beautiful few minutes of music I've heard in a long time. Des Grieux comes back and gives his own version of the future, the "Dream Song." Again, gorgeous music, perfectly sung. There is a knock at the door, and although she begs him not to answer it, des Grieux exits and is abducted. I've not seen this opera before. I didn't know what I was missing.

At intermission, I wander around and check out the nooks and crannies of the opera house. On the south side, there are a series of private banquet rooms that are restricted to members of the various opera entities. They are private bars, essentially.

Richly appointment and comfortable—in that turn of the century way—they are a nice perk for donations. On the Grand Tier level is the restaurant that is open to the public. Intermissions are relatively short. There's not enough time to be seated, order food, wait for it to arrive, and eat it. Instead, diners go to the restaurant before the opera and pre-order their food for later. When intermission arrives, they are seated at tables under the Chagall mural on the north side of the house and also along windows overlooking the reflecting pool facing north. Their food is ready and waiting for them. This is civilization!

I see something in the lobby that I've never encountered before at the Met, a woman with a seeing-eye dog. She is chatting with a house usher during intermission. I have no idea where she's sitting for the performance, and for that matter, where the dog's sitting. It's a handsome Labrador Retriever. I wonder if the dog goes inside to watch the opera. The Met and *Manon* have a rocky history with dogs singing. There was an infamous Renée Fleming mishap on September 26, 1997. During the festival scene of *Manon*, a Russian wolfhound named Pasha started to howl during Fleming's aria. The audience, of course, roared with laughter. Fleming was less amused. The *Times* chronicled the story, "After the first part of the aria, the handler who was on stage holding the dog for a tableau walked the dog off,' Ms. Fleming said. 'I told the director, 'It's the dog or me.'"[12] She ended up writing a retraction letter saying that her comment was tongue in cheek and that she was a longtime dog lover. Two puppeteers

Manon

who were onstage during the incident, Marshal Izen and Jim West, used the experience as the basis for a children's book about the episode titled, *The Dog Who Sang at the Opera* (Harry N. Abrams, 2004). There are no dogs onstage in this production.

Act III of *Manon* works toward a reconnection of Manon and des Grieux. He has suffered an unhappy romance and is about to become a priest. Manon learns of this and can't believe that he has forgotten her. She lurks in the shadows of Saint-Sulpice while des Grieux's father tries unsuccessfully to talk him out of the priesthood. The would-be priest thinks back to his life with Manon in the tenor touchstone aria, "Ah ! Fuyez, douce image." ("Flee, soft image") Vocally, it is another knockout. Massenet has set the vocal line as an echo of the organ music in the church. Very nice touch.

When she appears, des Grieux is angry at first, but he is softened by her reminiscences of their past. This is incongruous, because Manon is clearly in love with money and glamour more than anything else. I don't she how she imagines that des Grieux is going to be able to satisfy her. But that is the point of the tragedy. She convinces des Grieux to renounce his vows and fly away with him. Netrebko is having some vocal troubles. The soft singing is beautiful, but when she pushes her voice at all, her pitch wavers. The high notes are sometimes ragged.

For an opera as long as this one is, it is passing by quickly. After three hours, I'm gearing up for the story to get tragic, but during the last intermission, quite a few people sitting around me have left. It's possible that they moved someplace else—and better—but I suspect that they've simply had enough opera for one night. It's billed as an opéra comique, and Massenet keeps it somewhat light with the regular appearance of the three silly girls and their skirt-chasing, sugar daddies. That's fine for me because I want to hear more of Ginger Costa-Jackson. But the cards are stacked against the young lovers. Their money is running out, and Manon is no longer accustomed to living an impoverished existence. A plan is hatched to wager their remaining money. Manon and des Grieux are successful with a windfall of gambling profit, but they are accused of cheating and imprisoned.

The opera is based on a novel, *L'Histoire du chavalier des Griuex et de Manon Lescaut*. It was a morality tale that was very influential in its day. Published in 1731, it was controversial and banned in France—which made it intensely popular. The novel *is referenced throughout literature in works such as The Picture of Dorian Gray, Venus in Fur, Invitation to the Dance, The Lady of the Camellias, The Red and the Black, V., Finnegans Wake,* and so forth. This short novel was a story that anybody in Europe recognized during the 19th century.

Massenet's version ends with the broken Manon dying in des Grieux's arms, sentenced to deportation to America. In the Puccini version, *Manon Lescaut*, Manon is shipped off to New Orleans, and des Grieux sneaks onboard with her. In Puccini's Louisiana desert (yes, desert), Manon tells des Grieux that without water she cannot take another step. He goes to hunt for water while she laments her bad life choices. He returns unsuccessful in his search. They say farewell to each other, and she dies. He is overcome by grief and collapses on top of her.

To be honest, I haven't much cared for the sets of this production. I don't get it. I liked the church, but everything else hasn't made much sense to me. It all feels barren. I suppose that's where everything is heading morally, but it is an odd backdrop for such sumptuous costumes and a tale about excess. In the Massenet version, we are spared the trip to New Orleans.

The final act is played out on a road near the port of Le Havre with prisoners and guards. A plan to rescue Manon stalls. Alone together, she asks forgiveness for the shame she has brought upon des Grieux. He tells her that he forgives and loves her. And she dies.

I come away from the performance wanting to hear the opera again, right away. As we say in New York, "Who knew?" But, of course, this opera is no secret. It was just a secret to me. I feel the same way about Ginger Costa-Jackson. We haven't met yet, but I'm eager to hear more of her singing. Tonight's role was a tease of what is coming for her. Opera singers need personality to make the jump from supporting roles to leading roles, and I sense that she has something special that will take her far.

CHAPTER 10

I AM READY TO TACKLE THE REST OF THE *RING*. Tonight is *Das Rheingold*. The place is packed. Even at the elevated prices—my ticket has a fixed price and a "contribution" of 76% more tacked onto it—it looks like the Met could have hiked them even higher, and this for a Thursday night performance. The top price of the remaining tickets is $875. Even the cheap seats aren't cheap tonight. At the beginning of April, the Met began its first complete *Ring* cycle since May 2009. The Lepage *Ring* has been rolled out slowly, beginning with *Das Rheingold*, September 27, 2010, *Die Walküre* in April 22, 2011, *Siegfried* October 27, 2011, and *Götterdämmerung* this year, January 27, 2012. Odd that three of the four were premiered on the 27th day of the month. Maybe there's some Wagnerian superstition I don't know about. There's a lot about Wagner I don't know.

Not counting the roll-out of the *Ring* operas over two seasons, the Met will perform three complete cycles of the tetralogy before the 2011-2012 season is over and more next season when Wagner's bicentennial is celebrated. The first complete new Ring appeared over four weeks, ending April 24. Now the schedule compresses. The operas in the second and third cycles are performed almost back to back. The first three operas have one day separating them; the *Götterdämmerung*s comes two days after the *Siegfried*s.

Das Rheingold

I'm here for *Das Rheingold*. I have tricked myself into thinking that because it's only two and a half hours long, that it will be a breeze. I've forgotten to look at the fine print. There's no intermission. Historically, some productions of *Das Rheingold* take breaks between some of the scenes, presumably to change the set. One advantage—I question using that word—of the machine is that the transitions from scene to scene can happen almost instantly. I look at the estimated times in the program and calm myself down by remembering that I see movies that are that long, and I don't complain. Somehow popcorn increases stamina. Mental note: Take a letter. Dear Mr. Gelb....

There's a replacement tonight in the otherwise terrific cast. The role of Loge will be sung by Adam Klein. That's a name I wish Wagner were alive to see. Aside from singers who were also in the *Götterdämmerung* I saw in January—Erin Morley, Jennifer Johnson-Cano and Tamara Mumford as Rhinemaidens and Wendy Bryn Harmer who is singing the role of Freia tonight, the cast has Bryn Terfel as Wotan, Stephanie Blythe as Fricka, and Eric Owens as Alberich. Powerhouses all. Fabio Luisi is in the pit.

The lights go down, and the machine rotates into place, from a flat, horizontal plane to a steep ledge that the Rhinemaidens will climb. And here they are. The first words of the cycle are sung by Woglinde, Erin Morley. The maidens are in harnesses and they scale the ledge and "swim" around, teasing and taunting Alberich. In this production, they are presented as mermaids.

Alberich fools the maidens and steals their gold, which has the power to control the world if it is forged into a ring. There's a catch. In order for the magic to work, the owner of the ring must forebear love. Feeling spurned by the maidens, Alberich renounces love and grabs the gold.

The New York press has been making a fuss about the creakiness of the machine. (In all fairness, it couldn't possibly be as loud as the ballet dancers' toe shoes in *Manon* crashing against the wooden ramps without pause like herds of livestock walking up a stockyard gangplank.) This is not empty criticism. As the planks revolve, they make relatively loud grinding and shifting sounds. Come on, Met! Anybody have a Valhalla-sized can of WD-40? It's pretty distracting because quite a bit of the movement occurs between scenes, and this is also when the orchestra is playing interludes. Especially in the beginning of *Rheingold*, the music is tranquil. This makes matters worse. I'll be curious to see, eventually, an HD broadcast of these productions. Will the Met tweak the sound levels and mask the creaks? The audience appears to be devoted, regardless. Maybe they are more oblivious to the noise than I am. As the performance gets going, I notice that quite a few people have turned off their subtitle screens. The man in front of me is following along in German.

In the second scene (of four), Wotan, lord of the Gods, is on a mountaintop. He is played by Bryn Terfel, the Welsh baritone superstar. I've been waiting for this a long time. I was at Terfel's recital debut in New York, and I've followed his career rather closely. From the beginning, 20 years ago, people predicted he would be a terrific Wotan someday. In his first moments tonight, he sounds a bit uncomfortable, like he is pushing his voice in the lower register. But when he launches into a burst of high power, it is a thrilling sound. Wow, oh wow! He is matched superlative for superlative by the American singer Stephanie Blythe. She is playing Fricka, the wife of Wotan. The plot, stripped down to the essentials, is that giants have built for Wotan a magnificent castle. In payment, they demand Fricka's sister Freia (Wendy Bryn Harmer's role). Wotan tries to weasel out of the bargain and, upon hearing from a demi-god named Loge of Alberich's treasures, he hurries down into the middle earth with Loge while Freia is taken hostage.

The descent is pretty cool. The planks of the set become vertical, like a wall, and Wotan and Loge walk across them. This shifts the audience perspective to an aerial view. Their bodies are parallel to the stage floor. It looks like they are walking down steps. I assume that body doubles are harnessed from the rafters. Chalk up one for Cirque du Soleil.

The underground factory of the Nibelung dwarfs is all fire and smoke. Slaves mine and forge Alberich's gold. He has forced his brother Mime to make him a magic helmet named Tarnhelm (although in this production, it's a piece of fabric that the characters drape over their heads, like an oversized handkerchief) to transform into other shapes. Wotan and the wily Loge trick Alberich, who metamorphoses into a dragon and then into a toad, which Wotan traps and hauls back home. It's a lot of plot. But there are expanses of beautiful singing too. Loge is a wonderful role, and this singer is completely nailing it. And I've been reading in the papers about Eric Owens. Critics are calling his Alberich one for the ages. I don't disagree.

So far, the machine has been underwhelming. The projections onto it are mostly gray and bland. There was a clever effect of bubbles coming out of the Rhinemaidens mouths in the first scene, and I understand from articles I've read in the papers that there is an element of high tech sensors built into the set. They can react to the motion of the performers. Stones shift beneath Alberich's feet as he climbs up to the maidens. More interaction is happening, but if I hadn't seen *Götterdämmerung*, I would be wondering what all the fuss is about. In the scenes on the mountaintop, when the giants arrive, the planks shift into a position that can only be described as a gigantic lawn chair.

Wotan brings Alberich back to the top of the world. The Nibelungs are summoned to bring all his gold. Wotan lets Alberich keep Tarnhelm, but in a flurry of greed, he steals the ring. Moments later, the giants extract all of the gold, including the ring from Wotan, but not before Alberich curses the owner of the ring, and Erda, goddess of the earth, warns that possession of the ring will signal the destruction of the gods. The first victim of the curse is one of the giants. He is killed by his brother in a lust for gold.

Marvelous singing all around, as I expected. It's a high-wire act, even without the circus harnesses. The singers are required to stand on stage for long periods of time, looking appropriately intense, and then cry out impossibly loud, incredibly high notes, all over the din of an enormous orchestra. I can see rows and rows of horn players from my seat. They are wedged into the orchestra pit. There are six harps. Each of the singers responds magnificently to these demands. Except for a couple of extended scenes for Alberich and Loge singing, most of the characters cry out in short blasts and then take a breather.

Donner, one of Freia's brothers, dispels the horror of the giant's murder with a display of lightning and swirling weather. At last, the set comes alive. The planks tilt at a steeply raked angle. Donner brings down a crash of thunder (the lady next to me jumps, startled). With his staff, the clouds shift beneath his feet. The light projection is quite sophisticated. As Donner moves all about the surface, the clouds part below him. Very nice. And then the rainbow bridge appears that leads to Wotan's castle that he has named Valhalla. I love this effect.

Across a scrim behind the set, a color spectrum that is constantly shifting radiates. Perpendicularly to it, projected on the center planks of the machine, a band of morphing, colored lines that seem to be alive, forms a bridge. When the gods are ready to enter, the bridge tilts down and they scale the bridge (in harnesses) and then when it is nearly horizontal, they walk into Valhalla. Below them stands Loge who watches the gods and mocks their pride and foolishness. Valhalla will prove to be a real estate bubble, mark my words. And that is *Das Rheingold.*

Next up is *Die Walküre*. For today's Saturday matinee performance, I am standing at the top of the house. Yes, standing. As
it turns out, waiting until the last minute to get a ticket to a complete *Ring* cycle is a foolish strategy. I had hoped to get a $20 or-
chestra seat, as I had throughout the season. Silly man. The Met's
Ring aims to be a big money-maker, and they're not about to give
away seats. The day-of-performance lottery has been suspended.
I also try the Monday morning lottery system—at 10:00, you put
your name on a list for weekend performances, again subsidized.
But this near-freebie has been suspended too. I can't blame them.
They've spent so much on this thing; surely they feel compelled
to make it back as quickly as possible. Birgit Nillson, the great
Brünnhilde of yore, said the key to singing Wagner was comfortable shoes. I figure it can't hurt for watching Wagner either, especially if you've got a standing room ticket. I show up in
sneakers.

The woman sitting in front of me opens her program and goes
ballistic—I mean, a foot-stamping, fist-shaking tantrum. She is
holding a little slip of paper inserted into her program. I hadn't
noticed it, "In today's performance of *Die Walküre*, the role of
Siegmund will be sung by Frank van Aken, replacing Jonas Kaufmann, who is ill."

That is lousy news. Kaufmann is the young, handsome, German tenor of the moment. He seems to be everywhere. The Met
gave him a rare, solo recital in October and the lead in a new production of Faust in November. He is one of a few artists around

whom the Met appears to be building its future. It's been a meteoric rise to fame for him. During this season, he has been all over the world—which is the same story for many of the Met's stars—but look at his range of recent roles: Lohengrin and Florestan in Munich, Werther in Vienna and Paris, Cavaradossi in London, Vienna, Milan, Berlin and Zurich, Don José in London, Don Carlo in London and Zurich, des Grieux in Chicago and Vienna, Alfredo in Paris, and recitals in Paris, Vienna, Munich, London, Berlin, Baden-Baden, Athens, Brussels, Hamburg, and Essen. His cancellation is a big disappointment. This is bad.

The house is packed, and I assume that every one of them is fuming. Saturday matinees are a big deal to the Met. The 80 continuous years of radio broadcasts on Saturday afternoons has staked the claim that Saturdays—granted, for a certain segment of the American population—is for listening to opera from the Metropolitan. Unlike other performing arts in New York that think of Saturday matinees as something of a throwaway, as a placeholder between the big-ticket, glamorous performances of Friday and Saturday evenings, the Met programs these matinees carefully and casts them luxuriously. It's their brand. A lot rides on these matinees because they are heard worldwide. When Peter Gelb walks out onto the stage with a microphone before the performance begins, I worry that there are more cancellations to come. But maybe this is good news for me. Nina Warren is the Brünnhilde understudy. Maybe....

Gelb tells the story of Kaufmann's withdrawal from the performance. Yesterday, the tenor was stricken with a virus. On such short notice, the Met searched for a replacement. (I can't imagine that it didn't have one already, so I assume Gelb means a "suitable" replacement for the radio broadcast.) As it turns out, the Sieglinde at today's performance, Eva-Maria Westbroek, is married to a Wagnerian tenor who has sung the role before. He was planning to be in the audience cheering his wife on, Gelb says, but instead will be making his Metropolitan debut as his real-life wife's brother/husband, Siegmund. (How incest-intrigued Wagner would be loving this!) Gelb asks the audience's encouragement for Aken. His final words are that he hopes the machine will be kind to him.

The opening of *Die Walküre* is terrific theater. The scene is a snowstorm, and the music echoes the ending of *Das Rheingold*. It is taut, wiry, and exciting, the operatic equivalent of the *Mission: Impossible* theme song. The panels of the machine move, first to create a flat plane onto which images of swirling snow are projected, and then the panels separate and become vertical. They tilt at slight angles to resemble trees of a forest. Onto each pillar, an image is projected that shapes the planks to appear like separate trees. Men with glowing lanterns weave through the trees on their search for something or someone. I'm loving this. To my mind, this is the most exciting moment of the *Ring* so far. Lepage is smart for staging these orchestral preludes. In the score for *Die Walküre*, Wagner doesn't have any stage directions during the storm. His notes appear when Siegmund, the object of the hunt, arrives at Sieglinde's hut. She is Hunding's wife.

The plot of *Die Walküre* is simple. Siegmund and Sieglinde meet. They fall in love. Sieglinde's husband Hunding and Siegmund are enemies, and the gods get involved with their fight. Wotan wants to help Siegmund and Sieglinde (both mortals are his children), and he asks his Valkyrie daughter Brünnhilde to defend Siegmund. But Wotan's wife Fricka forbids it because she is the goddess of marriage and can't tolerate infidelity. Wotan is trapped because he must enforce the law even though he knows he will lose the ring forever if he does. Siegmund and Sieglinde run away together, realize that they are in love, and that they are also brother and sister.

In the battle, Brünnhilde defies Wotan, but he appears, allows Siegmund to be killed by shattering his sword, and then kills Hunding with the wave of his hand. Brünnhilde takes Sieglinde and runs from Wotan. As Wotan nears, Brünnhilde sends Sieglinde, who is pregnant, into hiding. Wotan punishes Brünnhilde by causing her to sleep in a circle of fire on a mountaintop until a brave hero can awaken her. Wotan kisses her eyes with sleep and realizes that the gods are likely doomed.

The audience today is really pulling for the last-minute Siegmund. You can feel the goodwill. And he sounds great, if occasionally hesitant. Several of the performers have iffy moments. Wotan's spear falls to the floor with a crash and rolls downstage, threatening to impale the orchestra. Siegmund makes some tentative entrances vocally. On the plus side, there are marvelous musical touches throughout the work. When Siegmund takes a drink from Sieglinde, for example, he stares at her, and the orchestra goes silent except for a single cello that plays a beautiful theme of love. Wagner's intentions are to let the audience experience what the characters are thinking and feeling by listening to the orchestra. It becomes an emotive proxy for them.

My feeling about *Das Rheingold* was that it is an extended setup of exposition. There are few moments when a character sings at length. It's almost a chatty opera. This opera, in contrast, is full of long, arching lines of melody. It is all about love. Doomed love, impetuous love, love for fathers and daughters, brothers and sisters, love of the law and duty. Wagner wrote the libretto (he called it a poem). He finished the text in 1852. But the music came somewhat slowly. *Die Walküre* was composed by 1854, and then he took another year to orchestrate it. He had written an 11-page paper, "The Nibelung Myth: as Sketch for a Drama," earlier, in 1848.

It would be 30 years more before the complete cycle would be performed. *Die Walküre* was the first of the *Ring* cycle to be performed at the Met, in 1885, during the second season of the fledgling company. By 1889, the complete *Ring* was heard in New York. The program notes a fact that I find startling: "The complete cycle was presented eight times in the spring of 1889, including tour performances in Philadelphia, Boston, Milwaukee, Chicago, and St. Louis. The uncut cycles conducted by Franz Schalk in 1898-1899 began a sequence of 19 consecutive seasons with Ring cycles."

In the first act, my favorite singing comes from Siegmund's two arias about his sad background and about spring. Each of these in the score runs for pages and pages. In the second scene, Sieglinde says that she'd like to know who he is. Siegmund responds with an aria 108 lines long. In the orchestral score, it's 17 pages of mostly-uninterrupted singing. The last lines, in English, are "Woman, you asked; now you know why I am not called 'Peaceful.'" That's a lot of singing, and almost all of it intense, loud and high. Frank van Aken gets through all of this with heroic strength. As he sings about the sword that his father promised he would find one day (it is waiting for him to pull out from a tree later), I feel so happy for this singer. A hero indeed. Siegmund's love for Sieglinde is blooming, and in an extended aria, the two lovers sing about spring. This, being Wagner, is long and, however self-indulgent, beautiful.

The two characters circle around the fact that they are soon-to-be incestuous siblings. Siegfried pulls the sword from the tree (Freud would smile at that), and announces his love for Sieglinde, "Braut und Schwester bist du dem Bruder - so blühe denn, Wälsungen-Blut!." (Wife and sister you'll be to your brother. So let the Volsung blood increase.)

When the husband and wife team appear in front of the curtain at the end of the act for applause, the house erupts in cheers. Imagine stepping in to a role like this. I'll confess that a little tear trickles down my cheek for them. What a perfect moment.

Frank van Aken grasps his wife's hand and brings it to his lips. He puts his arm around her and brings her close. They walk off-stage together triumphantly.

I walk downstairs onto one of the tiers above the lobby. It smells like a delicatessen. I don't know if it's just because I'm up in the Balcony and Family Circle, but these folks are brown baggers. Everyone looks to be eating leftovers, from Tupperware containers, sandwiches wrapped in wax paper, veggies pulled from pockets in Ziplock bags. There's coffee too, naturally, in Wagner-sized cups, of course. The opera started at 11:00, so it's lunchtime. It's a celebratory bunch. There's a guy wearing those short German pants. What are they called? Lieder-hosen. No, lederhosen. And, believe it or not, several people are wearing plastic Wagner helmets, with horns sticking out. The horns light up, red on one side, blue on the other. Of course they do. I walk down another few levels to the magnificent bar with the Chagall mural above it. Not that anybody is looking at art right now; we need food. I get a sandwich, and it's pretty good. Others are having champagne, and lots of it.

I walk outside onto the terrace. Tables have been set up, and people are having a great time. A section of the terrace is designated as a smoking section, but no one has bothered to alert the wind about the imaginary partition. I go back inside. All too soon, intermission is over. I make the return climb to my standing room spot. It's pointless to scope out empty seats with the hope of swooping in and inhabiting them when the lights go down.

These are hardy people. A five-hour opera performance is nothing. They would probably stay for the entire *Ring* in one orgiastic day if it were offered to them.

Before the lights go back down, I hear a lot of orchestra musicians practicing. It's not unheard of, but the amount of playing now is unusual. Particularly the horns are going through music soon to come, Brünnhilde's famous "Ho-jo-to-ho!" What a spectacular brass section the Met has! And they're certainly being put through their paces with this score. There is nothing like the telltale sound of a horn mistake, that awkward bleating, like a voice cracking. Happily, there's none of that today.

Right out of the gate in Act II, Wotan and Brünnhilde arrive. For a bass-baritone, Wagner certainly pushes the upper reaches of the singer portraying Wotan. It vocal line just hangs out there, high, fortissimo, with plenty of high Es. Bryn Terfel dispatches all of the challenges as if he were wantonly swatting away flies. His high notes, not only the single notes, but the complete phrases that are high, sound like a young man is singing them. They are free of the worn-out sound that I associate with Wagner bigwigs. He is as good as I'm ever likely to hear in this role.

Brünnhilde, who was not in *Das Rheingold*, lets fly with the most famous music from all of the Ring, "Ho-jo-to-ho!" (English translation: "Hojotoho!") These are the first words out of her mouth. Wagner is specific in the score regarding what he wants. The playbill describes it concisely, "The first two syllables ("Ho-jo") are a single phrase, followed by a sixteenth note ("to"), then the last syllable ("ho") to be held for five beats, followed by a single beat rest...Wagner asks the soprano to sing the final "ho" on two notes, separated by an octave leap but connected smoothly, ending on high Bs and then high Cs. He also asks her to trill—nonstop—for almost two measures before launching up to a high B and holding it for two measures."

Katarina Dalayman is today's Brünnhilde. She has a sizable following of fans. I consider her first "Ho-jo-to-ho!" to be a disaster. The high notes are shrieks, the octave scoops are bizarre sonic explosions, the trill is nonexistent (sorry; a wobbly vibrato is not a trill), and when she gets to the last note, a high B natural, she cuts it off sharply and prematurely, after only a couple of beats. Yikes. Either she hasn't warmed up, or this is going to be one long afternoon for her.

This puts me in a critical mood. Funny how that works, a logjam of being particular. I'm finding that these productions by Lepage have a crucial problem. It isn't the machine. Actually, I think the hulking thing is at a scale that matches Wagnerian ambition. It's flexible, and although there are creaks here and there, it certainly makes scene changes exciting and fluid. There's no need to bring down the curtain, drag in a new set, and begin again. I respond to that. If anything, it is sheepish in that the projections on it are a bit static. Every once in a while, the images are interactive, meaning that a character will step on it, and the imagery will react, but for the most part, it's a backdrop.

For me, a bigger dramatic problem is the dead space between

the machine's rotating panels and lip of the stage on the floor. Directly over the orchestra pit are a series of panels that are somewhat steeply raked. Action happens here from time to time. It's a big space, from side to side and also in depth. Maybe it's 15 feet or so deep. Then, when set pieces appear, they are situated onto a hydraulic lift between this front space and the machine. It's not terribly deep. Enough for a table, a chair, a fireplace. It is on a different level from the lip of the stage, and it presents something of a barrier for dramatic action. Singers trip on it as they pass from space to space. It's like a boring, black hole. I'm reminded of World War I trenches. There is a claustrophobic element to them, and in this opera, a lot of exposition happens in this trench. To my mind it's a design mistake.

In Act II, Wotan and Fricka fight. This is a glorious sonic battle of equals. Stephanie Blythe and Bryn Terfel: a cage match of the ages! Fricka wins (again), and the seeds are sown of the god's eventual destruction. Afterwards, Brünnhilde is swayed by Siegmund to defy Wotan. Vocally, Dalayman is warmed up now. Whew! But unfortunately, van Aken's voice is giving out. His character is going to die soon, and I hope his voice lasts long enough to avoid the demise being literal. I have heard singers with isolated patches of trouble before, but this is worse. It sounds like he's simply pushed it too far, too fast. He's run out of gas. There are cracks in his notes, and not particularly high ones either, and the gravely roughness lasts for entire phrases at a time. Still, this has been an incredible day for this singer. Meanwhile, Terfel's voice seems to be gaining even more power, if that's possible. By the time he lifts his arm and kills Hunding with a wave of his hand, I am convinced that if he wanted to, Terfel could blast a note at him and knock him dead.

As the black curtain falls to end the act, I don't wait for applause. I race down the stairs, and then down five flights more of winding stairs to get to the List Hall auditorium below ground level. It is time for the Opera Quiz, and I am determined to get in. We New Yorkers, although we don't drive our own cars much, know how to maneuver through traffic. I zip past human roadblocks on the staircases and maneuver like a studio stunt car driver through the lines that are forming to get into restrooms and to water fountains. Just as I arrive at List Hall, the usher on one side starts to close the door. She yells to the other side's usher that she's full. I'm not panicking yet, but I am determined. What would Wotan do? I stop short of tripping the old lady in front of me, but I do lean in, like a sprinter at the finish line's tape, and my shoulders get through the doors as the usher closes them behind me. Not that there are any empty seats, but at this point, what's the problem with standing for another half hour? Happily, an usher waves me over to her side, and I find a place on the aisle.

List Hall is the place where latecomers to the opera are exiled until the next intermission. Woe be to the ticketholder who arrives after the curtain has gone up. You're not getting in; they don't care who you are or where you're sitting. *Off to List Hall for you, buddy.* The space is not as big as I thought. There are only 144 seats facing a small stage. Today, I see a large banner proclaiming this to be the 80th year of radio broadcasts. Toll Brothers, the home building conglomerate, is the current bene-factor. For many years, it was Texaco. How many times have I listened to the opera quizzes at intermission on the Saturday broadcasts? Hundreds? But I've never been in this hall before. In front of me, there is a concert-sized piano on stage right, against the wall, and a very large accompanist ready to play it.

Three panelists are sitting on one leg of a v-shaped line. On stage left, each of them sits at a small table with their names dis-played in front of them: Rob Levine, Susan Ashbaker, and Robert Marx. Across from the panelists on the other side are two tables with the host, Ken Benson sitting behind one, and the tenor Jay Hunter Morris (the Met's Siegfried), at the other. A man talks to us, and he gives us the ground rules for the radio broadcast: when to applaud, when not to talk, when to call out answers to the quiz, when to leave, etc. The program is already underway for radio listeners. The Siegmund and Sieglinde are being inter-viewed backstage, upstairs, and their comments are piped into List Hall.

This is a day that Westbroek and van Aken (both of them are Dutch) will never forget. They describe to their interviewer the events of the last 24 hours. They were sitting down to dinner last night when van Aken received the phone call to substitute for

Kaufmann in *Die Walküre*. It was like a thunderbolt. Although he had sung the role before, it had been a couple of years since van Aken performed it. He told the Met, no. It was too crazy a thing to ask. The tenor had never sung at the Met before, and van Aken had never even been in the United States before. He didn't say how the Met twisted his arm—this is an agent's dream come true to have leverage like that—but van Aken agreed. The tenor says he didn't sleep a wink all night. The advice his wife gave to him was to "keep breathing". That sounds like smart counsel to me.

The two of them have sung together before, in Frankfurt, and they are scheduled to sing *Tristan und Isolde* in Dresden. They met in high school. The people all around me are sighing and cooing as if they are looking at photographs of beagle puppies at play. Admmittedly, it is a pretty great story. The interviewer asks them what they're going to do now. Westbroek responds with a laugh that she still has some singing to do in Act III, and that her thoughts are on the big farewell lines that she gets to sing. Van Aken is going to watch the rest of the opera with the General Manager. The two of them are planning to celebrate by going out to dinner with some people from the Met.

Now it's time for the opera quiz, and I dutifully applaud when I'm given the signal. There used to be lots of shows like this on the radio. I grew up in the television age, but living in a rural part of the country, I listened to the radio a lot as I traveled around in a car. The opera quiz on Saturday afternoons is the only live quiz show still on the radio today, at least that's what they tell me in List Hall. Over the years, as I listened to the broadcasts, I doubted whether it was actually happening live or if parts of it were prerecorded. It is live.

After a brief bit of calendaring—the Met season ends with *The Makropulos Case* and *Billy Budd*—the host asks the panel a question. He mentions that the *Makropulos* librettist was a pioneer of science fiction. He asks us to imagine being lost in the woods and listening to a scary opera. (Why would I want to do that?) But the question is to name an opera that one could talk about over a campfire in the woods. Susan Ashbaker lists the Peter Maxwell Davies ghost story opera, *The Lighthouse* (1980). She tries to make a case for it as an underappreciated work. The rest of the panelists and the moderator shrug. They haven't heard it. Bob Levine's choice is *Così fan tutte*. I can't figure out how that Mozart work is scary, but Levine says it gets people arguing, and that would be good for a campfire. He doesn't look like the kind of guy who's even been camping, but maybe I'm wrong. The last panelist, Robert Marx, chooses *Lulu*. Now that's more like it—murder, sex, intrigue. It's even got Jack the Ripper, the moderator quickly adds.

The next question is with the piano. It is sent in from a listener who is also a pet-lover. Although the moderator doesn't say exactly how many dozens of cats she owns.... The accompanist plays quotations from operas, each one a scene with music representing a horse. The panelists are to buzz in with the correct answer. Well, they don't have buzzers, but they raise their hands like grade schoolers. The first excerpt is from *La fanciulla del West* (Susan gets it right). Second is *Der Rosenkavalier* (Rob). Next is *Carmen* (Susan, again). Poor Bob looks frustrated that he hasn't been able to get any answers yet. He lifts his hands up to his temples. After the fourth excerpt, the panelists are stumped. The moderator tries to give them hints, but short of spelling it out, the panelists aren't going to get this one. The audience is asked if we know it. A wisenheimer yells out, "*Lohengrin.*" Correct. The last excerpt of this horse-play is *Les Troyens*. But it takes a while and plenty of big hints to get to it—"it's a big horse but it doesn't walk, it rolls." Finally Bob cries out the right answer proudly, as if he were winning the Nobel prize for Opera Trivia.

The main feature of the quiz is an interview with Jay Hunter Morris, who is making a big splash in the *Ring* cycle as Siegfried. He's a tall, lanky man. He looks like a cowboy. And when he opens his mouth to speak, his Texas drawl confirms it. Benson asks him what his schedule is like when he's singing a big role like this. How does he do it? What does he do between performances?

He says that he feels fine when the curtain goes up, but then he looks out into the abyss. At that point he goes into a cocoon. He says that when he is getting ready for a role, even between performances, he studies as much as he can, as long as he can. As he puts it, "As long as I can stay awake." I like this guy. There's something about the twang, of course, that feels funny coming from a heldentenor, but he comes across as such a normal guy. A really hard-working average Joe...who happens to have lungs of steel. He *is* Siegfried.

The quiz goes to another round of trivia, this time with Morris asking the questions about parents in opera. He notes that he's a dad, and the quiz is made up of advice that parents give their children in opera. It's fun and funny because some of the advice is moderately terrible parenting. The panel is doing pretty well until they get into Russian territory. I'm not sure of the right answer, exactly, but the moderator says the advice comes from Pushkin, and he asks us if we know the answer. I call out, "*Eugene Onegin?*" Correct. And hey, my 15 nanoseconds of fame are over.

Back to interviewing Hunter, Benson notes that last year's performance of Siegfried—when Hunter took over the role from other tenors who bowed out—became his big break. Hunter downplays the overnight-star aspect of it. He's been at this for 23 years, he says. He went to Juilliard and then began singing roles in regional theaters in the U.S. and being a perpetual understudy. I happen to know that he's sung a lot of contemporary music and premieres of new operas, including Captain Ahab in *Moby Dick*, Mitch in *A Streetcar Named Desire*, Unferth in *Grendel*, as well as Lennie in *Of Mice and Men*, Sam in *Susannah*, Anatol in *Vanessa*, and the title role of *Peter Grimes*. He sang two performances in *Jenůfa* (which I saw, in 2007), and then nothing until last year's *Siegfried* and this January's *Götterdäm-*

merung. He's asked about the key to his singing, and his answer is one word, "composure."

I really like his explanation, "Whether you're a 12-year old singing at church or a grown-up at the Met, you want to do your best. I've managed to stay composed to do my best." He explains that preparation is key to his ability to feel at ease. He thinks of every one of his performances, however small or in remote places, to have been necessary for him to be where he is now. I also get the sense that he is constantly studying. I really like what he's saying. I'll be hearing his Siegfried next Monday.

To end the quiz, the panelists are asked what qualities they look for in a Wagnerian singer. Ashbaker says that more than anything else, she wants a beautiful voice. Her advice is, sing "Mozart, Mozart, Mozart!" Levine defers to Wagner who said that the Italians have music in their blood, but the Germans have to work at it. He quotes from a letter that Wagner wrote, which is housed in the New York Public Library, that said Wagner wanted good Italian-style singing in his operas. Morris chimes in to say that at his Juilliard audition, an English lady who was a judge said about his singing, "I can't hear you over the piano. I think that's going to be a problem." That gets a big laugh from the audience. Volume isn't a problem for him any longer.

The chimes ring that intermission is ending. These chimes are played throughout the house to get patrons back in their seats. They aren't prerecorded. Today, a young lady holds a mini-xylophone in her arm and plays a brief excerpt from *Die Walküre.*

Die Walküre

The radio host signs off, and we scramble back to our seats as the lights dim overhead. I convince myself, as I climb ever higher, that I am seated close to Valhalla.

Act III of the opera includes the cool "Ride of the Valkyries." It's staged by Lepage with each of the eight sisters astride one of the machine's planks, holding onto long reins. The planks rise up and down randomly, like teeter-totters. It sounds a bit silly, but I'm really into it. The thing that keeps it from being a bad idea is the scale of it. Everything is larger than life. It's the equivalent of riding thirty-foot tall horses. The music is driving, pulsating. There's a ton of sound.

Each of the Valkyries has a voice as big as Brünnhilde. One of them is the LDS singer, Wendy Bryn Harmer. I'm not sure which of the blond beauties in shining armor she is, but after they slide down the entire surface of the machine and have moments of singing individually, I can easily make out Harmer's piercing voice. She is thrilling and all of her sisters together are practically overwhelming in power and impact. I wish that people who have never been to an opera could spend ten minutes at the Met watching, listening, and feeling this. It's huge.

The plot points are hit one by one, Sieglinde is rushed off into the woods (where she will bear her son Siegfried and then die). In her final lines of the opera, she talks about the baby in her womb, and the orchestra plays Siegfried's theme and the love theme intertwining. Beautiful touch, Herr Wagner. The final scene is one of the glories of all of the operatic literature. Wotan knows that Brünnhilde disobeyed him and also that she did what he wanted all along. He is torn between following the rules or his heart. Wagner always claimed that he cared as much about the libretto as he did about his music. It's clear, as I listen to this heartbreaking scene, even in English translation, that he wrestles with all of these contradictions artfully. Although she pleads for mercy, Wotan can't give it to her. She will be placed on a rock, and anybody who finds her will get her. Brünnhilde wins a compromise that, at least, some kind of barrier be placed around here as a deterrent to all but the most courageous men. She has defied the gods, and now he is renouncing her. His favorite son, Siegmund is dead, the magic sword is broken into pieces, Brünnhilde is lost to him, and without them, there is no chance of Wotan recapturing the ring and saving his race of gods. With his kiss, Brünnhilde becomes mortal.

Terfel is impossibly good here. It's not all blustery, Wagnerian rant. This is a tender and confused father singing from his heart. He is resigned to fate if a bit hopeful that somehow it can still work out. His voice is superb. During the intermission, Morris made a crack about singing Wagner, noting that when it comes right down to it, Wagner chews up your voice. Nobody can last more than a few years. "To do it you have to be, well, Bryn Terfel," he said.

The production ends with the planks of the machine arching up to form the jagged edges of a remote mountaintop. For some silly reason, the director hangs Brünnhilde—actually, a limp, life-sized Raggedy Ann doll—upside down from the center crevasse. As the unseen Loge brings fire to the mountain and encircles her, the orchestra plays a hint of what will happen shortly, when Valhalla falls to pieces. It's a gorgeous moment. And I'm completely exhausted.

As a ramp up to the complete cycle performances, the Met is more successful getting coverage for the productions. On April 23, the *Times* runs an article that centers on the changes that director Robert Lepage has made to the tetralogy since they premiered separately over the course of more than a year. The staff writer, Daniel J. Wakin, quotes Lepage in an interview saying that he had restaged "a lot of stuff", mostly small details. He notes that Fabio Luisi, after taking over for James Levine as conductor of the orchestra, became more involved in decisions involving singers and the way they move around the stage. Initially, for example, the gods made their entrances in *Das Rheingold* by sliding down the panels of the machine. That's gone now, Wakin reports. They simply walk on stage now.

Lepage is aware of the criticism of the production. He acknowledges that there are flaws, but he also points out that there's "a lot of good stuff." The singers have changed, as well. There are different singers in some of the roles, but the article notes that as the performers have more time onstage in the productions, they are becoming more relaxed and engaged. Bryn Terfel, who plays Wotan, returned to the Met this spring having lost

30 pounds. Lepage reports that as Terfel's appearance changed, so did his interpretation of the role. He is a philandering husband, Lepage reminds us, "The Wotan he does in 'Rheingold' looks much younger and hunkier, so the whole aging of the character comes into play." To his critics, Lepage reiterates that he is not interested in a staged concert version of the opera.

He says he was trying to cater to operagoers "who love the spectacle of opera, who love the magnifying of the ideas you can't see in the eyes of the singer." He ends the interview by talking about *Ring* productions in Europe and how the Met's cycle is different,

> The "Ring" is always dipped in these layers and layers of sociopolitical stances. People in Europe have to try to get even with Wagner.
>
> He said all these wrong things about the Jewish people in his days. One of his greatest fans is Hitler. We know all that. Europe is trying to get even with him. I said: That's all your stuff. Let's strip all of that from the 20th century and go back to the 19th century.[1]

Three days later, the chief music critic of the *Times* weighs in on the complete cycle. Anthony Tommasini's review is mostly dismissive of the productions, although he notes the director's changes that are improvements. He says flatly, "The Met's new 'Ring' is the most frustrating opera production I have ever had to grapple with. The machine represents a breakthrough in stage technology. There are breathtaking moments...But on balance the effects achieved are not worth the distractions they create." Regarding the music itself, Tommasini writes, "Two singers from the cast will enter the annals of 'Ring' greatness: the bass-baritone Eric Owens, for his chilling and uncommonly dignified Alberich; and the mezzo-soprano Stephanie Blythe, for her sympathetic and vocally magisterial Fricka." The critic says he likes Terfel, Voigt, and Dalayman, with some reservations. "The surprise of this 'Ring' is Jay Hunter Morris in the title role of 'Siegfried.' Though he is not a heldentenor by natural endowment, he has found his own way to sing this voice-killing role with youthful verve and a somewhat lighter yet full-bodied sound." He ends the review oddly, by acknowledging something that others haven't: the absence of James Levine in the pit, "Would this 'Ring' production have turned out differently, including some of Mr. Lepage's intrusive details, had a healthy Mr. Levine been fully engaged as the Met's music director through the project?"[2]

In an unrelated, by to my mind associated, article published on the same day, the *Times* reports that the National Endowment for the Arts has made "sweeping cuts" in PBS programming. Lincoln Center has been hit hard. In one case, "Live from Lincoln Center," the grant that was $100,000 last year was cut to zero this year. "Great Performances at the Met" telecasts' grants were chopped in half. WNET, the New York PBS station saw its support nearly wiped out, from $400,000 last year to $50,000 this year.[3]

In light of these facts, I can forgive the Met for trying to reach as many paying customers as it can. I question whether the naysayers of the Ring productions understand that the adverse publicity trickles down to public support for all the performing arts. That's not to say that negative criticism is out of place, but there are consequences for a community of artists when the reviews tip from reasoned criticism toward mockery and humiliation. I, for one, want to see more risks taken, not fewer.

For me, the *Ring* ends tonight or, depending on the tempos of the conductor, early tomorrow morning. The performance of *Siegfried* is scheduled to run from 6:00-11:30 PM. I saw *Götterdämmerung* in January, and I don't think I need to see it again to get the whole thing. Luisi is conducting, and I notice in the program that James Levine is still listed as Music Director. I wonder if he will ever return to full strength. He has withdrawn from the 2012-2013 season already. There's been absolutely nothing about his condition in the press or, for that matter, his participation in his duties at the opera house. Is he auditioning singers? Is he in communication with the General Manager about future productions, creative teams and casts? It's entirely possible that he's tottering around Lincoln Center, and it is also possible that he's completely elsewhere.

Throughout the *Ring*, I've tried to imagine what Levine would have been like in the pit. I wish that I knew the scores well enough to judge the differences between Luisi and Levine, but that's not something I can manage. There is definitely an avoidance of the Levine question, so to speak. In this vacuum—this *Ring* has become about the machine rather than the music—discussions about the orchestra's role seem to have been skirted. It's weird. I mean, it's not as if the critics loved the last *Ring* cycle either. As I recall, they called it retro and too literal. But the discussions in the press quickly turned to the musicians. This go round, it's not the same story arc. The Met has constructed a 45-ton scapegoat.

Of the four operas, *Siegfried* is the funny one. I don't know the music very well. There's an orchestral work by Wagner, "Siegfried Idyll", and I assume I'll hear it at some point tonight. The story of its premiere is one of my favorite tales in all of music. Wagner wrote the 20-minute work as a birthday present for Cosima, his second wife, after the birth of their son Siegfried, in 1869. (Their daughter's name was Isolde.) Within the music are several quotations from lullabies and other personal references that would have been recognizable to his family when the music was first played, on a Christmas morning, to wake up his wife. (Now, that's a good present!) I find my spot as the lights are dimming. Here comes *Siegfried*.

Each of the four opera productions in the Lepage *Ring* begins the same way. It's a nice, unifying touch. The planks of the machine are angled to form a continuous slope from the lip of the stage upward. Then, as the orchestra begins to play—and each opera has an orchestra prelude to set the scene—the planks rotate. In this case, the planks form a wall, and onto it is projected a vibrant image of soil, roots and little critters of the earth scampering about it. Next, the entire surface flips upside down to create another image in the forest, the hut of Mime. Since the end of *Die Walküre*, Sieglinde has died giving birth to Siegfried. The baby has been raised by Mime, whom we met in *Das Rheingold*— the brother of the evil Alberich. The reason that *Siegfried* is a comic opera is the relationship between Mime and Siegfried: they hate each other's guts. Siegfried is a spoiled, teenage super-hero. He is afraid of nothing. He's not exactly the smartest guy in the forest either. It has just occurred to him that he doesn't look like the dwarf Mime and probably isn't his real son. The running joke between the two is that Mime makes swords for Siegfried, but he breaks them all. Well, it's funnier in German.

There's no love lost on Mime's side either. He has determined that Siegfried is his best and only shot at getting the ring back from Fafner (the giant whom Wotan awarded treasure for building Valhalla). Fafner now lives in a cave in the forest and has transformed himself, using the magic Tarnhelm thing, into a dragon to guard the gold. Mime believes that Siegfried, knowing no fear, can slay the dragon. Or better yet, Siegfried and Fafner can kill each other, leaving him with the magic loot. Siegfried doesn't know his true heritage. The only thing he possesses is a sword that has been shattered into pieces. Mime comes clean— sort of—and tells Siegfried about his mother. He promises to repair the sword.

Siegfried

In the second scene, Wotan appears, dressed as a human being called the Wanderer. For no real purpose other than to review the plot of the first two operas, Mime and the Wanderer enter a riddle challenge. When Mime loses, he is told that Siegfried will fix the sword. Siegfried returns to the hut and in a fascinating passage of music, grinds the broken sword, melts it down, and reforges it anew.

Wagner calls upon Siegfried to sing very tough music and now, to bang onstage tools like a blacksmith to the specific counts in the score. I'm really impressed with Morris and also Gerhard Siegel who is portraying Mime. The crazy thing about this opera is that even though it's five and a half hours long, there are never more than two characters singing onstage at any time. Each of these scenes—some are nearly an hour in length—is an elaborate duet. Because the characters are so fiery, sarcastic, biting, and bitter, the demands on their singing voices is extreme. But so far, a couple of hours into it, they are fresh as daisies. They're just warming up.

Act II will introduce a female voice into this testosterone-a-thon. Erin Morley is singing the role of the Forest Bird. It is incredible to me to think that these LDS singers have been onstage in every one of the *Ring* operas. Even a few years ago, it would have been inconceivable to imagine such a deep bench of Mormon talent at the Met. Morley's part tonight is an off-stage role.

Siegfried, having defeated the dragon, tastes its blood and suddenly understands the singing of the Forest Bird. It warns

Siegfried that Mime will try to poison him. When Mime offers him a potion to satisfy the hero's thirst, Siegfried kills him. Then, the bird tells him of a beautiful maiden named Brünnhilde asleep on a mountaintop, encircled by fire. Siegfried sets off on a new adventure. The Forest Bird's music is incredibly beautiful. For a singer it's a tricky challenge because the woodwinds in the orchestra have been playing the tune and then suddenly, a voice must replicate it. The moment can be magical, like a veil being removed.

Morley is spectacular. Again, not a large role, but a pivotal one. The vocal line is utterly exposed. A single mistake is a glaring problem. Tonight, it goes off without a hitch. She has quite a lovely spin to her voice. I'm reminded of Kathleen Battle. At the curtain call for Act II, Morley appears in front of the curtain in a black dress, with a little yellow hand puppet that she waves at the audience as if to say, *Hey folks, I was the bird.* Next to all of these big men, Morley looks like a waif. She's done for the night.

It's a tag team play. Now it's time for another woman to appear, Erda, the goddess of the Earth. Wotan asks her about his fate, but she is evasive. It appears that the gods' only hope rests with Siegfried and Brünnhilde. As Siegfried approaches the ring of fire, the Wanderer appears and blocks his way. They fight, and Siegfried smites the Wanderer's magic spear. He is defeated, and we won't see him again. It's a good bit of psychological writing. Siegfried has taken the sword of his father who was killed by his father, and made it his own by melting it down. Siegfried is his own man. Ultimately, a human has defeated a god.

The Siegfried Idyll is played now, in bits and pieces, in the orchestra. Siegfried approaches Brünnhilde, but he's never seen a woman before. He has to cut off her armor to discover her truth nature. Having spent his life searching for fear, he is now overwhelmed by it. She is awakened with a kiss. It's inevitable that they'll fall in love, but Wagner takes his time, building themes that circle round and round, spiraling ever higher.

I have to say that Morris' singing is super-human. How anyone can be singing this freshly more than five hours into Siegfried is beyond me. It's not just that he's hitting all the notes, but more than that, it's a youthful, virile sound. Part of me hopes that he'll stop singing Wagner and save his voice, but on the other hand, who else is there who can do this? It's a wonder. Finally, Siegfried and Brünnhilde vow eternal love (over-hastily, since I know what's going to happen in *Götterdämmerung*), and the opera ends.

On May 1, the multimedia feature dedicated to the *Ring* on the Times website posts a brief, human interest story on the last-minute substitution of Frank van Aken at the Saturday matinee. The site remains a major disappointment regarding the public's participation. Although the Met posts reviews, feature stories, follow-up interviews, human interest stories, scholarship appraisals and more, the readers are not adding value by posting their own views. They don't appear to care. Normally, readers flood opportunities like this. We New Yorkers are not shy about offering our opinions. But after nearly a month of posts by the newspaper including great photographs of the productions, readers have posted a mere 75 comments to the site. To put this in some context, an article over the weekend that revealed the ways that Apple manipulates its finances in the U.S. and abroad garnered 1,370 reader comments on the day that the exposé was published.

The operas of the *Ring* are to be shown in movie theaters, one each week, beginning May 9. These have been broadcast separately over the last two seasons as part of the HD series, but for those wanting a compact *Ring* experience, seeing them back to back (sort of) replicates the experience of going to the Met to see the entire cycle. As a kick off to the HD Ring, the Met screens its new documentary, *Wagner's Dream: The Making of the Ring*, on Monday night, May 7. The film was part of the recent Tribeca Film Festival, but it is now receiving wide release around the country for one night only.

In Manhattan, it's being shown at the AMC theater on 42nd Street. Having purchased my $15 ticket on Fandango, I arrive at the theater five minutes early, expecting to stroll to a kiosk, print out my ticket and head upstairs. When I open the front door, I see that the entire lobby is packed with people. This is my local movie theater. I've been here dozens of times over the years, and I've never seen anything like this. There is a line that snakes back and forth from the ticket counter and extends into the lobby and out the front door. The building itself was a condemned

Broadway theater that was rehabilitated and turned into a movie house. The lobby where I'm standing was once the orchestra of the theater. The balcony above me is decorated as it had been one hundred years ago. This is standing room only.

Is it possible that all of these people are going to the *Ring* documentary? I know that there are lots of Wagnerites in town right now, but I can't imagine.... As it turns out, my first impression is wrong. The movie *The Avengers* opened over the weekend and raked in $200,000,000.00 in three days. These people, mostly, are trying to squeeze into any available showing of the action movie. Sorry Wagner, wrong super-hero movie. But when I do step into the screening room for *Wagner's Dream*, I find the large room packed full of people. I end up sitting on the front row, unable to see the width of the screen without craning my neck.

The premise of the documentary—made by the same in-house Met video team who created *The Audition*—is simple: Wagner would have loved the new Met production. It strains to make the point that 19th century stagecraft was incapable of realizing the composer's vision. Finally, the Met states breathlessly, we have the perfect *Ring*. I roll my eyes. This is going to be a tough sell.

The documentary opens with interviews of people on a standing room ticket line in August 2010. They are there to purchase tickets to the first opera of the Met's new *Ring*. They are a bit nutty (and also typical, as I know firsthand from standing in lines like these). They use words to describe the *Ring* like "unstageable."

The story jumps back to the first day of rehearsals for *Das Rheingold*. Gelb stands in front of the company and introduces them to Robert Lepage. General Manager Gelb says that he is trying to stage the Wagner operas with modern tools but respectful of tradition. He calls Lepage "one of theater's great visionaries." Gelb sees himself as a rescuer of the Met. The documentary quotes him saying that when he arrived, the opera house was in decline, with aging audiences and tired productions. He says the physical facilities were 20 years behind the times. It was his aspiration to force the Met to upgrade. The *Ring* is a conscious attempt to create a symbol of his artistic vision.

The film jumps farther back, to January 2008, in Québec City, where Lepage and his team have built a small, wooden model of the *Ring* set. It's only 15 inches or so tall, but the system is already conceptualized just as I've seen it in production. The model is not automated. It moves when fingers push at it. Lepage says something interesting about the genesis of the set. After he was engaged to develop the *Ring*—it was one of Gelb's first projects—Lepage went to Iceland. There, he encountered an exhibition of Icelandic myths, and he decided that although the *Ring* is German, at its heart, it is more ancient than that. He was inspired by the glaciers of Iceland, particularly the moment when they move and break apart. The machine of the Met's *Ring* came, not from an image of Teutonic women in breastplates, but from the earth's tectonic plates.

One year later, Lepage and his team have constructed a full-sized section of the machine. It will have 24 panels eventually. They have created four panels. To test it, they have harnessed an acrobat to stand in for the Rhinemaidens. He is hoisted up, just as the Rhinemaidens will be at the beginning of *Das Rhein-gold*. At this point, everyone is very pleased with themselves. They say they have the vision that Wagner had. I'm not buying this question of intent from any angle. I don't think Lepage is channeling Wagner's intent, but at the same time, I'm not inter-ested in slavishly following it either. If Wagner had somehow left da Vinci-esque drawings of a future machine for the *Ring*, I'd hate to think we would feel obligated to use it exclusively. That's just not how art works. But this is not about such highfalutin ideas. The Met is simply trying to justify the production. This is all spin, after the fact.

For some crazy reason, the Met takes its message directly to the least receptive organization it can think of, the Wagner Soci-ety of New York. They are traditionalists with a capital T. In the documentary, some of the society members claim to have seen 35 complete *Ring* cycles. Unsurprisingly, they doubt Wagner would approve of the new Met productions. Lepage argues in front of the group that just as the composer wrote leitmotifs than morph and change, the design for the opera also needed to be a single set that could constantly shift into something else. No one is swayed. It's a tough crowd.

Meanwhile, the clock is ticking in Canada. The Lepage team frets that once the machine leaves its in-house development, they will no longer have control of it. There is a hint that the Met's union contracts will preclude them from fine-tuning on site. No one knows what to expect. They simply know that the thing isn't ready and may not be ready in time.

In July of 2010, eight weeks before *Das Rheingold* is to open the new Met season, the word backstage is simple, "It's not going to work." The Met was told the machine would weigh 50,000 pounds. When it arrives, it tips the scales at 90,000. They are compelled to reinforce the floor of the Met to handle it. The stage itself is strong enough, but the machine can't be readily disassembled. To store it when it is not in use—and because the house uses a repertory system of rotating performances, it will not be in use half of the time, at least—the Met's gigantic wagons will pull the machine offstage to a holding area that is the equivalent of another Met stage.

In the documentary, the machine is repeatedly described as a living, quirky being. Maybe it's just the French being French, but it is almost as if they are expecting the set to be capricious. If so, it is a self-fulfilling prophecy. It jams. It sends error messages as if it has its own mind. It locks itself down.

The fun thing about the documentary is a behind-the-scenes view of the machine in action. It is not as I imagined. The machine is not nearly as fully-mechanized as I was giving it credit for being. Instead, behind the 24 planks stand a fleet of stagehands, wearing black clothing and black ski masks. To make a plank rotate, these hands grab a rope and pull. There are balance mechanisms too, but essentially, it is the tiny wooden model exponentially enlarged. If that makes it more user-friendly, I don't know, but the singers are absolutely terrified by it.

The Rhinemaidens are the first to test it. This is a pretty funny scene of the documentary. The three women wear elaborate harnesses. You can see it in their eyes: they are scared to death. But one of them—and I recognize her as Tamara Mumford—is completely up to the task. While the others are tentative, she is fearless. Suspended many feet above the stage, she is already "swimming" and smiling. There are only four days before the premiere. Gelb stares into the camera and says, "If it doesn't work, then...I will leave the country." At a dress rehearsal with orchestra, James Levine watches the Rhinemaidens take flight. With the panels directly behind them, their voices sound resonant. Levine says, "The set has good acoustics."

Opening night arrives accompanied by a torrent of rain. Outside in Lincoln Center and also in Times Square, dejected but determined fans sit in rain ponchos to watch the broadcast of *Das Rheingold*. At the end of the opera, the gods (actually, stand-in acrobat doubles) are supposed to enter Valhalla by scaling a tilting rainbow bridge. The machine has not been working properly in rehearsals, and on opening night, it locks up completely in this final scene. Stagehands are shown in near-panic trying to decide what to do as the orchestra plays past the point of their cue. Finally, the singers are told to simply walk off stage. The audience watches a colorful bridge that just sits there. The next morning, the critics revel in the failed mechanics of the show. The *Times* headline reads, "The Gods Are Stranded as Set Misfires." (It's an interesting exercise, by the way, to go back and read the reviews of the first, new *Ring* performances. The critics were very supportive of it, loved the singers, praised Levine to high heaven, were excited about the set, and said that, given the complexities, it went off better than expected.) None of that critical support is shown in the film. It prefers to paint the Met as the embattled underdog. The documentary shows the ending of the second performance, when all goes fine with the bridge.

The rest of the documentary follows a similar narrative path. Each new production is tested. The glitches are worked out. The singers freak out—in *Die Walküre*, one of the Valkyries says that she's "scared out of my head"—critics toss cold water on it, and audiences respond with measured enthusiasm.

Much of the second half of the long documentary follows Brünnhilde, Deborah Voigt. To my mind, it's unfortunate that she gave the filmmakers such intrusive access. She is singing her first Brünnhilde. The soprano is openly anxious about being compared to historic singers. Although she doesn't try to throw around excessive influence, Voigt is aware that a lot is riding on her performance, and she is filled with self-doubt. Vocal coaches, dressers, and assistants who are indulgent yes-men surround her.

On opening night of *Die Walküre*, Voigt goes to make her entrance, which calls for her to scale the machine, and she trips and slides to the floor with a crash. It's an embarrassing moment—humiliating, even—and the backstage cameras follow her like jackals after her exit from the stage. She deals with it as best she can, even humorously, but she announces that she wants a blocking change. (She doesn't get it; Gelb won't back her up.)

Meanwhile, excerpts are shown from the opera. It's great seeing the singers' faces. They are so dramatically prepared. I'm especially impressed by Bryn Terfel, whose voice is like a category 5 hurricane of power. Voigt never approaches that degree of brilliance in the documentary. It shows her struggling with high notes and interpretation. She is an all-American girl, and I suspect that her willingness to be self-deprecating and emotionally exposed opens the door to the filmmakers' exploitation of her. I'm saddened that the Met—this is a Met-produced documentary, after all—is throwing her under the bus this way. They would never do this to Anna Netrebko.

The documentary shifts after the first two operas of the *Ring* are premiered. As Levine cancels, first a few performances, then more and more, and finally cancels the entire season (and the foreseeable future, for that matter), the filmmakers completely dodge the associated issues of losing the conductor. Luisi is shown only briefly. For the most part, *Wagner's Dream* is about a machine and the actors who tame it. The orchestra might as well be pre-recorded. To the filmmakers, the drama is above the pit. And granted, there's plenty going wrong on stage.

With four days to go before the premiere of *Siegfried*, the tenor lead pulls out. Into the movie gallops the American tenor from Paris, Texas, Jay Hunter Morris. It is incredible to see his naïve openness to the experience. He reassures everyone around him that he's just fine, not to worry about anything. He is the opposite of the fretting sopranos. Having seen his performance of Siegfried last week, I'm astounded at Morris and his can-do attitude. Gelb states that in the world there are two, maybe three people who can sing the role. Morris is shown in excerpts to be about as perfect for the part as can be.

Finally, *Götterdämmerung* premieres. Voigt has had a chest infection. She is emotional and frightened. She calls singing the role, "Mount Everest". I'm touched that she acknowledges that the role was something that everyone expected her to tackle someday, and now that it is here, it is still a work in progress. As excerpts from the opera are heard, the cameras follow Gelb outside, onto the balcony overlooking the plaza. He calls the *Ring*, "The hardest project of my life." He says that given its complexities, he's unable to sit back and watch it without anxieties.

I enjoy the behind-the-scenes aspects of the documentary without actually liking the film very much. Still, it's fun to see the performers up close. I'm happy to follow three of the LDS singers in the film. It makes me want to see the HD recordings of the *Ring*. The documentary/commercial for the *Ring* has achieved that goal, at least. At the end of the showing, the audience in the movie theater applauds loudly.

CHAPTER 11

TONIGHT IS, FOR ME AT LEAST, the last performance of the 2011-2012 Metropolitan Opera season. There are still four more performances that will culminate on Saturday with the conclusion of the *Ring* cycle. But having seen all the works that are being presented from Wednesday to Saturday, I am left with one opera. It's something I've dreaded for, well, a long time. I plan to go back to *The Makropulos Case*.

But before that, I am taken on a tour backstage of the opera house. This is my opportunity to imagine what it would be like to be at work in the opera house. I've been curious to know what the day-to-day routines are for the Mormon singers. This should provide a glimpse into their workspace.

My guide is Lois Rappaport, a volunteer with the Opera Guild. We start at the stage entrance, appropriately enough. Lincoln Center is undergoing a multi-million dollar facelift, and the underground parking and paths have been restructured. Today, I enter a door marked "Do Not Enter" and walk up a few short stairs to a corridor lined with metal lockers on one side that leads to a reach a small vestibule holding a few old chairs, a security guard with two computer screens at face level, and assorted other workers behind desks. I am wearing a visitor's pass. We stride past him.

Our first stop is the stars' dressing rooms. I've been in them before, but my mind has played tricks on me. Either they have been drastically shrunk in the remodel, or the glamour of the events artificially increased their size in my mind. The stage manager assigns singers to dressing rooms. Each show has five stage managers. The row of dressing rooms—men to the right, women to the left—are identical: a small rack for costumes, an upright piano in the corner, a tri-fold, floor length mirror, a vanity encircled with lights, a private bathroom, one extra chair, and a wall of windows that are covered with inexpensive-looking blinds. When the building was constructed, I'm told, the dressing rooms were situated with windows on Amsterdam Avenue. The thinking was that singers would enjoy the fresh air. Apparently, those people making the decisions hadn't spent much time on Amsterdam, the primary route for large trucks entering and exiting the city. It is loud and dusty. The windows remain closed. If I had to estimate the size of these dressing rooms, I'd guess that they are about 200 square feet in total. For the singers who are sharing a dressing room, that's not much space.

I look at the costumes for tonight's performance. The green evening gown that Karita Matilla will wear in the role of the 337-year old opera star is next to a light blue pants suit that she'll have on as she enters in Act I. I notice that there's a designer label at the base of the inside collar. It doesn't say Chanel, it reads, aspirationally, The Metropolitan Opera.

Lois and I walk to the elevator to descend to the bottom of the opera house. The building has ten stories, not including the extendable fly space above the stage. Six floors are above ground.

The four below are, as my guide says, "Where the magic happens." We exit on the C Level. The walls and floors here are the same as on the Stage Level backstage: painted cinderblocks for walls and industrial rubber mats on the floors. As we wander down the narrow corridors, we occasionally pass a small office. These are coat closets with a computer screen in them. They fit exactly one person, no more. All space is at a premium here.

When it was designed—by Wallace Harrison, the same architect who designed the United Nations building and Rockefeller Center—these lower floors were to hold an entire season's sets and costumes. The facilities were so magnificent that set designers decided to push the limits of what a stage could hold. To make a long story short, the Met can now hold only a week's worth of staging in the building. That's how big all of the productions have become.

We walked by the *Ring*'s machine on the way to the dressing rooms. It has been parked offstage until tomorrow night. It is enormous. The Met main stage is two full-sized basketball courts placed side by side. Behind and to the sides of the main stage are three more stages that are roughly the same dimensions. One has a full-sized turntable capable of rotating an entire set. The main stage is on hydraulic elevators that can lift parts or all of the stage to allow vertical set changes in mid-opera. From the C Level, we see one of the elevators at work.

These are cavernous spaces, empty in the middle but filled to the rafters along the walls. Everything is carefully marked with the name of the opera. Here are steps, crates, pillars, walls, roofs, house fronts, slopping mountainsides, and much, much more. This is hoarding at a *Citizen Kane* level, except it is only a week's worth of opera sets. Stagehands roam everywhere around us. They work in shifts 24 hours a day. After an opera ends, usually around midnight, a shift arrives to strike the set and store it. It prepares for the next day, not the set for the next performance, rather the set that will be on the main stage during the day for rehearsals. Another crew will put the next performance's set in place sometimes only a few minutes before the curtain goes up. I am surprised to report that all of the workers I see—they are all men wearing jeans and t-shirts, for the most part—are exceptionally nice. New York union carpenters saying "Excuse me, pardon me" as they pass by? These are not the breed of wolf- whistling, beered-up construction workers common to the streets of the city.

We walk by rehearsal rooms. These are very large, about the size of a high school gymnasium. I've been in these rooms before. Years ago I sang with a big choir in the city, and we rehearsed here a few times with the Met orchestra. Again, nothing fancy about these rooms. Wood floors, mirrored walls like a dance studio, some risers, scattered chairs. The only nod to the significance of the building is a very good piano in the corner.

We scamper through the halls like rats in a maze. I am officially lost. Every hallway looks the same to me. I ask my guide if people get lost around here, and she tells the story of the singer who couldn't find the person assigned to get him from the dressing room to the stage. He got lost, and in a panic made his stage entrance through the scene's fireplace. I feel his pain. We hop onto an elevator. It opens on the A Level. The smell of food floods over us. This is the floor where the cafeteria is located. I've been here too. My wife used to work at the Met's Grand Tier restaurant, and a time or two, I joined her for a meal here before she went to work. I never liked it, though. I was too distracted by people watching. I couldn't eat a sandwich while Placido Domingo ate a salad at the next table. It felt wrong. I literally couldn't eat.

All the props and costumes at the Met are built on-site. I walk through the carpenter's shop on the fourth floor, and I expect to see people packing things up for the season. Instead, there are panels being tested for next year's *Maria Stuarda*. A carpenter tells me that they are trying to find the right colors and haven't hit on it yet. The walls look like wood but are actually lightweight rubber pressed with the texture of wood. On worktables sit the chairs for next season's *Rigoletto*, set in the 1950s. They're appropriately cool. The carpenter tells me that they bought the chairs but have recovered them with fabric created at the Met. He encourages me to touch them. "You can feel them. Look, people are going to be sitting them, you know." The shops work all year around. If anything, I'm told, the summer months are the shops' busiest time. Lumber is stacked along the walls. I ask about the beautiful paper lanterns hanging from a rack along one windowed wall. They were made for a production but got cut. "We never throw anything away."

There's a laboratory in the corner, filled with sinks, nozzles, hoses and surgical supplies. Unlike the rest of these shops that are mostly open spaces, this room has a series of tall draperies that divide it into quadrants. I point to it, and I'm told that this is where the costumes are distressed: blood smearing, dirt caking, drips, dyes, scratches, rips and tears. We walk next past a shop with lumber stacked up many feet high all around us. This is where construction happens. I wonder if I will find a bent nail here, a symbol of good luck for performers. The floor itself looks like a Jackson Pollack-splattered canvas, but after I home in on the sight, I see nails, and bent nails, everywhere. There is the unmistakable smell of sawdust although the floors are swept mostly clean. It strikes me that elsewhere, other than the cafeteria floor and the woodshop, the Met doesn't smell like anything.

If it resembles anything in the wild, it's a rabbit's warren, enlarged to industrial size. I scurry through long, dark tunnels and emerge in hangar-like dens. It is midafternoon, and there are fewer people in the building than I imagine to be the case in mornings and evenings. Still, there is working proceeding around every corner. I watch as a vocal coach puts a singer through her paces in a small rehearsal room.

We continue up to the costume shop. I examine a few of the wigs as my guide tells me about their construction. A mold is taken of each performer's head. A fine mesh covers the mold, and the wigmaker knots human hair, one delicate strand at a time, through each opening of the mesh. In the back of the head, the mesh's grain is slightly larger. Three strands of hair can be tied at once there. A wig requires approximately 40 hours of labor to complete. The exception to human hair is a wig that is gray. For those pieces, the Met uses yak hair. When I look closely at the wigs, I see the mesh extends in front of the hairline a half-inch or so. I'm told that for HD broadcasts, wigmakers trim back the mesh as closely as possible.

Next-door is the costume shop. Inside three women are working with fabric-draped mannequins. There is a staff of 30 seamstresses at the Met. Aside from the tools of the trade that would be found in any atelier, the Met's costume shop is a living library of fabrics and textiles. Tubes of fabric are stacked all the way to the ceiling alongside every available wall. The Met has several fabric scouts on full-time retainer. They travel the world looking for unusual textiles that will become opera costumes.

Each year, the Met creates up to 2,000 costumes. Most of them are unique. That is, one costume for each role. I ask how they negotiate the costumes when a role is shared by singers of different sizes. Many of the costumes are extremely flexible and can accommodate singers of markedly different proportions. This is accomplished with hooks, laces, Velcro and other hidden closures. A long dress, for example, might appear from the audience as a single piece but is actually a separate top and skirt. The bodice might have lacing up the back, underneath a panel, and the skirt might have a mechanism inside that allows it to be pulled up or let down, depending on the height of the singer.

In addition to creating new costumes, the department is continuously refurbishing older costumes. Laundry facilities are located in the building. When a costume is decommissioned, it is donated to the Theater Development Fund, the same organization that runs the half-price ticket booth in Times Square for Broadway shows and other events. TDF rents costumes to schools and nonprofit organizations at a steep discount from what they would cost otherwise.

We pass by the rooms for the Children's Chorus. In addition to the adult chorus, the ballet, the soloists, and orchestra, the Met runs a school to train children. Several operas each season require children's voices. The choral program is free and meets twice a week, in the afternoon, during the school year. There is a beginner's, intermediate, and advanced class. When the Met needs a child's voice for a production, children in the advanced class audition and selected vocalists are invited to perform in the production. I have a friend whose daughter is currently in the Met's children's choral program. She told me that one day, when she went to pick up her daughter after class, there was a tall, handsome man who was kneeling down and talking to her. She approached him and said hello. He was very nice and friendly, she reported. It was Jonas Kaufmann, who had given a solo recital at the Met—an exceptionally rare occurrence—the weekend before.

The Met has a problem with security. Although there are

guards placed at the main entrances of the auditorium—both the street level at below ground—the gates are like funnels. Thousands of people pour through two spaces that are only a few feet wide. At performances, there is a cursory check for explosives by a small security team that shines penlights into women's handbags. But for a patron requiring high security (rather than the opera house trying to protect itself), the Met is inadequate. On my backstage tour, I walk past the only outside door that is secure. It is a small opening on the south side of the building, right off of the main stage. It is also the entrance for animals to be transferred from their carriages parked on 60th Street, through the south plaza, and into the opera house. The entrance, on the inside, is comprised of a small stair and a ramp for horses. For a visiting head of state, for example, who needs to enter without the security nightmare of dozens of anonymous people pressing against him, it's an underwhelming solution. Compared to any fine hotel in New York—with their secret elevator systems, emergency exits, and private security details—the Met's security facilities are antiquated.

But for such an enormous enterprise, it is extremely well organized. I suppose it would have to be this way. Anything else would be chaos. I am given a daily rehearsal sheet for the Met. Today, the rehearsal areas and main stage are scheduled, nearly down to the minute. And I'm told it's a relatively light day because the season is coming to a close. There must be fifty different rehearsal items on the day's list, scattered throughout the building. Somewhere in this place, there's a lot of cooperation and planning going on. This level of communication impresses me.

I see the teamwork in action as I walk onto the main stage. It is bustling with activity. Today, there have been rehearsals for next season's *Rigoletto*. On the turntable stand towers of neon signs evoking Las Vegas of the 1950s. In the updating of the opera, Rigoletto runs the Duke's casino. It looks great. When the curtain goes up next fall, this set will get applause, I'd wager. And close up, the scale of it is huge. Some twenty stagehands are lined up hoisting a light track that is the size of a skyscraper's I-beams and runs the entire width of the Met stage. I look up. In addition to multiple tracks of lighting, there are scrims and backdrops that stretch higher than I can see. I stand in awe as these are raised and lowered simultaneously, like a shadow play of giants. Offstage sits a three-story battleship. It is for *Billy Budd*, which will be the final opera performed this season, on Saturday night. It will begin at 9:00 PM after the *Götterdämmerung* matinee—the final cycle of the *Ring* begins at 11:00am and ends at about 5:00 PM. I look around for the sets of *The Makropulos Case*, but I don't see them anywhere. It's possible that they're still downstairs, lurking somewhere.

From the stage, the house and its rows of seats look smaller than I would imagine. It's too big to lay a claim to being intimate, but there is a sense of coziness to it. Maybe it's the wood, velvet, and gold, but I'm reminded of a jewel box with separate compartments for various treasures. My last stop is to walk into the house itself. My guide points out the rosewood paneling that lines the entire house. I've heard before the story that it came from a single tree, and Lois repeats the story now. It is veneer, of course, a mere thickness of millimeters, so I suppose it's possible. She tells me that the importance of having the wood from a single tree has something to do with matching resonances. I don't understand the alchemy of acoustics. But she adds that there are no corners at the Met because it would negatively affect the sound.

Lois gives me other trivia: the velvet is plush enough to be comfortable without being too plush, which would dampen the sound. The ceiling is covered in one million 2-inch squares of gold leaf, chosen because gold doesn't tarnish. The fashion textile house Scalamandre created the gold curtain for $350,000. I don't know if that's a little or a lot to pay for a curtain. I get a kink in my neck looking up at the chandelier, given by the Austrian government. In 2008, the chandeliers throughout the Met were refurbished by Swarovski in Vienna at a cost of one million dollars. It was the first time since the opera house opened that the crystal had been repaired. Typically, the Met replaces burnt-out bulbs and gives the chandeliers a good cleaning each summer before the new season begins in the fall.

I peer down into the orchestra pit. The pit can be raised and lowered, says my guide, and it holds 110 musicians. There is a separate elevator for the prompter who is raised up into the prompter's box for each performance. There are five full-time prompters at the Met. All of them are women, I'm told. It's a job I don't quite understand. What does a prompter do, exactly? Lois explains to me that the prompter whispers the first line of each entrance for the singers. They also signal to the performers if their notes are sharp or flat. I'm told they have a little trick for getting the attention of a singer without having microphones pick up the sound: they make a kissing sound.

On the sides of the stage are large panels that hide lighting instruments from the view of the audience. Embedded into the side panels are also multiple television monitors with cameras keyed onto the conductor. A singer onstage can look at a monitor and always know what the conductor is doing. This is probably a good thing.

At the very back of the main level of the house is a glassed-in booth. Here sit sound technicians and others for the HD broadcasts, as well as the engineers who manage the subtitle systems. They are controlled live. The enclosed room itself is quite large. There are several desks with chairs and monitors. With the increasing presence of HD cameras throughout the house, I suspect that this room is becoming mission control. I walk out of the auditorium. I'm surprised how short the walk is. After a performance, with people creeping along up the aisle, a patron takes a few minutes to exit the room. By myself, it is over in seconds.

I'm appreciative to Ms. Rappaport for the tour. She tells me a little bit about her life and mentions that her husband was a musician in the pit bands of Broadway for many years before he retired. Throughout the tour, she has chatted with workers inside the Met. Everyone seems to know each other, somehow. As one woman passes us by, Lois waves her down and asks her how she is doing, adding, "I haven't seen you in a while." It is like a giant family, the Met is. The website's address is metoperafamily.org. Before today, I thought it was a gratuitous thing, the addition of the word "family". But now I am beginning to see it more literally. In my hand, I have some money that I plan to give to Lois as a tip for the two hours of our behind-the-scenes journey. As I turn over my visitor's badge that has been draped around my neck for the tour, I extend the cash to her, but she won't take it. She says, "Instead, why don't you make a donation to the Opera Guild?"

I have to say that I love the Met's outreach initiatives. Opera Guild is a part of that. Think about it: someone living in a remote cabin in the woods can view operas from the Met as frequently as the people who live across the street from Lincoln Center. (Since I know people who live in the apartment buildings across the street and never attend performances at Lincoln Center, I make that statement without fear.) I'm thinking specifically about the television broadcasts. The first *Great Performances* telecast occurred in 1977. In the 2006-2007 season, the Met began a partnership with the Met for a new series, *Great Per-formances at the Met*. Rather than filming the operas live using PBS as its producing entity, the Met began taping the HD broad-casts that they produce and show in movie theaters and together with PBS, they place the works on television primetime. Major corporate support for *Great Performances at the Met* is provided by Toll Brothers, which also produces the Saturday radio broadcasts.

Six operas were shown in the first season of *Great Performances at the Met*, and eight the following year. During this 2011-2012 season, *Great Performances at the Met* showed these six works: *The Enchanted Island, Satyagraha, Faust, Rodelinda, Don Giovanni,* and *Anna Bolena*. Of these, I saw all of them. Highlights for me were Jonas Kaufmann in *Faust*—there was a moment in the first act when he sang a high B natural fortissimo, and then he diminished the note to almost nothing, an extraordinary effect—and *Satyagraha*, the Philip Glass opera about Gandhi which I found to be moving and original. I enjoyed seeing operas on television that I had experienced in the opera house. I didn't dislike anything, although I have to admit that I fell asleep on my couch during *Rodelinda*. Still, it's pretty incredible to think that people across the country can see these things without leaving their living rooms. I don't know any fans of opera that didn't cut their teeth on radio and PBS broadcasts from the Met. A full subscription package to the Met is seven operas. This PBS programming is like giving a household hundreds of dollars worth of opera, a full subscription of the Met's best productions, for free.

The Met's series of operas shown in movie theaters, *The Met: Live in HD*, transmitted 11 operas during the current season: *La traviata, Manon, Siegfried, Götterdämmerung, Anna Bolena, Don Giovanni, Satyagraha, Rodelinda, Faust, The Enchanted Is-*

land, and *Ernani.* It also premiered the documentary, *Wagner's Dream.* Generally, each of these films is shown once, although in the summer, there are "encores"—this year there will be six repeat showings, and they include productions dating back to 2009. Next season, *The Met: Live in HD* will bring 12 new operas into movie theaters across the U.S. and Canada and to as many as 56 other countries.

I still don't have my ticket to the performance of *The Makropulos Case* tonight. The production got rave reviews in the press, so it's not very smart of me to procrastinate like this. I went online earlier in the week and noticed that there were quite a few tickets remaining, but that was before the reviews came out. After my tour, I walk past the queue for the $20 Weekday Rush Tickets. (I feel like I owe Agnes Varis and Karl Leichtman a thank-you note. Most of the operas I've seen at the Met throughout the season were subsidized by their generous program.) The line is already snaking back and forth. I worry that if I wait much longer, I'll be in trouble.

In line, I strike up a conversation with two people. The first is a woman who has already seen this opera two times in the last two weeks. Ultimately, she decides to pick up her guitar and heavy shopping bags and go home. The other is a man who asks me to hold his place in line as he does a headcount. He returns and says that we're number 84 and 85. Well, that's bad. There are 150 rush tickets, and each person in line can purchase two.

He says that we're on the bubble, but I suspect I'm on the wrong side of it. I ask him if he's done this before, and he responds that he's an old pro. He rattles off the titles of the operas this season that he's seen. It's probably seven or eight. And he notes the full-price tickets too. It sounds like he's here a lot, but he also tells me about plays, and rock concerts, and art exhibitions that he's seen recently. As self-congratulatory as it is to say this, to me he sounds like an average New Yorker.

I hadn't heard this before, but he also tells me about a gang that's been crashing the lines of these rush tickets, buying up as many as they can, and then going up onto the plaza and scalping them for $200 each, a 1000% markup. On one occasion, a group of men intimidated those in line into letting them slip in at the last minute. But the man I'm talking to—and he's probably six foot, 190—wouldn't stand for it. He told them off, and he went to get security guards. Scalpers stand in front of the Metropolitan Opera almost every performance. If you go frequently enough, you'll see the same faces. It's their profession.

Scalping is legal in the state. From time to time, legislators try to place caps on the percentage profit allowable, but it is a multi-billion dollar industry. These entities include big businesses like the ticket brokers, like Ticketron, Ticketmaster, and Live Nation, as well as individuals incorporated or not. Over the years, the resale of tickets has been legal and then restricted. In 2007, the state began a three-year experiment to permit it in an expanded form. The governor at the time, Eliot Spitzer, said,

"Scalping laws did not make sense. This will be good for the venues, good for consumers and good for the artists." But in 2010, Governor David A. Paterson presided over a legislature unable to extend the law beyond its three-year trial. It was a contentious issue, but the main problem was the new bill's inability to address paperless ticketing. As it currently stands, New York State law allows paperless tickets only if consumers are offered with an alternative form that is transferrable.[1]

Every state has its own regulations, and some of them are wacky. They include restrictions on the resale within 200 feet of the box office, hefty license taxes for anyone reselling tickets, and a declaration that it is illegal to sell tickets in public but permissible from home. New Jersey, for example, limits the face value of a scalped ticket sold by a non-registered broker to $3 or 20% of face value. It also prohibits the original sellers from holding back more than 5% of the tickets. Many states don't permit resale of tickets at all.

In New York, resale of tickets is dependent upon the size of the venue. For an event in a hall or stadium larger than 6,000 seats, the charge for a ticket can be up to 45% above the original face value (20% above if less than 6,000 seats). Bribes, bonuses, and commissions paid to operators at a venue are illegal. Ticket resellers have to be licensed and post a bond against fraud, extortion or violation of the ticket broker law. Brokers can tack on a "reasonable service charge" to ticket sales, although the specifics remain undefined. Finally, it exempts charities from the law if they use the profits toward their chartered purposes.[2] To my surprise, I manage to get my \$20 ticket to *The Makropulos Case*. I briefly consider scalping it, but twenty percent of \$20 isn't very much profit.

Leoš Janáček was born in Brno, Moravia in 1854 but did not see wide success in music until he was 62 years old. He is one of the few opera composers of the 20th century to have multiple works performed regularly at the Met. Of his nine operas, the Met has staged four of them: *Jenůfa, Káťa Kabanová, The Makropulos Case* (sometimes titled *The Makropulos Affair*), and *From the House of the Dead*. The City Opera has a fine production of his opera *The Cunning Little Vixen* (1924), as well.

Janáček's orchestral and chamber music is somewhat well known outside of the Czech Republic, but his reputation rests mostly on his operas. This is even more surprising because he doesn't fit into any composition category very neatly. It's not romantic music, it's post-Wagner, it's kind of modern, but not really, it's sort of melodic, but again, not entirely. Most musicologists refer to Janáček as a forerunner of what would come after him. He became very interested in Moravian folk music, and like Bartok, Stravinsky and others who would latch onto similar source material, Janáček found freshness in the traditions of his people.

In his operas, words are set to music in an unusual way. He was the librettist for all of his later operas. In his operatic works, the sounds of spoken language dictate, in part, the composition. The inflections, nuances, cadences, and accented lilts of the language are translated by Janáček into the music. He sounds like no one else. This parity of language and music makes perfect sense, but we forget how original a concept it is. As an experiment, notice how your own voice musicalizes words. Out loud, say, "I don't know. What do you think?" Say it again, slowly. Notice how the pitch rises and falls. There are accents and rhythms inherently in the phrases of words. We are composing music when we speak. This composer relished those found objects, the music that already exists in spoken language. That is one of the things that makes him modern.

Unfortunately for its audiences, the Met has presented Janáček's operas in languages other than Czech until quite recently. In 1924, the Met gave the U.S. premiere of *Jenůfa*, in German. At the same time, he was working on his final, great operas, and his music was being championed throughout Europe. That was not to be the case in the U.S. Here is an excerpt of the 1924 review by Irving Weil of the *Evening Standard,*

> Why Mr. Gatti-Casazza ever came to look hopefully upon "Jenůfa" would be a mystery if one did not happen to think that he has in his company a Bohemian conductor, a Bohemian ballet master who, nevertheless, is given to offering advice, and a Moravian prima donna. Probably all three were too much for him and therefore, "Jenůfa."

> But no one ought to take it into his head from this that

"Jenůfa" is the worst opera we have ever heard. As a fact, it is a long way from that. The unforgettable "Mona" of Horatio Parker, the "Cyrano de Bergerac" of Walter Damrosch, "The Polish Jew" of—who was it wrote that one?—were immeasurably worse. Indeed, now we have begun cataloguing, we can think of a score or so far, far worse. But "Jenůfa" is quite worse enough.[3]

Fifty years passed without any more Janáček at the Met at all. When Ariel Bybee performed a role in *Jenůfa* in 1985, she sang in English. But in the early 1990s, the Met rolled out four new productions by the composer. How to account for the sudden rediscovery of Janáček? I think there were two reasons. The first is the advocacy of conductors and singers who believed in his music strongly and could perform these works in their native language. The second is the arrival at the Met of the subtitle system that permitted everyone to understand the texts. I suspect that part of the problem with presenting Janáček in English and German (and that's what the Met did for many years) was that it just didn't sound very good. If the music is built upon the idiosyncrasies of the Czech language, I can't imagine that a translation in English or German would be completely effective.

The Makropulos Case I saw on January 1, 1996—it's listed as an Act I fragment in the Met archives—was to be sung in English by Jessye Norman. I suppose it's a lot to ask of a singer to learn Czech for a role. There are a few other works in the language, operas by Smetana, Dvořák, and Martinů; but they are rarities. Still, non-native speakers have performed these operas, and my soprano tonight, Karita Mattila, will be singing it in Czech. She is a Finnish singer who prides herself on the strength of her acting. I happened to be in the house when she made her Met debut in 1990, as Donna Elvira in *Don Giovanni*. At the time, her voice struck me as one of the most beautiful things I'd ever heard. It was such a clear sound. There was power to spare too, but at the heart of it was directness and purity. To sum it all up, she was the epitome of control—acting, phrasing, breathing, moving, and singing. Her career began in 1983 when she won the inaugural Cardiff Singer of the World competition. Thirty years have passed since then. I've heard her a few times, and I found each portrayal a marvel. The role of Emilia Marty is her third Janáček role at the Met.

I take my seat with some surprise. The house is full. Mattila is a big star at the Met. Her breakthrough role was *Salome*, a performance received with what can only be described as shock and awe. The critic Anthony Tommasini wrote,

> …And I use the word exposed literally. For her slithering and erotic interpretation of Salome's 'Dance of the Seven Veils,' cannily choreographed by Doug Varone and sensually conducted by Valery Gergiev, Ms. Mattila shed item after item of a Marlene Dietrich-like white tuxedo costume until for a fleeting moment she twirled around exultant, half-crazed and completely naked. (No wardrobe

malfunction here.)

Given the physical and emotional toll of her portrayal, that she could also sing this daunting role with such gleaming power, eerie expressivity and, most remarkably of all, beguiling lyricism was stunning. When the opera ended and Ms. Mattila appeared alone before a black curtain, looking spent and dazed, she seemed almost frightened by the vehemence of the audience's applause and shouts of 'Bravo!'[4]

The critic described her voice in a way that I think captures Mattila's allure as an artist,

The actual nudity may have taken less courage than the psychological nudity Ms. Mattila exposed in the final scene, when, delirious with power, she held Jochanaan's head in her hands and sang Strauss's soaring phrases with Wagnerian thrust and unflagging energy. At times her sound in the top notes was earthy and strange, even raw. But I'm not quibbling here, just describing Ms. Mattila's vocally and physically audacious performance.[5]

Makropulos begins with a staged prelude. I vaguely remember it from having seen it before. The main feature visually is a large billboard with Mattila's face (Emilia Marty's face) in a glamorous headshot, something like Warhol's Marilyn Monroe without the vulgar coloration. When the story moves to Act I (there are three short acts), I recognize the lawyer's office. There, on stage left, are the endless rows of grey cabinets. The tenor Alan Oke begins to sing about an unresolved legal case, 100 years old. He sings the line about people who live too long, and another, about each of us returning "dust to dust". I hadn't remembered that moment which was so full of irony in a performance with a singer moments away from his death. I'm uneasy during this scene. Muscle memory, I guess. The queasiness is ameliorated by the fact that the staging has been reworked. The tenor no longer scrambles up the ladder as he sings. In fact, there is no ladder at all. While it makes no visual sense to have an entire wall of file cabinets without any way to open them, I'm happy to see it gone.

At the place in the opera when I watched the tenor suffer a heart attack and collapse onstage, I nod my head for a second or two. And I realize that we are only two minutes into the opera. Maybe three. I had forgotten that. It was only beginning.

With this baggage now out of the way, I feel free to experience the opera without reservations. Mattila makes a big entrance— the soprano is a glamorous woman, and this part fits her like a glove. Almost before I know it, the first act is over. After the experience of Wagner and his unhurried pacing, this opera that began at 8:30 and will end shortly after 11:00 (including two intermissions) is passing by in a flash.

The plot is about a baron's estate. One character claims to be the heir, but it is contested by another. Such as it is, this is the drama of the opera. Emilia Marty is an opera star. As the story progresses, we learn that she was given a recipe to extend her life 300 years. She is a sexual magnet for all of the men she sees, and by the time the opera ends, she will have seduced, rebuffed, destroyed, and toyed with all of them. When one of the men commits suicide because he loves her without hope of requital, she dismisses the tragedy out of hand. Marty is the stereotype of an opera diva, and the role has been played that way, by real-life divas. It's a powerful part, but not an especially taxing one, vocally. And if I dare say it, Marty's a perfect role for an aging opera singer to play. Brünnhilde, it is not.

In Act III, Matilla really shines in an extended revelation about her past. We learn that as a young girl, Marty was given a potion by her father, a court physician. He had been ordered to create a magic elixir for the emperor. The potion was tested on Marty. When she fell into a coma, her father was imprisoned as a fraud. Later, Marty awakened and began her long life. The 300-year extension is wearing off now, and she helps solve the estate case in order to gain access to the chemical formula that is buried among its legal papers. She confesses to all her story, and exhausted, she says she no longer has any will to live. Another character in the opera, a singing protégé of Marty, takes the formula and sets it on fire. As she does, Marty falls to the floor and the giant portrait of the diva also bursts into flame.

The *Times* said,

As much as Puccini's "Tosca,'" Verdi's "Aida" or Berg's "Lulu," Janáček's 1926 opera, "The Makropulos Case," comes across as the stunning masterpiece it is only if a production has a soprano who can inhabit the lead role. Here that character is Emilia Marty, the mysterious prima donna at the center of this suspenseful thriller, set in Prague in 1922. On Friday night Karita Mattila sang Marty when the Metropolitan Opera brought back the sleekly modern and inspired 1996 production by Elijah Moshinsky, last seen in 2001.

Before we meet her we learn that Marty is a sensational opera singer, mesmerizing on and off the stage. And at her first appearance, in which Marty shows up unexpectedly in the office of Dr. Kolenaty, a lawyer, Ms. Mattila was electrifying before she had sung a note. The lighting captured the luster of her blond hair, pale blue dress and knowing smile. This is what you call charisma. Ms. Mattila's voice may have lost some of the bloom, security and power that made her the Salome of our time at the Met in 2004 (repeated in 2008). But her singing was commanding: cool and cagey one moment, intense and chilling the next.[6]

Memory is a magician. Its sleights of hand—what an experience felt like, looked like, sounded like—conceal workaday routines. The opera is about that, and my experience of revisiting *Makropulos* is about that. The beauty (and the frustration) of a live performance is the eventual acknowledgment that any memory of it can never be fixed as fact. Where are the metrics for its evaluation? Even a taped performance reduces it to the perception of the camera, and much eludes recording. As I listen to Mattila, I am hearing notes and phrases, but it is through the prism of my experience. The question, how does she sound, is distinct from but connected to this: how *did* she sound? And if the voice isn't what it was, can a listener weed through the problems to hear beautiful qualities obfuscated by aging?

Mattila isn't the only singer tonight that I've heard before. The main tenor who is singing the role of Albert Gregor (the chief plaintiff in the case) is sung by Richard Leech. In the late 1980s, he emerged as a potential superstar. He is American, and at the height of the Three Tenors craze, many looked to him, Neil Schicoff, and Jerry Hadley as U.S. alternatives. It was not to be. Leech, in particular, was dogged by a great review. *The New York Times* wrote about his Met debut in La bohème in 1989, "Other than Pavarotti on his best night, I can't think of another tenor I'd rather hear in the part."[7]

He's had a great career, but not a stellar one. The comparison to Pavarotti was fair and flattering but ultimately burdensome and unkind. Tonight, I have a hard time hearing the Leech I used to know. He's put on a lot of weight, his voice is still powerful, but it's shouty and stiff. Without seeing his name in the program, I'd never believe that he was the same tenor I heard years ago. Mattila, on the other hand, is as radiant as ever. Her voice doesn't behave like it used to, but I tend to like voices that feel lived-in.

At the end of the evening, I exit the opera house feeling a bit sad. The season is over. This experiment of going to lots of opera performances, reading reviews and news stories, talking to performers, and digging through research in a concentrated amount of time is done. I doubt that I'll ever give myself over to opera in this way again. The themes of *Makropulos* are weighing on me too. On Sunday, Mother's Day, I tried to remember my mother, and it is becoming increasingly difficult to recall specifics. Both of my parents were unafraid of dying. They talked to me of their views of legacy and living wills when they were in their early 50s—that's my age. If someone offered me 300 extra years of life on earth right now, I don't think I'd take it, either.

CHAPTER 12

THE SEASONS ENDS. The LDS singers are set to go their separate ways. It will be a busy summer for them. Erin Morley sings the soprano soloist in *Carmina Burana* with the New York Philharmonic, Rafael Frühbeck de Burgos conducting, and the third symphony of Carl Nielsen, Alan Gilbert conducting, at the end of May and the middle of June. Then she goes to Santa Fe Opera for a leading role in *King Roger* by Karol Szymanowski opposite Polish baritone opera star, Mariusz Kwiecien.[1]

Nicholas Pallesen is singing the role of Pluto right now at the New York City Opera in Telemann's *Orpheus*. *The New York Times* lauded his performance, which continues through mid-May. Pallesen is a winner of many competitions, awards, and career grants. The most recent and most prestigious is the 2012 Richard Tucker Career Grant of $10,000. He goes to Santa Fe this summer as well, in a workshop of Theodore Morrison's *Oscar*, in July. The newly-commissioned opera based on the life of Oscar Wilde will premiere in 2013, and Pallesen takes the role of Walt Whitman. In the fall, he returns to the Met covering the role of Sebastian in the opera *The Tempest* by Thomas Adès, and Marullo in *Rigoletto* in early 2013. Next April, he will tackle the title role of Rigoletto at Shreveport Opera, where he was named Singer of the Year.[2]

Tamara Mumford travels to Los Angeles at the end of May

for four performances of the world premiere of John Adams's oratorio based on the Passion, *The Gospel According to the Other Mary*, at Disney Concert Hall, libretto by Peter Sellars from the Bible and contemporary Latin American poetry. She will be singing the contralto part of Martha. Gustavo Dudamel conducts the L.A. Philharmonic. Mumford will be a soloist with the Billingham Festival of Music (Washington) in July (Mozart, *Mass in C Minor*) before returning to New York to sing the alto soloist in Mahler/Schoenberg, *Das Lied von der Erde* (chamber orchestra version arranged by Schoenberg) with the New York Philharmonic and Emanuel Ax, pianist, in November. She takes the title role of Rossini's *La Cenerentola* in January 2013 at the Seattle Opera, and then reprises the Adams oratorio on tour with the L.A. Philharmonic in Paris, Lucerne, London, and New York in the spring.[3]

Opera-goers at the Met will have many more opportunities to hear Ginger Costa-Jackson in the 2012-2013 season. But first she sings *Nixon in China* at the San Francisco Opera in June. At the Met next season, she will sing Mercedes in *Carmen* (September, October and February, March) and Smaragdi in *Francesca da Rimini* (March) and she will cover Cherubino in *Le nozze di Figaro* (October and November) and Ascagne in *Les Troyens* (December and January).[4]

It isn't too surprising that during the upcoming Wagner biennial next year, Wendy Bryn Harmer will be performing multiple *Ring* cycles. At the Metropolitan in April, she will sing in *Das*

Rheingold and *Götterdämmerung*. In August of 2013, she will sing the same, multiple roles in Seattle.[5]

Nina Warren is engaged to sing Mrs. Lovett in *Sweeney Todd* in the fall before going to Palermo, Italy for *Die Walküre* in February and March. She'll be back next spring at the Met covering the *Ring* cycle Brünnhildes. The Met will perform three complete cycles in April.[6] There will be a lot of Nibelungs around the world. But Nina Warren writes in an email to me that perhaps she will step away from some of these engagements. This is where real life enters into the picture for these LDS singers. In Warren's case, she has a family to think about. Her twins are now entering college, and her elderly father is ailing. When the children were younger—the twins were practically born on the stage of the Met—they loved to travel the world, and wherever Nina sang, her husband and children tagged along. But their youngest daughter is now entering high school, and Nina wonders whether uprooting her is the right thing to do. She writes to me about the hardship of being in New York this season, far away from her teenage children.

That dilemma—the lifestyle of the international opera singer and the consequences for their families—is worth exploring in the context of these LDS singers. The young singers at the Met are flexible enough to be able to travel wherever the work is. Having watched this phenomenon for 25 years, I see a certain pattern. The LDS opera singer comes up through the ranks. If they become established enough, they have a big choice to make:

do they settle down in one place, or do they jet set? Ariel Bybee, for the most part, planted her feet at the Met. She had a husband and a daughter, and they lived a relatively normal life diagonally across the street from Lincoln Center. Others have traveled a different route. They have made a name for themselves and then, when children arrived, they moved to an academic environment, as voice teachers who continued to take singing roles, sparingly. Not all of the LDS singers are married, nor do all of the married singers have children. But for those who have both spouses and children, this debate about lifestyle is a constant topic of anxiety for them.

In a way, singing at the Met is a pretty good gig for a young mother or father. Once the opening night is out of the way and all of the rehearsals are finished, performing at the Met is as easy as showing up two or three times a week for a few weeks, singing your role, picking up your check, and going home. Opera engagements don't include housing and living expenses, so it's burdensome for the singers to arrange for the necessary childcare and short-term housing in big cities. There's no single way to approach the challenges. Some LDS singers have lived in the suburbs and have commuted to work as needed.

The operatic LDS fathers have relied upon their wives for childcare. The operatic mothers seem to have a more complex set of circumstances. If they are based elsewhere, and their husbands work, they sometimes leave their families behind—if it is going to be a short engagement—or they bring a nanny along with them and the children. I know a few instances where their husbands became stay-at-home dads while the children were young and then developed careers of their own as the children entered school. In the case of one of the Met singers this year, her husband is a professor who had an arrangement with his university to spend most of the school year in New York.

The singers who are in the Lindemann Program tend to be permanently based in New York. They do a lot of covering of roles, coaching, and rehearsing, and as a result, they need to be close; otherwise, they'd spend their lives on a plane. But a few LDS singers are starting international careers without a home base.

The topic of women working is a lightning rod for Mormons no matter where you live. Obviously, all Mormon women work. Ask any LDS mother with young children if what they are doing is work. Better yet, don't ask unless you want a death glare aimed at your head. A cynic would say the question is not whether Mormon women should work but rather should they make money.

My mother ran a drapery business out of our house, and my sisters all had part-time jobs when their children were young and full-time jobs later. My wife works now. I'm sensitive to this issue, but I have no opinion for those who are trying to decide what is best for their families. I leave that to them.

A few years ago, I was speaking to a mother in one of the church congregations in Manhattan. She told me about her daughter who is a musician. As a young child, the girl showed exceptional promise on the violin. The parents supported her, gave her lessons and opportunities. She went to Juilliard as a pre-college student, and later, studied with Josef Gingold, the legendary violinist and teacher, at Indiana University. He took on two private students: her and Joshua Bell. She's a brilliant musician and a close friend. Her mother said to me, "What is a young Mormon girl supposed to do who has talent? She is taught to develop those gifts and that they come from God, but is she supposed to abandon them as an adult?" That's an excellent point.

And don't say tell me that playing in church once in a while and teaching music lessons to neighborhood children is going to satisfy these artists; it isn't. My heart goes out to those who are trying to figure out all of these things. It is more than a question of moneymaking. Artists at this level have well-defined identities as performing artists. How can you say to one of them, now go home and forget all of this?

Some time ago, I was helping the concert pianist Grant Johannesen write his memoir. He grew up in Salt Lake City, and on the occasion of his debut with the New York Philharmonic (George Szell was the guest conductor), many of his friends and family from Utah traveled to New York for the concert. Afterwards, people rushed up to him with their congratulations. There had never been an artist from the Church who was poised to have a career like this. And indeed, it was to become a world-class career; he was one of the great pianists of his generation. On the night of his debut, the ward bishop walked up to Grant after the concert and said, "I'm so glad that you've got this out of your system. Now you can come back and be our ward organist again." Grant told me this story with horrified disbelief some five decades afterwards. It still stung. And I believe it adversely affected his life.

The Mormon prejudice regarding sending its young people out into the world to have careers that are different than their parents' is something that I hope is diminishing. More than anything else, this limiting notion has held back Mormon artists in many fields, but particularly in the performing arts. It is a holdover from darker days in the Church's history, when outsiders were viewed as threats to the community's safety, when they circled the wagons. It is a provincialism that is at odds with a broader desire to engage with the population in the world, all of whom it sees as literal brothers and sisters. At the heart of the bias is a doubt that individual belief can withstand opposition. In the minds of many LDS parents, it's a scary prospect to send a child into an atmosphere that includes dangers. And the world of opera is potentially a scary one. Although I could say the same thing about Wall Street, the military, professional sports, or any number of professions, including the profession of not having one at all.

I sat down with one of the Met's Mormon singers and asked her about the issues involved with the perception of opera as a fit (or unfit) endeavor for a believing Christian. She told me that as a student, she encountered an attitude of, *Enjoy it now because it won't last; you can't have a career and a family.* But she once sang with the Mormon Tabernacle Choir as a soloist, and the director at the time, Craig Jessop, gave her advice that she continues to rely upon. Essentially, he said, "You will hear a lot of opinions from a lot of people. Don't worry about anything other than learning how to sing and staying close to the Lord."

I suspect that what these younger LDS singers need is a few years of flexibility. The arc of their careers will make some of these work/life decisions for them. Not all of the singers will still be singing in large venues ten years from now. Even if all of them (and the generation that is undoubtedly following in their footsteps) want full-time careers as performers, they are likely to have more scheduling flexibility once they leave the hothouse of apprenticeships and role covering. They will sing here for a role, and then there. They will become freelancers with its attendant freedoms. At that point, they can live anywhere they choose. They can turn down offers that don't align with their goals. They can dovetail family schedules with their professional calendar; at least, that's the hope.

John Taylor, the third president of the Church of Jesus Christ of Latter-day Saints made this prediction in 1857,

> You mark my words, and write them down and see if they do not come to pass. You will see the day that Zion

will be far ahead of the outside world in everything per-
taining to learning of every kind as we are today in regard
to religious matters. God expects Zion to become the
praise and glory of the whole earth, so that kings hearing
of her fame will come and gaze upon her glory....[7]

Spencer W. Kimball elaborated on this prophesy in a speech to
Brigham Young University faculty and staff in 1967. Later, it was
published in the Church magazines as "The Gospel Vision of the
Arts." It is something that all creative artists who are LDS—in
my experience—have taken seriously, and they quote from it like
a mantra. At the same time, unable to point to the artists of distinction from the Church, many also feel like it is perpetually,
tantilizingly close, but may never come to pass.

The Kimball article begins with opera, "With regards to masters, surely there must be many Wagners in the Church, approaching him or yet to come in the tomorrows—young people
with a love of art, talent supreme, and eagerness to create. I hope
we may produce men greater than this German composer, Wagner...."[8]

He asks whether there can be another Verdi or Bach from the
ranks of the Church. This speech was a wake-up call for creative
artists in the Church, but it's a misreading to limit it to composers,
painters and writers. Kimball, who was a baritone who sang a solo
at his high school graduation and loved singing before throat cancer destroyed his voice, cited opera singers in the article:

Is there anyone who has not been stirred by the rich

melodic voice of Enrico Caruso, Italian-born operatic tenor? Surely there have been few voices which have inspired so many. Considered to be the greatest voice of his century by many, year after year he was the chief attraction at the Metropolitan Opera. Would someone say that they produce singers best in Italy, in Germany, in Poland, or Sweden? Remember we draw our members from all of these places. The gospel attracts many and stirs their blood with the messages of the ages, and they sing songs of accomplishment, eternal marriage, exaltation.

He continues and talks of other great opera stars of the past, Adeline Maria Patti, Jenny Lind, and Mme. Schumann-Heink. He quotes the prophet Brigham Young, "Every accomplishment, every polished grace, every useful attainment in mathematics, music, and in all sciences and art belong to the Saints."

Next, Kimball talks about LDS singers,

As I have traveled throughout the Church, many times I have been entranced with sweet and lovely voices. I believe that deep in the throats of these faithful Saints of today and tomorrow are superior qualities which, superbly trained, can equal or surpass these known great singers. Members of the Church should be peers or superiors to any others in natural ability, extended training, plus the Holy Spirit which should bring them light and truth. With hundreds of 'men of God' and their associates so blessed, we have the base for an increasingly efficient and worthy corps of talent.

In a challenge to all creative artists in the Church, President Kimball next asked a simple question, "In the field of both composition and performance, why cannot someone write a greater oratorio than Handel's Messiah?" And he questions, flatly, "Why not?"

He makes a statement that must have seemed ludicrous at the time, and I'm quite sure that until the current election cycle, nobody gave it a serious thought. Kimball stated, "Perhaps growing up in a backwoods forest in Indiana or Louisiana or in Oregon or Illinois, there may be some little deprived boy doing his elementary math on a wood fire shovel and borrowing books from neighbors and splitting rails, who will find his way tomorrow to the knowledge and inspiration which will send him skyrocketing to fame and honors, *perhaps even to the White House*, and a man to be ever after heralded for his wisdom, bravery, conscience, humanity, leadership, and to be quoted till eternity." (italics added)

I wonder now how fully Kimball was imagining the years to come. Was he merely asking LDS artists to think bigger? Was he predicting the future? The speech has been parsed endlessly within the Church. But at its heart is a simple question: why not?

I don't wish to make too big a deal of this feeling that I have, but here are these singers of great accomplishment—six of them in a single year engaged by the Metropolitan Opera. They are not "the six" but rather six of many in their field who are achieving part of what President Kimball urged in this sermon that was published churchwide in 1977, after he became the twelfth president of the Church. What now? I think change is coming.

Yet, I'm not convinced that a singer's religious identity is of any interest to an audience. I know that New York Jets football quarterback, Tim Tebow is devoutly Christian, for example, and he gets praise and criticism for the unabashedness of his belief. He drops to his knees in prayer on the field after scoring a touchdown, he writes verses of the Bible on his face before every game, and so forth.

But I can't think of any great singers, even historical ones, whose religious views were especially important to their public. I could be wrong, but I can't think of exceptions. Nor do I want it, particularly. I'm not hoping that one of these LDS singers will wear a CTR ring at their next recital at Carnegie Hall or will write "Mor. 10:5" under their eyes in black liner before stepping before the footlights at the Hollywood Bowl. But change is coming in other ways.

Running parallel to the arrival of opera singers onto the current music scene—and concert pianists, symphonic and chamber artists, choral conductors, pop and rock stars, actos, and any number of other LDS performing artists—is an equally distinguished group of Mormon composers of fine art music. These men and women are practically unknown to members of the Church. I recently had a conversation with a Mormon opera singer about this. She is having a fine career: big roles at big opera houses, with glowing reviews trailing behind her. I asked her about contemporary Mormon composers. A blank expression fell over her face? "Are there any?" she asked.

For the next few minutes, I did my best to bring her up to speed by asking questions and then answering them myself. Have Mormon composers had their work performed by the biggest symphonies in the country? Yes. Have they been recorded by the top labels and with the best American conductors? Yes. Are they receiving commissions by the leading new music ensembles in the country? Yes. Do they win major prizes and awards? Yes. Are they graduating from the best conservatories? Yes. And are they studying with the most influential composers and teachers? Yes. Are the LDS students getting important fellowships, workshops, residencies, and grants? Yes. Do Mormon composers' works appear with the leading recording labels of new music? Yes. Are the composers who are also academics working at prestigious universities in the country? Yes.

I gave a list, as best as I could muster off the top of my head, of these Mormon composers' recent accomplishments, and I dropped all of the appropriate names associated with them: Chicago Symphony, National Endowment for the Arts, American Composers Orchestra, National Symphony, New York New Music Ensemble, Arditti String Quartet, Alameida Theater, O'Neill Music Conference, American Music Center, Aaron Copland Fellowship, American Academy of Arts and Letters Grant, the Academy of France Prix de Rome, Minnesota Orchestra, IRCAM, Albany Records, Capstone Records, Symphony Space, Utah Symphony, Harvard, Eastman, Juilliard, Indiana University, American Composers Alliance, Meet the Composer, Pew Charitable Trust, Hilliard Ensemble, Speculum Musicae, ASCAP/SCI, Barlow Endowment, Charles Ives Scholarship, Ensemble Inter-Contemporain of Paris, Dallas Chamber Orchestra, Seattle Symphony, Kennedy Center for the Performing Arts, Aspen Music Festival, Fulbright fellowship, American Music Center....

Enjoying my little game of Stump the Soprano, I then asked how many operas she could name written by Mormon composers. There was a long pause. I think she was hoping that I'd say zero, if only to make her feel better—she is an excellently-trained, brainy singer, by the way, who graduated from one of the nation's preeminent music schools before heading off to New York and the Met. I said that I'm not positively sure of the total number of Mormon operas ever written, but I know of 81. Her jaw fell slack. I knew what the next question would be, if she dared to ask it: are any of them any good?

Here's what I know about Mormons, opera, and Mormon operas. The genre, as it were, started a long time ago. The Mormon opera, *Deseret, A Saint's Afflictions,* appeared in New York in October 1880. Its composer, Dudley Buck, who was not a member of the Church, capitalized on the American hysteria about polygamy and fashioned a comedic melodrama of cavalry soldiers, native Americans, a Salt Lake City polygamist and his wives, one baby and an unscrupulous Indian agent.

I became aware of this opera only recently, when Darrell Babidge, Assistant Professor of Voice at Brigham Young University. In response to an inquiry about this opera, Janet Bradford, head of the Music/Dance Library at BYU, discovered a libretto for Deseret in the Harold B. Lee Library collection. She led us to a selection of arias that were published and are now housed, and available as PDF files, at the Library of Congress.

It's not a particularly subtle work. There is an operetta-like playfulness in its text. Think Gilbert and Sullivan's "I Am the Very Model of a Modern Major General" as you read this aria sung by the villainous character, Joseph Jessup:

"I fear that the Lieutenant may discover my duplicity,

And not believe that I was driven to it by necessity;

So I will git me up and git and fly from this vicinity,

And take with me a specimen of Mormon femininity."

I cringe when I say *Deseret* is a Mormon opera. Buck's opera (libretto by W. A. Croffut) and another opera named *Deseret* by Leonard Kastle (libretto by Anne Howard Bailey), which was commissioned and broadcast by NBC-TV in 1961, are Mormon operas in the way that the Puccini's *La bohème* is French. That is, not very.

So what about Mormon opera (translation: operas written by Mormons)? Until recently, I would not have dared to take a stab at a comprehensive list. I couldn't say whether there were 10, 20, or maybe even more. With a little extra time on my hands over the holidays last year, I found myself flipping through library card catalogs, online composers' sites, and talking to a few friends. Here's what I found.

I'm aware of 81 operas written by Mormons and a handful of other operas that have Mormon characters in them. The Mormons' operas range from works performed in the early days of Salt Lake City pioneers to the most recent by the Mormon composer Douglas Pew, *A Game of Hearts*, which will be premiered this November by the Washington National Opera at Kennedy Center as part of its inaugural American Opera Initiative.

I suspect the final tally of every opera by a Mormon composer, if we knew everything collecting dust in attics and elsewhere (or worse: unknown and lost), would be something north of 100 scores. These are not oratorios, musicals, cantatas, song cycles, or orchestral works with vocal soloists (that number would be very large indeed); these are operas.

This is an amazing number for a bunch of reasons. For all its patronage of music, the Church is not in the business of staging operas, although its universities have done it with some regularity. Opera composers have written these works without the kind of benefaction otherwise available to creative artists in LDS culture. Said another way, there are no operas on display at Temple Square in Salt Lake City. Operas are expensive to stage, take a long time to write, and carry high risks for all involved. An opera is an ante, upped. So the existence of any Mormon operas is something of a miracle. Repeatedly, as I talked to LDS composers in my research, they were surprised to learn that anyone else in the Church was writing opera. 81 is a big number.

Singers should not feel bad that they don't know much about Mormon opera. As Mormon scholarship goes, almost nothing has been written on the subject. I guess these composers are not the kind of pioneers that have attracted attention. Even specialists whom I would imagine to know such things are in the dark. Here's what I mean: go to a Church university and ask a vocal major or a composition major to sing something from a Mormon opera, and you'll get a blank stare. Ask an opera company with an LDS director or with Church members on its board if it has ever produced Mormon work, and they'll look at you like you're from Mars. Walk through a Church-friendly bookstore and look for a CD bin with the label "Mormon Opera." You'll be looking a long time.

I can give an overview of the Mormon operas I've found. Some of the Church's most-loved composers have tried their hands at opera, including Evan Stephens (*The May Queen or the Innocents Saved, Gypsy Maids*, and *Old Maids*, all circa 1880), Leroy Robertson (*Pegeen*, 1971, incomplete), Merrill Bradshaw (*Coriantumr*, 1967 fragment), and Crawford Gates (*Joseph! Joseph!*, 2005).

But here's something intriguing: more than two-thirds of Mormon operas have been written in the past 20 years. How to account for that? I'm not sure. Several LDS composers have written only one opera, but the bulk of Mormon operas have been written by composers who specialize in the genre. Three composers have written seven or more, and five other composers have two or more operas to their credit.

Christian Asplund, composer-in-residence at Brigham Young University, has written seven chamber operas to date, his most recent is provocatively titled, *History of Church, A Family Home Opera* (2006). I particularly love *The Archivist* (1996, libretto by Lara Candland), which I find mysterious and edgy. Asplund's operas bend expectations and rethink what music and drama have to say to each other.

Murray Boren's 10 operas (about the same number Puccini finished) are big, more traditional opera house scores. Starting as a student at BYU in the 1970s and then returning to its composition faculty later, his operas have alternated between religious and secular sources. His operas adapted from secular literature are based on medieval mystery plays, W. B. Yeats (*The Only Jealousy of Emer*, 1973), James Joyce (*The Dead*, 1993) and Willa Cather (*The Singer's Romance*, 1998). The librettists for his religious works have included Orson Scott Card (*Abraham & Isaac*, 1977) and Eric Samuelsen (*Emma*, 1983 and *Eliza*, 2004).

Two of Boren's operas have been heard in New York. After an extended excerpt from *Emma* was performed at Weill Recital Hall in 1986, the *Times* critic John Rockwell nudged producers to present the entire work in his concert review. The New York production in 1992 of *Emma* was reviewed in the *Times* by Allan

Kozinn, who described the music this way, "The orchestral music, conducted by Mr. Boren, had an eerie, clustery, interestingly textured sound, something like mid-1960's Ligeti, peppered with hints of Minimalist figuration."[9] The other Boren opera to be produced in New York was *The Dead*, which premiered Halloween night, 1993, at the Vineyard Theater.

Boren also crafted two operas from the Book of Mormon (*Mormon/Moroni*, 1987). For the bicentennial celebration of Joseph Smith's birth, Boren composed *The Book of Gold* (2005). (I was his librettist for *The Dead, The Book of Gold,* and *The Singer's Romance,* 1998.) The Joseph Smith opera was produced, recorded and telecast by BYU TV. It starred Metropolitan Opera singers Ariel Bybee and Jennifer Welch-Babidge. Darrell Babidge sang the role of Joseph Smith, Jr.

A number of the Mormon opera composers are quite young. For all the talk about the graying audience for classical music, young people are flocking to the dramatic intensity of the form, and its audience base is expanding, particularly through new media and innovative broadcasting. Young composers are drawn to the possibilities of opera. Young LDS composers have developed relationships with performance groups in their communities and a few have even founded theatrical companies themselves. Some of these entrepreneurial adventures are happening far from Utah, and perhaps for that reason, they are under the radar of many church members and its publications.

It won't surprise anybody to learn that many Mormon operas

have very little, if anything, to do with stories or characters overtly LDS. To my mind, that doesn't make them any less Mormon. Two thematic exceptions are recent operas by Harriet Petherick Bushman, *Long Walk Home* (2006) that tells the story of the Willie and Martin handcart companies, and Crawford Gates' *Joseph! Joseph!* (2005) that portrays the frontier prophet, both of which had performances in Salt Lake City in 2006. M. Ryan Taylor's *Abinadi* (2003) is the most recent composer to set a Book of Mormon story as an opera. A production was staged at BYU shortly after Taylor's M.F.A. graduation. Abinadi comes a generation after Merrill Bradshaw started (and then stopped) work on the opera *Coriantumr* (1967), based on a play by Clinton Larson.

The Mormon opera composers who are using secular texts are high-minded and literary. Their operas tackle writers such as Plato and Aeschylus (Peter McMurray, *A Rooster for Asclepius,* 2008), Nathaniel Hawthorne (Rowan Taylor, *The Birthmark,* 1960), Oscar Wilde (Jeanette Boyack, *The Birthday of the Infanta,* 1957), and Cervantes (William Call, *Camila o El Curiosos Impertinente,* 1987/2007).

For a time, these composers seemed to be waiting for patronage within LDS culture, if not from the Church itself. Perhaps they've thrown up their hands now and are going it alone. From my point of view, the most exciting news is that they are at work. Unlike many composers in the Church whose output seems restricted to rearranging hymns, all of these artists are creating something bold and new. To me, this is as it should be; it is what artists do.

In addition to the young turks, there are a number of operas by our most recognized composers. I attended a semi-staged reading with orchestra at Symphony Space in New York of Marie Barker Nelson's update of the Orpheus legend, *Orpheus Lex,* an opera completed in 2005. It was a marvelous evening. In her version of the classic story, Orpheus is a folk singer in Idaho. I also found operas for children on the list, particularly some of the operas by Charis Bean Duke that were written to be performed by children. I especially liked a sweet aria, "What a Girl" from *The Adventures of Tom Sawyer* (2008).

I came across the story of Leroy Robertson and his opera, *Pegeen* in his biography. He was at the end of his life. He had a bad heart, and his body was speedily failing, particularly his sight. He had spent a lifetime dedicated to music at the highest level. For a time, he was one of the most decorated composers in America. And he had committed his life to the Church and to church music. Robertson had been thinking of tackling an opera project for years and finally settled upon J. M. Synge's *Playboy of the Western World.* It would be his last composition. Despite near blindness, he made his own adaptation of the play and composed the first of three acts. Then, he showed it to colleagues in New York who were enthusiastic. He continued to write. This must have been a physically heroic undertaking. At the time of his death in 1971, the piano-vocal score for *Pegeen* was completed for the first two acts and much of the third. His manuscripts are in boxes at the University of Utah J. Willard Marriott Library, waiting.

Sadly, I haven't heard as much of these operas as I'd like. I'm no expert on them. But I am curious. I want to hear all of John Laurence Seymour's operas. I want to hear music from the group of dissertation operas, as I call them, works that were completed for a university degree by these composers, almost certainly were never performed, and hint at what might have happened had the composers had time, a little money, and somebody to tell them to keep going. I say it's not too late.

What is missing in Mormon opera is advocacy. Fortunately, some of this music is available online, and the composers are eager to oblige those whose are interested with access to musical scores. Libraries have more of this music than you'd imagine. The primary repository today for Mormon opera is the Music/Dance Library at BYU. It is becoming a major archive of LDS scores, recordings and documents in part because it let it be known to LDS composers that their music was welcome there. If I were an LDS composer, I would make a habit of sending one copy of everything I wrote to the library. Some composers have web sites with bits of their work available for free listening and download. Because of the costs of recording an opera in a studio, very few of these works are available commercially. I encourage Mormon opera singers and interested others to go exploring.

81 is a big number, but it's not the half of it for Mormon singers. For every one of these operatic works by LDS composers,

there are literally dozens of art songs, cantatas, oratorios, and other pieces of vocal music ideally suited for them. Many of the excellent, emerging class of LDS composers are writing vocal music, although a relative few are writing full operas. This is where it gets interesting. The economics of programming an opera is overwhelming. But for an opera singer who is putting together a recital or imagining a recording, for example, these young Mormon composers solve a key problem of an LDS singer's identity: how to portray spiritual belief from the stage?

I'm aware of many works by LDS composers that would be a perfect fit for Mormon vocal artists. And the next, progressive step after that is collaboration of new works. Almost all of the Mormon singers—certainly those at the Met—excel in contemporary music. The challenges of a modern score pose few restrictions to them. What would a match of Mormon composers and singers be like?

What would it mean to an LDS composer to know that a truly gifted LDS singer would be performing their new work? I guarantee that it would alter the level of the composition; it couldn't possibly be otherwise. These singers can simply do things technically that others can't. This would be a door-opener, creatively, for a composer. The by-product for the singer might be powerful, personal works that are specifically tailored to them.

This, I believe, is what President Kimball foresaw thirty-five years ago. I am not especially interested in presenting Mormon hymns and arrangements of them to the larger public. What I'm hoping for is the Mormon equivalent of Britten's *War Requiem,* Adams' *On the Transmigration of Souls,* Messiaen's *Saint François d'Assise,* Bernstein's *Chichester Psalms,* Reich's *Different Trains,* Barber's *Knoxville: Summer of 1915,* and Stravinsky's *Symphony of Psalms.*

It's dreaming big, I know, but to echo Kimball, I ask, Why not? What, exactly, is the missing component? Tell me. It isn't talent. My opinion is that the ingredients are all there. Who will combine them?

The opera season is over. The singers have left the building, so to speak. The four giant banners that draped the front windows of the Met announcing the *Ring* cycle have come down. The placards on display in front of the building have slowly given way to other interests. The bodies depicting tragic opera figures are now toned ballet bodies. The nomadic American Ballet Theater, which will perform at the Met until July 7, has moved in. ABT occupies the house for several weeks each spring, but it is not the Met; it's a subtenant of the Met. As for the employees of the opera house, some continue to work in the costume shops, the wig shop, and the carpenter's workshops. The rehearsal rooms—one of them with a newly refinished and bouncier floor for dancers— have different occupants now.

The Met is not touring this year. Last June, the entire company went to Japan for two weeks, some of them trembling for their safety. After the March 2011 earthquake, tsunami, and nuclear disasters, Met stars Anna Netrebko, Joseph Calleja, and Jonas Kaufmann all pulled out over concerns about their potential health. But this year, there is none of that drama. Instrumentalists scatter to various summer music festivals, hopefully to rediscover why the fell in love with music in the first place. The singers have jobs with summer opera festivals and other engagements. And the rest, presumably, are happy to have a vacation.

With the season over, what am I to make of it? First of all, it was a heck of a lot of fun going to so many performances and seeing people with whom I feel a personal connection. I think back to the beginning of the season and the Met's ad campaign "Any moment a great moment." I have to admit that despite my grammatical reservations about the tagline, it proved prescient. I experienced these surprises throughout the season in operas new and old. There were moments that I expected to be great and weren't, moments I didn't expect to be great and were, and moments that rose to a level of greatness, as promised.

After all the dust has settled, I'm not entirely sure what a difference this season brought, in the grand scheme of things. The worst news for the company itself was that Levine is out, potentially forever. He is not scheduled to return to conduct at the house where he holds the title of Music Director. I predict that he will never conduct again a full performance at the Metropolitan Opera.

I spoke with a friend who plays in the orchestra, and he said that Levine had sent them an email this week with the sentiment that he hoped to be able to return eventually. But Levine's close friends are not as hopeful. He hasn't been involved with the Lindemann Program this year as Gelb said he was. Maestro Levine has not been a presence at the opera during the season.

This is a titanic shift, akin to the New York Philharmonic losing Leonard Bernstein or the NBC Orchestra losing Arturo Toscanini. Fabio Luisi is a fine replacement temporarily, but it's a patch in a leaking dam. However adroit Peter Gelb is at getting works onstage, he's ultimately not a musical impresario capable of taking the Met to higher musical aspirations. Razzle-dazzle and showmanship aside, the Met is about music, and the expectations are sky high for its musical post. This problem will become more acute as time passes, because Gelb is overly sensitive to critics, and they're about to bring down the hammer on him for musical and artistic decisions, rightly or wrongly. Rich patrons are not especially happy to see critical rants in the papers, and so this thing could spiral out of control rather quickly. Even if Levine does return in 2014, if he's not in top form, the audiences and critics will, however graciously, feel they're being cheated. There will be financial consequences.

I wondered, at the beginning of the 2011-2012 season, whether I would witness any breakout performances of the six LDS singers I planned to follow. In my mind, Tamara Mumford in *Anna Bolena* and Wendy Bryn Harmer in *Götterdämmerung* come closest. I found them to be engaging actors and singers.

Erin Morley and Ginger Costa-Jackson fell into another category. Their roles were not quite as sizable, but both were perfect in their tasks. Erin, in particular, made the most of all three of her *Ring* operas. They are biding their time, essentially, until larger opportunities come their way. They are known entities, both inside the house and outside of it. It's a matter of time for all four of these women.

The two singers that I did not hear at the Met because they were covering roles—Nina Warren and Nicholas Pallesen—are in a separate category. Nina was inches away from going on as Brünnhilde in January. It was a huge "almost". Nina is in a different stage of her career than the others. She had her Met debut in 1992, in *Die Walküre*, and she's performed 24 times more at the Met since then. More significantly for her has been an extensive career elsewhere, singing the biggest roles that a soprano can tackle: Turandot, Salome, Lulu, Brünnhilde, Minnie, Leonore, Senta, Chrysothemis, and Tosca, as well as leading roles in other operas by Schoenberg, Tan Dun, Birtwhistle, Berg, Wagner, Strauss, Zemlinsky, and many others, on the world's biggest stages. It would have been great to hear her again, but I'm not worried for her.

Nicholas Pallesen is busy elsewhere singing, but his Met moment has yet to arrive. After his appearance at the Met National Council Grand Finals concert in 2007, Pallesen has been paying his dues—covering, singing in regional opera productions, racking up impressive awards and career grants. I'm not worried about him either. He's a baritone. Those lower voices are in no hurry, and he is likely to mature into the big-voiced Verdi repertoire. My prediction is that if he goes after it, he can have any kind of career he wants.

If only in my own mind, I debunked some of my prejudices during the season. Opera is not expensive. My average ticket price was about $20 (in New York, it costs $20 to see a movie in 3-D), and I sat in the orchestra section for almost every one of the performances. It was not particularly difficult to get seats either, except for the opening night of the season and end of the season's *Ring* cycle. Other myths? That opera is for an exclusive crowd. Not true. I repeatedly sat next to interesting people who were ordinary folks—not rich, not elitist. Opera isn't just for old people. The most fun I had was taking my 16-year old daughter to the mash-up of Shakespearean plots and Baroque tunes.

Finally, and specifically about the idea of exploring the seasons with LDS singers at the Met, there is something remarkable going on. It may be entirely possible that the Met 2011-2012 season will be seen as a tipping point for arts in the Church. It is a question of critical mass. For example, the singers this year at the Met hung out together, they shared dressing rooms and meals. At a large event in-house, there was an unofficial "Mormon table" of singers.

One soprano told me the story of going to her dressing room and finding the other LDS singer preparing her Relief Society lesson for the next Sunday. When they are together, they talk about home life and how they plan to manage marriage, children, and career. These are small, mostly insignificant anecdotes. And yet, think of what it must feel like for a Mormon singer to have a support system in place of people who are facing the same intense pressures as they are and who understand their religious values.

One of the problems that LDS artists have faced historically is the issue of "them vs. us." Imagine what it means to these singers to have other members of their church rehearsing and performing alongside them. It has to be huge. And then there is the question of how these Mormon singers are perceived by their peers.

It is already happening that others are making positive generalizations about Mormonism based on their interactions with these singers. A Mormon singer is no longer an outlier. There's no longer a novelty attached to it. I expect more and more LDS singers to emerge at the highest ranks of their profession. I almost guarantee it. Perhaps that is the biggest change of all.

I wonder if I dare tackle a bigger question, now: what does the Met singers' church membership mean to me? Can I articulate it as bluntly as to say that it affects my identity? Because at the root of it all, it does. I am a lot of things. I'm a white, male, middle-aged New Yorker. I am a Yankees fan, an opera fan, a gardner, a business owner, a husband and father. Any noun that follows the "I am" is part of me.

For many people of my religion, to say "I am a Mormon" carries the gravity of racial identity. It has to do with permanence. For many of us at church, it is as unlikely that we would change faiths as it is to change genders or skin color. Insults to our faith hurt like racial slurs, and breakthrough successes of those of our faith feel like something worthy of national pride.

The rural towns where I grew up had a single high school in each. The rivalries between the schools/towns were intense. It went beyond fun and games. These rivalries were hate-filled. I know about it first-hand because I moved from one town to its rival and then back again. Things have changed now, but back then, you wouldn't dream of dating or marrying anyone from the rival town. It wasn't done. Folks in my town would say, about the school one hour away, whose colors were red and gold, "I'd rather be dead than red." I grew up taking them at their word.

I think of this kind of inherited identity when I consider being a fan of something. Now, I live in a town where the Yankees fans hate the Red Sox fans, and vice versa. Once, I made the mistake of wearing a Boston Red Sox cap down the street because one of my brother's high school teammates pitched for the Red Sox, and he was going to play in Yankee Stadium. Let's just say I won't make that mistake again.

The passions that we bring to our leisure interests powerfully inform how we think about ourselves. In some ways, I wonder if these chosen characteristics are not even more commanding than inherited ones. The traits of being a fan—love, devotion, fidelity, commitment, passion, belief—overlap with religion affiliation, it seems to me.

What does this have to do with Mormon singers at the Met? I am affected by these singers the way that Jewish baseballs fans were when Sandy Koufax chose not to pitch in Game 1 of the 1965 World Series because the date fell on Yom Kippur. I imagine that for young Jewish boys in Brooklyn, where I used to live when I first moved in New York City, Koufax symbolized that anything was possible. Without doubt, the same thing is happening today with African Americans who follow Barak Obama's leadership in the White House.

For me, the professional accomplishments of Mormon opera singers point to an unusual overlap in things about which I'm proud. Over time, what will the consequences be? Like any breakthough, the individual achievement invites imitation to the point of acceptance and eventually, to a critical mass. I am aware of the changes that these singers might bring to the art of my culture, and I also have an eye on their symbolic importance. For a year, I have followed the performances of six Mormon opera singers in the larger context of a seaon at the best opera house in America. As individual nights in an opera house, they were of historical importance to a relative few.

But I am one of the few.

I walk out of the opera house for the last time this season with a heavy heart. I suspect that I will never devote such concentrated thinking about and listening to opera again. I'll be back. I am a fan, after all. But the Metropolitan has been a siz-able and probably unsustainable part of my life for the last year. The main entrance to the opera house is at ground level, directly inside the glass doors that exit onto the plaza. But there is an-other entrance one level below it, in the concourse. I finish the season by exiting there.

I look at the great wall of photographs that flank the doorway, some 1,000 black-and-white images of singers, directors, conduc-tors, and designers. They span the entire history of the Metro-politan, from 1880 to 2012. These pictures conjure such memories. How many hours have I spent in this building? This year I saw a dozen operas from the Met, but I attended a per-formance here for the first time 31 years ago. How many per-formances have there been for me altogether? A lot.

At the beginning of the season, during the first intermission on opening night, I walked down to these photographs and found the image of Ariel Bybee. At the time I wondered about the future of other Mormon singers at this institution. During the season, I followed the career developments of the six LDS vocalists en-gaged by the Met to sing roles and experienced a glimpse of the range of their talent. What will become of them?

I happen to know—although they are contractually obligated not to give details quite yet—that some of these singers will be performing starring roles in the great opera houses of the world like Vienna, Paris, London, and the Metropolitan in the next two years. This is a stunning achievement. Again, I'm compelled to note that it's unprecedented; it is a breakthrough moment in the history of my culture. And were it to combine with the championing of exisiting and new music by Mormon composers, it would alter the entire culture forever.

As I turn to leave the building, I notice that the Met has hung some new photographs in the alphabetical arrangement of the company's great artits. They have added the images of Wendy Bryn Harmer and Tamara Mumford to the wall of stars, two more LDS singers. They won't be the last.

Notes

Introduction

1. Raymond A. Ericson, Musical America, 3/1960

Chapter 1

1. The New York Times, 9/23/2011

2. The New York Times, 9/27/2011

3. New York Post, 9/27/2011

4. New York Daily News, 9/27/2011

5. The Wall Street Journal, 9/28/2011

6. The New Yorker, 10/11/2011

7. The New York Times, 9/24/2011

8. The New York Times, 10/11/2011

Chapter 2

1. The New York Times, 11/15/1986

2. The New York Times, 10/21/2011

3. The New York Times, 10/22/2011

4. The New York Times, 10/23/2011

5. The New York Times, 12/10/2011

6. The New York Times, 8/16/2011

7. The New York Times, 12/10/2011

8. The New York Times, 10/6/2011

9. operaphila.org

10. operaphila.org

11. The New York Times, 11/10/2011

12. nicomuhly.com

13. out.com, 11/28/2011

Chapter 3

1. Time, 2/4/1935

2. Berkeley Daily Gazette, 10/30/1934

3. The New York Times, 6/19/1934

4. Metropolitan Opera premieres during the Gatti-Casazza era were: La fanciulla del West (Giacomo Puccini, composer, 1910), Königskinder (Engelbert Humperdinck, 1910), Mona (Horatio Parker, 1912), Cyrano (Walter Damrosch, 1913), Madeleine (Victor Herbert, 1914), Madame Sans-Gêne (Umberto Giordano, 1915), Goyescas (Enrique Granados, 1916), The Canterbury Pilgrims (Reginald de Koven, 1917), The Robin Woman: Shanewis (Charles Wakefield Cadman, 1918), Il trittico (Giacomo Puccini, 1918) The Legend (Joseph Carl Breil, 1919), The Temple Dancer (John Adam Hugo, 1919), The Blue Bird (Albert Wolff, 1919), Cleopatra's Night (Henry Kimball Hadley, 1920), The King's Henchman (Deems Taylor, 1927), Peter Ibbetson (Deems Taylor, 1931), The Emperor Jones (Louis Gruenberg, 1933), Merry Mount (Howard Hanson, 1934), and In the Pasha's Garden (John Laurence Seymour, 1935)

5. The New York Times, 6/19/1934

6. Huntingdon Daily News, 10/20/1934

7. North Adams Transcript, 7/19/1934

8. The New York Times, 6/19/1934

9. Time, 7/2/1934

10. Time, 7/2/1934

11. Time, 7/2/1934

12. Ogden Standard-Examiner, 1/17/1935

13. Metropolitan Opera, archives.metoperafamily.org

14. Carlton Smith, Literary Digest CXIX, 1/1935

15. Cleveland Plain Dealer, 1/25/1935

16. The Salt Lake Tribune, 1/25/1935

17. Oakland Tribune, 1/25/1935

18. The New York Times, 1/25/1935

19. The New York Times, 1/29/1935

20. New York Daily News, 1/25/1935

21. New York World Telegram, 1/25/1935

22. New York Herald Tribune, 1/25/1935

23. Time, 2/4/1935

24. Time, 2/4/1935

25. The New York Times, 1/25/1935

26. "Foreword to a Life Story," unpublished manuscript, Harold B. Library, BYU, 1980

27. "Foreword to a Life Story," unpublished manuscript, Harold B. Library, BYU, 1980

28. The operas of John Laurence Seymour are: Antigone, Heroic Opera in Prologue and Three Acts, op. 4; The Snake Woman, Romantic Opera in 5 Acts, op. 5 (discarded version); Les Précieuses Ridicules (The Affected Maids), Musical Comedy in Oct Act, op. 6; The Devil and Tom Walker, Fantastic Opera in Three Acts, op.

7; The Bachelor Belles, an Operetta in Three Acts, op. 13; Vospi-tannitsa (A Protégée of the Mistress), Opera in 4 Acts, op. 15; In the Pasha's Garden, An Opera in One Act, op. 17; Rudens of Plau-tus, Opera Comique in 5 Acts, op. 18; Ramona, Lyric Opera in Five Acts and Epilogue, op. 34; Ming Toy, A Musical Comedy in Prologue and Two Acts (1949); Two Gentlemen of Verona, An Op-eretta in 2 Acts, op. 38; Golden Days, A Comic Operetta in Two Acts, op. 40; The Maid, the Demon, and the Samurai, op. 43; Tom Walker's Bargain, Fantastic Opera in 4 Acts, op. 66; Measure for Measure, Lyric Drama in 5 Acts, op. 69; The Lure and the Prom-ise, a Musical Play in Three Acts with a Prologue and an Epi-logue, op. 70; Aureng-Zebe, Heroic Opera in Five Acts, op. 71; Nephi, The Tender Bough, A Music Drama in a Prologue and Five Acts, op. 72; Ollanta, el Jefe Kolla, Opera Eroica en 4 Actos, op. 73; Atahuallpa, Opera Eroica en 5 Actos, op. 75; La Vida es Sueño, Opera Romántica en 3 Actos, op. 77; and Sappho, Roman-tische oper in 5 Aufzugen, op. 78.

29. Inez Cooper interview, Dr. John Laurence Seymour, 7/19/72

Chapter 4

1. The New York Times, 12/18/2011

2. The New York Times, 12/14/2011

3. Opera News, 12/2011

4. The New York Times, 1/1/2012

5. The New York Times, 1/18/2012

6. The New York Times, 1/21/2012

7. Joseph Volpe, The Toughest Show on Earth

8. Joseph Volpe, The Toughest Show on Earth

9. Joseph Volpe, The Toughest Show on Earth

Chapter 5

1. The New York Times, 2/29/2008

2. metoperafamily.org

3. The New York Times, 2/28/2008

4. The New York Times, 3/11/1889

5. The New York Times, 1/5/1889

6. www.metfamily.org

7. The New York Times, 1/1905

8. Deutsche Kunst und Deutsche Politik

9. Das Judenthum in der Musik

10. The New York Times, 1/28/2012

Chapter 6

1. The New York Times, 2/27/2012

2. www.reichelrecommends.com

3. Washington Post, 2/24/2012

4. The New Yorker 3/12/2012

5. The New York Times 2/24/2012

Chapter 7

1. www.icsom.org/settlement

2. www.metfamily.org

Chapter 8

1. The New York Times, 9/15/ 2003

2. Author's correspondence with Jamie Peterson 5/9/2012

Chapter 9

1. Deseret Evening News, 2/5/1902

2. http://history.utah.gov/findaids/B00097/B0097.xml

3. www.michaelballam.com

4. The New York Times, 2/1975

5. The New York Times, 3/31/2012

6. The New York Times, 3/27/2012

7. The New York Times, 4/4/2012

8. The New York Times, 4/17/2012

9. Salt Lake Tribune, 4/23/2012

10. Correspondence of the author, 4/12/2012

11. The New York Times, 8/23/2011

12. The New York Times, 9/13/1997

Chapter 10

1. The New York Times, 4/23/2012

2. The New York Times, 4/26/2012

3. The New York Times, 4/23/2012

Chapter 11

1. The New York Times, 3/7/2012

2. NYACA § 25.01 - 25.35

Evening Standard, 12/1924

3. The New York Times, 3/17/2004

4. The New York Times, 3/17/2004

5. The New York Times, 4/29/2012

6. The New York Times, 10/2/1989

Chapter 12

1. erinmorley.com

2. nicholaspallesen.com

3. tamaramumford.com

4. costajackson.com

5. wendybrynharmer.com

6. http://encompassarts.com/artist/nina-warren

7. Sermon, September 20, 1857; see The Messenger, July 1953

8. Ensign, July 1977

9. The New York Times, 7/14/1992

Made in the USA
Charleston, SC
24 November 2012